Palgrave Studies in Audio-`

Series Editor
K.J. Donnelly
University of Southampton
Southampton, UK

The aesthetic union of sound and image has become a cultural dominant. A junction for aesthetics, technology and theorisation, film's relationship with music remains the crucial nexus point of two of the most popular arts and richest cultural industries. Arguably, the most interesting area of culture is the interface of audio and video aspects, and that film is the flagship cultural industry remains the fount and crucible of both industrial developments and critical ideas.

Palgrave Studies in Audio-Visual Culture has an agenda-setting aspiration. By acknowledging that radical technological changes allow for rethinking existing relationships, as well as existing histories and the efficacy of conventional theories, it provides a platform for innovative scholarship pertaining to the audio-visual. While film is the keystone of the audio visual continuum, the series aims to address blind spots such as video game sound, soundscapes and sound ecology, sound psychology, art installations, sound art, mobile telephony and stealth remote viewing cultures.

Advisory Board
Philip Brophy, Australia
Michel Chion, University of Paris III: Sorbonne Nouvelle, France
Sean Cubitt, Goldsmiths, University of London, UK
Claudia Gorbman, University of Washington Tacoma, USA
Lev Manovich, Graduate Centre, CUNY, USA
Elisabeth Weis, Brooklyn College, CUNY, USA

More information about this series at
http://www.springer.com/series/14647

Emilio Audissino

Film/Music Analysis

A Film Studies Approach

Emilio Audissino
University of Southampton
Southampton, UK

Palgrave Studies in Audio-Visual Culture
ISBN 978-3-319-87135-6   ISBN 978-3-319-61693-3 (eBook)
DOI 10.1007/978-3-319-61693-3

© The Editor(s) (if applicable) and The Author(s) 2017
Softcover reprint of the hardcover 1st edition 2017
This work is subject to copyright. All rights are solely and exclusively licensed by the Publisher, whether the whole or part of the material is concerned, specifically the rights of translation, reprinting, reuse of illustrations, recitation, broadcasting, reproduction on microfilms or in any other physical way, and transmission or information storage and retrieval, electronic adaptation, computer software, or by similar or dissimilar methodology now known or hereafter developed.
The use of general descriptive names, registered names, trademarks, service marks, etc. in this publication does not imply, even in the absence of a specific statement, that such names are exempt from the relevant protective laws and regulations and therefore free for general use.
The publisher, the authors and the editors are safe to assume that the advice and information in this book are believed to be true and accurate at the date of publication. Neither the publisher nor the authors or the editors give a warranty, express or implied, with respect to the material contained herein or for any errors or omissions that may have been made. The publisher remains neutral with regard to jurisdictional claims in published maps and institutional affiliations.

Cover credit: © gmutlu/Getty

Printed on acid-free paper

This Palgrave Macmillan imprint is published by Springer Nature
The registered company is Springer International Publishing AG
The registered company address is: Gewerbestrasse 11, 6330 Cham, Switzerland

Preface and Acknowledgements

The spur to develop what I present in this book came from a practical need. For my previous monograph on John Williams I needed to study his film music not as 'music', as mine was not a research in musicology, but in films history and stylistics. I also needed to analyse the role of his music in films, and Williams's music, is mostly in the area of what would be called 'accompaniment' music, not 'comment' music. More than tools to interpret its meaning, I needed tools to analyse its formal agency. I came to the conclusion that Neoformalism was the right approach for my scope. As a former film-maker, when I watch a film that has some effects on me—perceptive, affective, semantic, ideological—what intrigues me most is to understand how those effects have been produced and induced. In general, I find Neoformalism a stimulating way of analysing films because it entails a sort of reverse engineering: from the finished artefact, one has to reconstruct and examine the creative steps that led to the result. Specifically, I have also found Neoformalism to be very helpful in investigating what music can do when combined with visuals. Since it has proven very handy to me, I resolved to develop a Neoformalism-based method to the study of music in film.

I call this method 'Film/Music Analysis.' The slash sign between 'film' and 'music' is not intended as a frill, a pretentious coinage—well, not only. If I say that I perform a 'film–music analysis' the general understanding is that I am going to dissect musicologically a piece of music written for the screen. The slash sign in film/music analysis is to be interpreted as a relational sign: this is an instance of film analysis in which particular attention is placed on the music as to its interaction with the other components of the film. And the order is also important: in 'Film/Music Analysis' *film* analysis is the first concern, as it stems from a film scholar's perspective.

The work is articulated into three parts. Part one is the *Pars Destruens*, in which I present a review of the issues that I think make most past and current approaches incomplete or biassed. Part two is the *Pars Construens*, in which I present my theoretical frameworks of reference, mainly Kristin Thompson's Neoformalism. But film music is also *music*, and even if the method I propose does not entail in-depth harmonic analysis or descriptions of the contrapuntal design and it strives to keep the references to the musical text to a minimum, some concepts from Music Studies are to be brought in. These are drawn principally from Leonard B. Meyer's music theories and connected to Neoformalism with an overarching framework based on Gestalt Psychology. Then, I propose a method to analyse music in films based on the spheres of mental activity in which the film-viewer is engaged: perception, emotion, and cognition. As guidelines for the analysis, I finally offer a set of three functions that music can fulfil in films, based on those three spheres of mental activity. The third part could be called *Pars Demonstrans*. One chapter consists of a set of case studies focussed on single topics and musical agencies: an examination and criticism of Stilwell's 'Fantastical Gap' in *Laura*, *The Witches of Eastwick* and *The Sea Hawk*; a discussion of Chion's 'anempathetic effect' in *Hangover Square* and *A Clockwork Orange*; a look into how songs and lyrics operate in films, with examples from *Breaking Bad* and *Casablanca*; an analysis of how music combines with the other cinematic elements in the opening-title sequences to set the tone for the narrative and prefigure future developments, with examples from classical Hollywood films and a more extended analysis of the opening sequence of *The Hateful Eight*; a study of the macro-emotive function of the music in *The Umbrellas of Cherbourg*. The closing chapter is a full analysis of *Close Encounters of the Third Kind* and *E.T. The Extraterrestrial*, focussing on how the score cooperates with the other filmic elements to produce the local and global design of the narration, and also comparing my film/music analysis of this pair of films with other recent analyses by musicologists.

The research for this study was financed with a Vice Chancellor's Award in Film from the University of Southampton, and the bulk of this was written during my stint in their Film Department. I would like to offer my warmest thanks and appreciation to Kevin Donnelly, my always friendly and helpful supervisor, with whom I had a number of extremely pleasant and enlightening consultations—namely, he pointed me to Gestalt Psychology as a perhaps better fit than Cognitivism for my work. My thanks also go to Francesco Izzo and Miguel Mera for their musical advice. And I also extend my appreciation to all the other nice people I had the opportunity to work with at Southampton: Tim Bergfelder, Mike Hammond, Sally Keenan, Lucy Mazdon, Paola Visconti, and Michael Williams. For making this book possible, I am grateful to Palgrave Macmillan, and in particular to Lina Aboujieb and Karina Jákupsdóttir, who assisted me in the development phases.

I would also like to acknowledge the Worldwide Universities Network that awarded me a Research Mobility Programme grant to spend a period of study as Visiting Scholar at the University of Wisconsin-Madison, USA. I was graced with the opportunity of penning the parts about Neoformalism there, in Neoformalism's birthplace. I would like to express my sincere gratitude to David Bordwell, Kristin Thompson, and Jeff Smith, who were so kind as to welcome me in their academic community during my visit and to offer me invaluable advice and seminal directions for my research. The good parts in the following pages are the fruits of such consultations; any bad part is to be imputed solely to my misunderstanding.

Finally, a due acknowledgement to my stable family—my parents Silvia and Vittorio and my sister Sara—who have always borne with my travelling around, my appearing and disappearing, and with my strange occupational status during these years. Grazie!

Imperia, Italy
May 2017

Emilio Audissino

Contents

1 Introduction: Who Is Entitled to Study Film Music? ... 1
   Notes ... 9
   References ... 11

Part I Pars Destruens

2 The Not-so-fantastical Gap Between Music Studies and Film Studies ... 17
   Film Music in Music Studies ... 17
   Film Music in Film Studies ... 25
   Notes ... 36
   References ... 38

3 Recent Attempts to Bridge the Gap and Overcome a Separatist Conception ... 45
   Proposals to Overcome the Separatism ... 45
   Communications Model Vs. Perception Model ... 53
   Notes ... 61
   References ... 62

Part II Pars Construens

4 The Neoformalist Proposal   67
   Neoformalism: An Introduction   67
   Neoformalist Film Analysis   77
   Neoformalism and Music in Films   85
   Notes   88
   References   90

5 Film/Music Analysis I: Music, Gestalt, and Audiovisual Isomorphism   95
   Music as Music   95
   Music and Gestalt Qualities   100
   Analysing the Filmic System: Macro and Micro Configurations   110
   Notes   118
   References   121

6 Film/Music Analysis II: Functions and Motivations of Music   125
   Music and Motivations   125
   Functions   130
   Notes   151
   References   152

Part III Pars Demonstrans

7 Five Illustrations of Film/Music Analysis   157
   Are All Gaps 'Fantastical' and Meaningful?   157
   Anempathetic Effect, Proper   162
   Tell It with a Song: Cognitive Function of the Lyrics   167
   Opening Credits, Prefiguration, and Title Music   173
   Music as the Connective Tissue of Emotions: The Umbrellas of Cherbourg   180
   Notes   185
   References   187

8	*Close Encounters of the Third Kind* and *E.T. The Extraterrestrial*: **The Bonding Power of Music**	191
	Close Encounters of the Third Kind *(1977)*	192
	E.T. The Extraterrestrial *(1982)*	205
	Conclusions	213
	Notes	214
	References	218
9	**Recapitulation and Final Thoughts**	223
	Notes	228
	References	229

Filmography 231

Index 237

List of Figures

Fig. 2.1	The father's guilt	21
Fig. 6.1	Pauline waters the flowers, *Pauline et Paulette*	140
Fig. 6.2	The set of functions	151
Fig. 7.1	Nazis singing 'Die Wacht am Rhein'/The peoples singing 'La Marseillaise', *Casablanca*	171
Fig. 7.2	'Those ferocious soldiers…are coming right into our arms…', *Casablanca*	172
Fig. 7.3	Opening credits, *The Hateful Eight*	177
Fig. 7.4	Gentle rain/Frigid snow, *The Umbrellas of Cherbourg*	184
Fig. 8.1	Comparison between *Pinocchio* and *Close Encounters of the Third Kind*	205
Fig. 8.2	Ascending perfect fifth in the *E.T.* score, transcription from *E.T. The Extraterrestrial*, John Williams music published by USI B Music Publishing (1982 BMI), administered by Songs of Universal [Used in compliance with the U.S. Copyright Act, Section 107]	212

CHAPTER 1

Introduction: Who Is Entitled to Study Film Music?

Film music is a complicated field because it is a composite subject matter. It is about music and it is about film, which means that two separate disciplines can claim they are entitled to study it. Film music is part of the film, and so film scholars have (should have) an interest in it. But film music is also music, and so musicologists have (should have) an interest in it.

Compared to other 'composite' disciplines, with film–music studies one often gets the impression that the disciplines involved have fairly different scopes and targets if compared to, say, Psychomusicology, for example. In Psychomusicology the psychologists are interested in how the human brain perceives and elaborates music, and the musicologists are interested in how music is perceived and elaborated by the human brain: both, though from different perspectives, share the same target, that is, to gain a better understanding of how music and the brain interact. I have the feeling that this is generally not the case with film music.

Books and publications on film music can be traced back to the very beginnings of the craft itself—for example, Leonid Sabaneev's (1935) handbook or Kurt London's (1936) monograph, not to mention the many treatises and anthologies penned during the silent era (Erdmann et al. 1927; Rapée 1924; Zamecnik 1913–1914). Until the late 1980s, there had been three types of publications. One was the 'How to do it' handbook, which provided descriptions of the trade and practical advice to those interested in its technicalities—for example, the orchestration

© The Author(s) 2017
E. Audissino, *Film/Music Analysis*, Palgrave Studies
in Audio-Visual Culture, DOI 10.1007/978-3-319-61693-3_1

manuals by Hugo Friedhofer and Henry Mancini (Friedhofer and Atkins 1977; Mancini 1986). Another one was what can be called the 'Politique des Autheurs' chronicles, in which a historical survey of the art and craft of film music was offered, articulated through and with a strong focus on the composers that shaped its course—for example, Tony Thomas's books on Hollywood music (Thomas 1979, 1997)—or biography/autobiography focussing on a single author (Rózsa 1989). Finally, there was the appreciation (or deprecation) essay that defended (or attacked) the aesthetics of film music—examples are, respectively, Prendergast (1977) and Adorno and Eisler (2007). Almost all of these publications were penned by practitioners: Friedhofer and Mancini (orchestrators and composers in Hollywood); Thomas (music producer specialising in film music); Prendergast (a music editor with a string of Hollywood collaborations); Hanns Eisler (film composer for Bertolt Brecht and Fritz Lang).[1] The same happened in most countries, for example, in Italy or France, where some of the earliest books on the topic were by the film critic Ermanno Comuzio (1980) and the film-maker and composer François Porcile (1969). Film music was seen merely as a craft, a subsidiary practice without any artistic merit, and therefore something of interest only to those who practised it, or to some enthusiasts with peculiar musical tastes.

In 1987 Claudia Gorbman published *Unheard Melodies* (Gorbman 1987). This is considered the first major scholarly examination of film music, somewhat the foundation of 'serious' film–music studies. To follow, two other books strengthened the academic profile of this field: Kathryn Kalinak's *Settling the Score* (Kalinak 1992) and Caryl Flinn's *Strains of Utopia* (Flinn 1992). Interestingly enough, the academic study of film music was launched by film scholars—Gorbman, Kalinak, and Flinn—not by musicologists. Maybe in the music departments the Adorno/Eisler authoritative condemnation of film music as a merely derivative collection of clichés still resonated quite vigorously.[2] Today, things have exactly reversed. In the meantime, such disciplines as Ethnomusicology and Popular Music have entered the academe, moving Music Studies away from the somewhat stiff canon-centred/*Absolute Musik* approach that was still exerting some influence in the twentieth century (Neumeyer et al. 2000, p. 21).[3] Film music has become a legitimate object of study and, as a consequence, musicologists and music theorists have conquered the field. The four leading journals today—*Music and the Moving Image*; *The Journal of Film Music*; *Music, Sound, and the Moving Image*; *The Soundtrack*—have a majority of musicologists on their editorial boards, and major annual conferences on the topic are typically organised by and held in music departments—for example, the *Music and the Moving Image* conference at the Steinhardt School of Music, New York University, and the *Music for Audiovisual Media* at the School of Music, University of Leeds. Another sign that music departments are leading the game is the current tendency to assume that the fact of writing about film music equals being a musicologist. After I published a film–music monograph, I have been regularly mistaken for a musicologist, receiving emails by book editors or music students looking for contributions or advice of musicological nature. My book is clearly classified as a Film Studies book, listed in the 'Wisconsin Studies in Film' series. Yet, when it is acquired by universities, it is acquired by music departments[4]—not film departments—and has been mostly listed in the new release sections of Music Studies websites and societies.[5]

Having founded the discipline, now film scholars seem to have retreated to a somewhat 'uncomfortable' minority position. Why 'uncomfortable'? Because music is difficult to verbalise. Musical analysis involves a plethora of technical terms, dedicated jargon, and skills in music reading and a considerable ear training that are not so easy to secure. One can describe a given lighting pattern or a costume in a film even if he is not a full-fledged photographer or costume designer. Visual elements seem to be easier to translate into verbal descriptions, probably because of the visual predominance in our sensory system (Posner et al. 1976). Trying to describe a piece of music featured in a film might prove daunting if one is not in possession of the analytical and descriptive tools required—more daunting than describing any of the visual elements, more daunting than reporting dialogue—after all, dialogue is verbal communication and reporting it presents no problem for the layperson. Even dealing with the more complex sound-effects track (Altman 1992; Kulezic-Wilson 2008) might be easier than dealing with music. I can describe a peculiar noise in the film by comparing it with our encyclopaedic knowledge of the world, the database that is common to most—for example, when Quint is eaten by the shark, we hear a gory gurgle coming from his blood-pouring mouth, like the sound of water drained down into a half-clogged sink. Most sounds are related to some real-life action or object and trigger automatic visual associations. Music is a more abstract sound realm with no direct correspondence with the real world.[6] The result of verbalising music by employing a layperson's common-sense database risks sounding naïve, impressionistic, or even risible to the ears of a trained musicologist. For example, one could describe the main melody of Waldteufel's *The Skaters' Waltz* (1882) as having a first part where the skaters slide on the ice describing long and arched figurations, and a second part in which they execute smaller circular spins; not a very detailed and telling musical analysis indeed. For intellectual honesty, many film scholars lacking a musical background prefer not to touch music lest they might cut a bad figure. However, music is one of the elements operating in the film, and neglecting it can impair the completeness of a film analysis or even engender mistakes. Peter Larsen, for example, reports that Raymond Bellour's analysis of *The Big Sleep* (1946, dir. Hawks) presents a wrong segmentation because music is ignored altogether (Larsen 2005, p. 118).

Film criticism for a broader audience also shows this symptomatic 'selective deafness' for music in films. Take *Jaws* (1975, dir. Spielberg), a film where the music *is* the shark—'The music...does not merely signify [the shark's] presence, it *is* its presence.' (Donnelly 2005, p. 93)—or the shark *is* in the music (Biancorosso 2010), a film whose success, according to Spielberg himself, has been due to the music by a 50% (Bouzereau 2000, p. 8). The article for its twentieth celebration printed in the 1995 issue of *Empire* never mentions, not even in passing, neither John Williams nor the role of the music (Salisbury and Nathan 1995, pp. 78–85). Another outstanding instance is the special issue of *Film Review* devoted to Steven Spielberg (Anon 2001). In this ninety-eight-page 'Your Complete Guide to Spielberg!', composer John Williams is named one time, only cursorily (p. 70). Again, no mention here of Williams's music in the *Jaws* section (pp. 16–17)—and no mention either as regards *Close Encounters of the Third Kind* (1977), a film where the music has a very central and conspicuous role in the narrative (pp. 18–19). No nods to music at all even in the detailed six-page coverage of *E.T. The Extraterrestrial* (1982), as if it were a Bresson film, but precise accounts are provided on all the visual elements involved—cinematography, special effects, set design, even hairdressing (pp. 82–87). The only part in the 'Spielberg Special' where the music is mentioned is a review of the unsettling opening sequence of *Saving Private Ryan* (1998): 'There's no music to *interfere* with the pictures and the dialogue is mostly drowned out by the noise of the battle' (p. 70, emphasis mine). Quite tellingly, music is acknowledged when it's absent, when it does not 'interfere.'

If film scholars and critics are uneasy in coping with music and its jargon, they cannot be completely blamed. Musicologists are sometimes quite harsh when they defend the exactitude of their terminology and the borders of their discipline from amateurs. It may happen—and has happened—that when some film scholar ventures into some film–music analysis, musicologists promptly expose her/his inaccuracy. In his review of film scholar Anahid Kassabian's book, the musicologist James Wierzbicki points out:

> Not so convincing, alas, is most of what Kassabian has to say about music. In her Prologue, she notes that she has 'chosen to avoid the technical language of music studies wherever possible' (p. 9). [O]ne suspects that Kassabian eschews musical terminology largely because her understanding of music is benighted....[There is] a raft of sweeping generalizations that reveal a skewed perception not just of music as a whole but of how music is regarded by persons to whom it matters. (Wierzbicki 2006, pp. 461–462)

And William Rosar thus comments on some non-musicologists that embark on studies of film music: '[I]n former times it was deemed extremely bad form and even the height of impertinent arrogance for a scholar in one discipline to presume to work in another, at least without adequate (academic) preparation, let alone tender opinions as to how that discipline should conduct itself' (Rosar 2009, p. 103).[7]

Yet, cinema too has its technicalities. A superficial knowledge of the film medium can be often detected in musicologists that is comparable to the superficial knowledge of music detected in film scholars. For example, Robynn J. Stilwell writes 'Like the red, green and blue which combine to form the process colour of the film's image, dialogue, sound effect[s] and music together form the film's soundscape' (Stilwell 2001, p. 167). Stilwell is talking here about the 'additive colour system' (RGB), which is the one used for TV screens and video projectors, in which three coloured lights add one another to form the colour images. Additive colour system was used for films during the early colour experiments in the silent era—like the Chronochrome Gaumont and the Technicolor Process No. 1.[8] But since the 1920s film, projection has been employing a different system: the 'subtractive colour system' (CMYK).[9] Only in recent years has the additive colour system been used for film projection again—with HD digital projection replacing the traditional film stock—but when Stilwell wrote her piece (2001), she just manifested an approximative knowledge of film technique. Yet, such film-technique mistakes are rarely pointed out as often as musical mistakes are—possibly because film technique is not of much interest to film scholars either.

This hegemonic position of the music departments might have been favoured by the very fact that Film Studies has a reputation for being an easy academic enterprise, a sort of pastime if compared to other disciplines in the Humanities such as, say, Germanic Philology, Medieval English Literature, or Music Theory. Film Studies possesses no such precise and consolidated terminology as Music Theory. Where exactly does a 'Medium Close Up (MCU)' begin to be a 'Close Up (CU)'?[10] There is also disagreement as to how to call those instances in which two or more lines of action run at the same time exerting some influence on each other and the narration cuts back and forth from one to the other—is it 'cross-cutting' or 'parallel editing'?[11] This lack of exactitude is likely to make Film Studies look like a 'soft' discipline and lead people from other disciplines to think that getting ready to teach or analyse films is something anyone without a proper education in film can do anyway—after all, everyone has happened to watch some films. It is not difficult to tell a Close Up from a Long Shot, once you have gotten familiar with these few terms. The plots of narrative films can be summarised and verbalised without any particular discipline-specific requirements. Indeed, it is quite frequent to see musicologists with an interest in film music engage in film history or film analysis.[12] So do scholars from other disciplines in the Humanities, most typically Literature, perfectly comfortable in giving film classes alongside classes in English Poetry, Twentieth-century Novels, or Critical Theory. On the contrary, if someone wanted to teach music history and engage in an analysis of, say, a Mahler symphony or a Bach fugue, reading a couple of books in a few weeks would not be enough: a proper musical education takes years. I don't know of any film scholar—or English Literature scholar—daring to give classes in musical analysis.

Film Studies is still a young academic discipline, launched in the Literature or Aesthetics departments in the 1960s/1970s. So there might still be the idea that it is a subsidiary of the Literature departments. But this reputation of Film Studies as a sort of 'trump card' that anyone in the Humanities can play without a specific background may also be due to Film Studies having insisted for a long time on 'readings' and critical interpretations, especially in the 1970s. Films are used to talk about something else—society, politics, gender, race, and so forth—giving the idea that anyone in the Humanities can use films as a pretext to talk about their interests. In 2000 David Bordwell lamented, 'People believe that film belongs to everyone in the Humanities and that we in Film Studies are supposed to hold the doors open for lit professors to put *Blade Runner* and Baudrillard together and dub it a film course' (Quart 2000, p. 41). This tradition has produced the consequence that the discussion of the 'content' (or the meaning) is much more important than the discussion of the form and style. In Bordwell's words again:

> For many educated people, the most important question about cinema revolves around its relation to culture....In no other domain of inquiry I know, from the history of science and engineering to the history of music, literature, and visual art, is there such unremitting insistence that every significant research project must shed light on society. Scholars can freely study iambic pentameter, baroque perspective, and the discovery of DNA without feeling obliged to make vast claims about culture's impact on said subjects. Is cinema important and valuable solely as a barometer of broad-scale social changes? (Bordwell 2008, p. 30)

Anyone in the Humanities can talk about 'contents'. For example, we all agree that *The Birth of a Nation* (1915, dir. Griffith) is extremely (and embarrassingly, for today's standards) racist in its meaning/content. This film can be used in a class as a pretext to talk about racial prejudices in early twentieth-century America—this is something a sociologist or a historian can do, employing the film as a mere specimen of that historical and cultural context. Film scholars should be the ones able to comment on the films' technical, formal, and stylistic features as well. In the case of *The Birth of a Nation*, a film scholar's interest should be (also and at least equally) focussed on the *analysis* of the film's formal and stylistic innovations, not only on the *interpretation* of its racial discourse.

'Analysis' and 'Interpretation' are two different stages of investigation, possibly integrating one another to give a full view of an artwork. 'Analysis' typically refers to the close examination of the formal and stylistic traits of an artwork, while 'Interpretation' is the broader critical baring and explanation of the artwork's more or less implicit meanings and connotations. 'Analysis' requires the use of discipline-specific tools and a more technique-oriented approach, while 'Interpretation' employs broader critical and hermeneutic skills. Quite significantly, in Film Studies, 'Analysis' tends to be confused with 'Interpretation'. And musicologists have taken notice of that:

> In the most recent edition of the venerable *New Grove Dictionary of Music and Musicians*, the term 'analysis' warranted an essay of nearly fifty pages....In the recently published *Oxford Guide to Film Studies*...the term rarely appears and is wholly absent from section labels and titles for the sixty-two individual essays. Instead, one finds 'film interpretation', 'critical approaches', and 'theoretical frameworks'. (Neumeyer and Buhler 2001, p. 17)

This over-attention to interpretation, content, message, and cultural significance has probably caused Film Studies to gain a reputation of a broadly 'humanistic' discipline without really specific tools and expertise. When musicologists became interested in film music, they took the lead because they had stronger discipline-specific tools to offer.

Given these premises, the research question from which all this study takes the move is: How can we analyse music in films from a film scholar's perspective, be as discipline-specific as possible, and take into account a gamut as large as possible of the types and range of agency that music can have (that is, not only *interpret* but also *analyse* music's agency)? The answer that I propose in the following pages is to use a formalist method. Contrary to most approaches from Music Studies, my approach seeks to handle film music not so much as music (a musical text) but as one of the many elements that construct the film (a cinematic technique). It considers music as an internal and interdependent part of the film's system, not as something external that is either in competition or in compliance with the film—see the traditional category of 'counterpoint' and 'parallelism' in film–music studies. Contrary to most approaches from Film Studies, it aims to cover all the range of functions that music can perform in films—not only the cases in which music jumps to a foreground position and thus evidently offers a 'comment' and obviously prompts interpretation and readings. I am also interested in those instances in which music does not 'signify' anything but 'merely' performs some formal function. To give a solid ground to my proposal, in the next two chapters I start by presenting a selection of problems and limitations that I detect in the current approaches of both musicologists and film scholars.

NOTES

1. Hanns Eisler composed the music for the Brecht project *Kuhle Wampe* (1932, dir. Dudow) and Fritz Lang's *Hangmen Also Die!* (1943).
2. One of the first musicologists to publish a book on film music was Brown (1994).
3. On the prejudice against film music based on the Romantic distinction between Absolute and Applied music, see Audissino (2014).
4. For example, my book is available in the Lewis Music Library at MIT, USA (http://library.mit.edu/item/002220914); in the Music Library at the University of Leipzig, Germany (https://katalog.ub.uni-leipzig.de/Record/0012916378); and in the Mills Music Library at the University of Wisconsin-Madison, USA (http://search.library.wisc.edu/catalog/ocn856579584), and in the Denis Arnold Music Library at the University of Nottingham, UK (http://aleph.nottingham.ac.uk/F/MHBJCI3GGUAY86MYR1LQK5MC453NCXA5C7861JN1GFYPMDCY2G-08428?func=full-set-set&set_number=006348&set_entry=000001&format=999). Accessed 18 November 2016.
5. In November 2015—eighteen months after the book's release—there was no trace of it in the website of the SCMS (Society for Cinema and Media Studies) (http://www.cmstudies.org/search/all.asp?c=0&bst=%22emilio+audissino%22), while the book had already been listed in the website of the AMS (American Musicological Society) in their section 'New Books in Musicology 2013–2014' (http://www.ams-net.org/feeds/newbooks/). Note that I am not a member of either societies.
6. Of course, there is onomatopoeic music (as the horse-like trumpet call at the end of Leroy Anderson's *Sleigh Ride* [1948]) and also a consolidated musical associationism (e.g., solemn pipe organ music conjures up images of churches and sacred liturgies). But in the former instance, music becomes concrete because it mimics a sound, and by doing this it exits the abstract realm of music to enter the real-life realm of noises; in the latter, musical associationism is not a direct 'natural' relation as that between a sound and its source, but a conventional construct consolidated through repeated use in time.
7. This article criticises the typical interdisciplinary approach to film music. Interdisciplinarity is seen as typically creating a middle ground with new terminology and tools shared by two main fields of studies—in our case, film and music—in a sort of compromise where the disciplines involved renounce part of their rigour in order to meet the other one(s).
8. See Cherchi Usai (2000, pp. 33–39).
9. In the subtractive colour system three dyed layers on the filmstrip (Cyan, Magenta, Yellow, Key [black]) are traversed by the projector's white light,

which reproduces colours by subtraction of said CMYK layers from the white spectrum of the projector's light beam. See (Anon 2007, p. 24).
10. There is a widespread disagreement as to how many shot sizes there are. Yale University's teaching materials for 'Film Analysis' list the following scale of shot sizes: Extreme Long Shot (ELS); Long Shot (LS); Medium Long Shot (MLS); Medium Close Up (MCU); Close Up (CU); Extreme Close Up (ECU): Online, http://filmanalysis.coursepress.yale.edu/cinematography. Accessed 24 October 2016. Bordwell and Thompson provide the following: Extreme Long Shot; Long Shot; Medium Long Shot; Medium Shot; Medium Close-Up; Close-Up; Extreme Close-Up (Bordwell and Thompson 2010, p. 195). On the Cinemetrics website, Barry Salt offers a list with more terminological variations: 'Big Close Up (BCU) shows head only, Close Up (CU) shows head and shoulders, Medium Close Up (MCU) includes body from the waist up, Medium Shot (MS) includes from just below the hip to above the head of upright actors, Medium Long Shot (MLS) shows the body from the knee upwards, Long Shot (LS) shows at least the full height of the body, and Very Long Shot (VLS) shows the actor small in the frame.' http://www.cinemetrics.lv/salt.php. Accessed 25 October 2016.
11. David Bordwell and Kristin Thompson call that 'cross-cutting' and provide the typical Griffith-like last-minute rescues as an example (Bordwell and Thompson 2010, pp. 246–248). Tom Gunning calls the same last-minute rescues 'parallel editing,' as if the two terms were synonyms (Gunning 1994, p. 126, n. 53). Yet, 'parallel editing' is often nuanced with a different meaning. In 'cross-cutting' the lines of actions cross, which means that they come into contact. In 'parallel editing' they run parallel, and two parallel lines never cross and never come into contact. Hence some use 'parallel editing' only for those instances in which editing makes a parallel between situations/images that have no spatio-temporal relationship, in order to make a comparison with a commentary function. Such instances are the parallel narratives from different ages in Griffith's *Intolerance* (1916), the comparison between the violent repression of the strike and the slaughter of cattle in Eisenstein's *Strike* (1924), or the shot of the gossiping old ladies meaningfully followed by a shot of clucking hens in Fritz Lang's *Fury* (1936). 'Cross-cutting' and 'parallel editing' are not synonyms in Italy and France, for example. The Italian film scholar Sandro Bernardi in the Treccani 'Enciclopedia del Cinema' distinguishes between 'montaggio alternato' (cross-cutting) and 'montaggio parallelo' (parallel editing) ('Procedimenti narrative,' online entry, http://www.treccani.it/enciclopedia/narrativi_%28Enciclopedia_del_Cinema%29. Accessed 23 November 2016). In France the same distinction translates

into 'montage alterné' and 'montage parallèle' (for example, in http://www.cineclubdecaen.com/analyse/montageparallele.htm. Accessed 26 November 2016).
12. A recent example is Buhler and Neumeyer (2015).

REFERENCES

Adorno, Theodor W., and Hanns Eisler. 2007 [1947]. *Composing for the Films*. London and New York: Continuum.
Altman, Rick. 1992. The Material Heterogeneity of Recorded Sound. In *Sound Theory. Sound Practice*, ed. Rick Altman, 15–34. London and New York: Routledge.
Anon. 2001. Steven Spielberg Special. *Film Review*, Special #36.
Anon. 2007. *The Essential Reference Guide for Filmmakers*. Rochester, NY: Eastman Kodak Company.
Audissino, Emilio. 2014. Overruling a Romantic Prejudice. Forms and Formats of Film Music in Concert Programs. In *Film in Concert, Film Scores and Their Relation to Classical Concert Music*, ed. Sebastian Stoppe, 25–44. Glücksstadt, Germany: VWH Verlag.
Biancorosso, Giorgio. 2010. The Shark in the Music. *Music Analysis* 29 (1–3): 306–333.
Bordwell, David, and Kristin Thompson. 2010. *Film Art. An Introduction*, 9th ed. New York and London: McGraw-Hill.
Bordwell, David. 2008. *Poetics of Cinema*. New York and London: Routledge.
Bouzereau, Laurent. 2000. Jaws, CD Booklet. Decca, 467 045-2.
Brown, Royal S. 1994. *Overtones and Undertones. Reading Film Music*. Berkeley, CA: University of California Press.
Buhler, James, and David Neumeyer. 2015. *Hearing the Movies: Music and Sound in Film History*. New York: Oxford University Press.
Cherchi Usai, Paolo. 2000. *Silent Cinema: An Introduction*. London: BFI.
Comuzio, Ermanno. 1980. *Colonna sonora: Dialoghi, musiche rumori dietro lo schermo*. Milan: Il Formichiere.
Donnelly, K.J. 2005. *The Spectre of Sound: Music in Film and Television*. London: BFI.
Erdmann, Hans, Giuseppe Becce, and Ludwig Brav. 1927. *Allgemeines Handbuch der Film-Musik*. Licherfelde, Berlin: Schlesinger'sche Buch.
Flinn, Caryl. 1992. *Strains of Utopia: Gender, Nostalgia, and Hollywood Music*. Princeton, NJ: Princeton University Press.
Friedhofer, Hugo, and Irene Kahn Atkins. 1977. *Arranging and Composing Film Music*. Washington, DC: Microfilming Corporation of America.
Gorbman, Claudia. 1987. *Unheard Melodies: Narrative Film Music*. London and Bloomington: BFI/Indiana University Press.

Gunning, Tom. 1994. *D.W. Griffith and the Origins of American Narrative Film: The Early Years of Biograph*. Urbana, IL: University of Illinois Press.

Kalinak, Kathryn. 1992. *Settling the Score: Music and the Classical Hollywood Film*. Madison, WI: University of Wisconsin Press.

Kulezic-Wilson, Danijela. 2008. Sound Design is the New Score. *Music, Sound and the Moving Image* 2 (2): 127–131.

Larsen, Peter. 2005. *Film Music*, trans. John Irons. London: Reaktion Books.

London, Kurt. 1936. *Film Music: A Summary of the Characteristic Features of Its History, Aesthetics, Technique; and Possible Developments*. London: Faber & Faber.

Mancini, Henry. 1986. *Sounds and Scores: A Practical Guide to Professional Orchestration*. Van Nuys, CA: Alfred Publishing.

Neumeyer, David, and James Buhler. 2001. Analytical and Interpretive Approaches (I): Analysing the Music. In *Film Music: Critical Approaches*, ed. K.J. Donnelly, 16–38. New York: Continuum International Publishing.

Neumeyer, David, James Buhler, and Caryl Flinn. 2000. Introduction. In *Music and Cinema*, ed. James Buhler, Caryl Flinn, and David Neumeyer, 1–30. Hanover, NH: Wesleyan University Press.

Porcile, François. 1969. *Présence de la musique à l'écran*. Paris: Editions du Cerf.

Posner, Michael I., Mary J. Nissen and Raymond M. Klein. 1976. Visual Dominance: An Information-Processing Account of Its Origins and Significance. *Psychological Review* 83 (2): 157–171.

Prendergast, Roy M. 1977. *Film Music: A Neglected Art: A Critical Study of Music in Films*. New York: W. W. Norton.

Quart, Alissa. 2000. David Bordwell Blows the Whistle on Film Studies. *Lingua Franca* 10 (March): 36–43.

Rapée, Erno. 1924. *Motion Picture Moods for Pianists and Organists: A Rapid Reference Collection of Selected Pieces, Adapted to Fifty-Two Moods and Situations*. New York: Belwin.

Rosar, William H. 2009. Film Studies in Musicology: Disciplinarity Vs. Interdisciplinarity. *The Journal of Film Music* 2 (2–4): 99–125.

Rózsa, Miklós. 1989. *A Double Life: The Autobiography of Miklós Rózsa, Composer in the Golden Years of Hollywood*. New York: Wynwood Press.

Sabaneev, Leonid Leonidovich. 1935. *Music for the Films: A Handbook for Composers and Conductors*, trans. S.W. Pring. London: Isaac Pitman.

Salisbury, Mark, and Ian Nathan. 1995. Jaws: 20 Year On. *Empire* 73 (July): 78–85.

Stilwell, Robynn J. 2001. Sound and Empathy: Subjectivity, Gender and the Cinematic Soundscape. In *Film Music: Critical Approaches*, ed. K.J. Donnelly, 167–187. New York: Continuum International Publishing.

Thomas, Tony. 1979. *Film Score: The View from the Podium*. New York and Chicago: A. S. Barnes.

Thomas, Tony. 1997 [1973]. *Music for the Movies*. Beverly Hills, CA: Silman-James.
Wierzbicki, James. 2006. Review of Anahid Kassabian: Hearing Film: Tracking Identifications in Contemporary Hollywood Film Music. *Journal of Film Music* 1 (4): 460–463.
Zamecnik, John Stepan. 1913–1914. *Sam Fox Moving Picture Music*, vol. 3. Cleveland: Sam Fox.

PART I

Pars Destruens

CHAPTER 2

The Not-so-fantastical Gap Between Music Studies and Film Studies

Music scholars and film scholars approach film music from different angles, obviously. Yet, it is not simply a matter of considering film music as something more pertinent to Music or more pertinent to Film; within Music Studies and Film Studies there are further subdivisions as to how to tackle film music. This chapter offers an overview and articulation of the typical ways in which film music is dealt with by the two disciplines (for the sake of clarity of argumentation, the types of approach of the two disciplines have been separated, even if they often overlap, specifically regarding the culturalist and the semiotic approaches) and proposes some reflections on the typical drawbacks that make the current approaches from both disciplines somewhat incomplete.

FILM MUSIC IN MUSIC STUDIES

When tackling film music, music scholars are often interested in it as 'music' that happens to be in some film. The first manifestation of this 'disciplinary bias' is what can be called 'score micro-analysis.' In these instances, the centre of interest is the film score as it appears on paper: the sheet music. Such micro-analyses typically present insightful musicological examinations, offer accurate reproductions and transcriptions from the score, and also relate the particular film score at hand to the overall production of its composer. A fine example is Ben Winters's *The Adventures of Robin Hood* (Winters 2007b) in which the context and period of Korngold's life when the *Robin Hood* score was written are reconstructed; manuscripts were retrieved from the archives and extensive excerpts are featured; the general architecture of the score is examined, both in terms of Korngold's adaptations of previous concert pieces of his and, in turn, subsequent adaptations of parts of the film score into concert pieces. Another example is Charles Leinberger's monograph on *The Good, the Bad, and the Ugly* (Leinberger 2004), which also features an *ad-hoc* interview with Ennio Morricone.

A different approach can be called 'architectural analysis.' It favours the examination of the overarching construction principles or ideas over minute accounts, and seeks to unveil the unifying principle of the score, for example a musical idea that runs throughout the score. This is the case of David Neumeyer's analysis of *The Trouble with Harry* (1955, dir. Hitchcock). Schenkerian analysis is applied to unearth the common *ursatz* (fundamental structure) of the thematic materials and to illustrate the tonal design of the score (Neumeyer 1998, p. 121). Another recent trend in music theory and musicology that addresses the overall design and development of a score is the study of triadic transformation, mostly under the Neo-Riemannian theory.[1] It employs analytical tools that depart from the traditional functionalist/hierarchical chordal theory of diatonic music to relate chords directly to each other without the tonic as a reference point. Neo-Riemannian theory has been used in film music to classify the typical chordal progression used to communicate situations and feelings—exotic locales, mystery or magic, romance, and so on—and also to explain by what musical means film music sounds like film music.[2] Alternatively, the unifying principle can be a narrative idea rendered in music. Such an instance is James Buhler's 'Star Wars Music and Myth,' in which he convincingly shows how the scores to the first *Star Wars* trilogy can be thematically divided around two poles, one excluding the 'Dominant-Tonic' move and represented by Darth Vader's Theme (the 'Imperial March') and one flaunting it and represented by the Force Theme (also associated with Obi-Wan Kenobi). One of the narrative themes of the trilogy is the contrast between Force and technology, a contrast between the natural order and an artificial order imposed by the violent use of technology. The Force is a natural, almost religious spiritual energy, and it is the main weapon of the Jedis—the good ones— who fight with the rebels against the imperial dictatorship. Technology is, on the contrary, the Empire's instrument of domination, alongside the evil version of the Force, the 'Dark Side'—something similar to 'white magic' versus 'black magic'. Darth Vader is the symbol of this dichotomy:

he is a renegade Jedi who joined the 'Dark Side' and, with most of his body replaced with bionic prostheses, is now more a machine than a man. Buhler argues that the score renders in music such contrast of technology versus Nature (Buhler 2000).

All these 'architectural analysis' approaches go beyond the close analysis of the score and also link the music to the extra-musical elements. Indeed, it must be signalled that in the last years Music Studies has moved from the traditional formalistic focus on the score to a wider consideration of performance contexts and audience reception—moving from the 'trace' (the score as it is) and the 'poietic dimension' (the reconstruction of the compositional process and the composer's intention) to an 'esthesic dimension' (the analysis of the work from the vantage point of the audience/listeners), to use Nattiez's vocabulary (Nattiez 1990, pp. 10–37). Philip Tagg's studies on popular music are precisely aimed at superseding the strictures of the '*Absolute Musik*' ideal and the canon-centred elitism of old musicology and relocate music from the abstract realm of tones, harmonic relations, and formal structures to that of concrete audience experiences (Tagg 2012; Tagg and Clarida 2003). Another example of this broader focus that addresses music as an event rather than as a text is the recent history of opera by Carolyn Abbate and Roger Parker, which comes with absolutely no musical examples or references to the scores:

> [S]cores encourage elaborate attention to particular aspects of a strictly musical argument, above all those involving harmonic and melodic details on the small and the large scale, aspects that have tended to figure too prominently in musicological writings about opera. In other words, scores encourage the idea of opera as a text rather than as an event. Memory, on the other hand, goes back to an event....Hence the musical descriptions in this book were written almost entirely on the basis of memory. (Abbate and Parker 2012, pp. 3–4)

This event-based approach for opera is a very interesting one for film scholars, as the musical descriptions of the films are also typically carried out from memory or from a broader medium in a similar way as the one described by Abbate and Parker. This lesser importance given to the scores comes as reassuring to film scholars: close musicological analysis is not really necessary to address film music.[3] Yet, there is at least one *difference* and one *problem*.

The *difference* is that an opera composer does not generally compose the music with such a clear idea of what the staging is going to be. There might be staging indications in the score, but an event-based analysis of, say, a Wagner's opera would describe the interaction of the music with that singular and specific performance, and that analysis would not be valid for another performance—and, obviously, Wagner did not compose the music having *that* one particular performance in mind. Opera is a performing art, never stable from one event to the other. On the contrary, film events—the screenings—are much more stable, as the screened film is a reproducible artwork with a fixed form. Film composers write their music with one precise film in mind, and the music is designed to fit that film and then is mixed with the other sound elements, forming an interlocked whole with the visual track. The music/visual interaction of a film score can be, more or less, attributed to the composer's intention and design, while the music/performance interaction of an opera changes from one event to the other and is to be attributed to the director of that particular performance rather than to the composer. Also, unlike opera, when dealing with film music, the composer's musical choices are to be thought of as more dependent on all the other extramusical elements in the film.

The *problem* of this opera-based approach, because of the aforementioned difference, is that it does not provide specific tools to analyse how the music operates in connection with the other cinematic elements. Operas tell stories and their music can be analysed in terms of storytelling—the same can be said of ballet music, symphonic poems, incidental music for theatre, and any other type of applied composition. A film is not just a story being told and staged. A (narrative) film is a story told and staged through cinematic devices—mise-en-scene, camerawork, lighting, editing, optical effects, sound effects, and so forth. Even when it engages with the film, a musical analysis inspired by the procedures of opera analysis is prone to restrict its focus on narrative structure and mise-en-scene (staging). An analysis of film music conducted with this approach might read as an analysis of any other form of applied music. As Claudia Gorbman warned, 'to judge film music as one judges "pure" music [*and opera music, I would add*] is to ignore its status as a part of the collaboration that is the film. Ultimately it is the narrative context, the interrelations between music and the rest of the film's system, that determines the effectiveness of film music' (Gorbman 1987, p. 12). For example, consider the following piece of analysis

Fig. 2.1 The father's guilt

applied to the musical transcription presented in Fig. 2.1: 'The music aptly conveys the father's sense of guilt for having forced the woman to separate from his son. It conveys this thorough a repeated fragment of ascending/descending chromatic scale in the violas, celli, and contrabasses (back and forth from E2 to A2), as to depict the guilt incessantly drilling the father's conscience'.

This could be an interesting remark about a narrative contribution from a film score. Yet, the passage I have analysed is not from a film score but from Giuseppe Verdi's *La traviata*, when Germont Sr. visits the dying Violetta and, belatedly, acknowledges that he has done her wrong (No. 11, 'Finale Ultimo', bars 39–45: 'Oh, mal cauto vegliardo! Il mal ch'io feci ora sol vedo.' ['Oh, incautious old man! Only now I can see the wrongs I have made!']). Similarly, the aforementioned Buhler analysis of *Star Wars*, though insightful, could be the analysis of a ballet score where the technological villain is paired with mechanic music and the good heroes with natural-sounding music.

One of the leading sites for a music-oriented approach is the *Journal of Film Music*, whose mission is to be 'a forum for the *musicological* study of film from the standpoint of *dramatic* musical art [emphasis mine].'[4] Note the use of 'musicological' and 'dramatic', which respectively betray a strong importance given to score analysis and, in those instances in which the music is examined in relation to the film, a limited focus on narrative level and staging. In a recent issue, two articles are indicative of this perspective. Peter Moormann's 'Composing with Types and Flexible Modules' takes *Jaws* (1975, dir. Spielberg) as a pretext to survey the use of the *ostinato* not only in film-music history—for example, Bernard Herrmann's *Psycho* (1960, dir. Hitchcock)—but also in general music history (Moormann 2012). Apart from a quote from Williams explaining why he chose an ostinato as the shark's motif, there is no attempt—because there is no interest—to demonstrate how said ostinato works within the film itself. For example, the fact is not considered that the shark's motif not only accelerates and gets louder as the shark accelerates and decelerates and gets softer as it decelerates—thus communicating the off-screen movements of the shark—but also the thickness of its instrumentation changes according to whether the shark comes up to the surface or goes down into the abyss; instrumentation thickens as the shark approaches the surface and conversely thins down when it goes down. The ostinato works efficiently in the film by using many musical parameters in a very complex way, rendering the movements of the shark both on the horizontal axis (through variations of the music's tempo and dynamics) and on the vertical axis (through variations of the music's texture) (Audissino 2014, pp. 111–118).

In the same journal issue, Frank Lehman analyses the Ark's Theme in the Map Room sequence of *Raiders of the Lost Ark* (1981, dir. Spielberg). I have conducted somewhere else a thorough analysis of how music works in this very film (Audissino 2014, pp. 145–182). The comparison of Lehman's take and my take makes a good point about the 'disciplinary bias' I have been dealing with in these pages. Lehman is interested in in-depth musical analysis—with a Neo-Riemannian approach—and describes the harmonic transformations that the Ark's Theme undergoes, an analysis I don't have the expertise and skills to do:

> The theme…is highly chromatic, constructed almost entirely from non-diatonic transformations acting on purely minor triads. Particularly salient is the theme's *leitharmonie*, a tritonal oscillation between tonic and the triad T6 away. The theme thus draws on centuries' worth of associations with dark magic, and implies to the audience that this is a dangerous MacGuffin, best left untouched by humanity's grasping hands. (Lehman 2012a, p. 184)

My interest is more in film analysis and my description of the Ark Theme goes like this:

> The mysterious and ominous tone of the Ark leitmotiv is given by both the minor-mode harmonic instability between distant keys…and the nature of the melodic intervals….The motif moves downward within a perfect fifth…within which can be found the 'dreaded' augmented-fourth interval—the tritone…, typically…associated with disturbing, ominous events. The Ark is a magnificent and powerful object, but it is also a treacherous and deadly one. (Audissino 2014, pp. 159–160)

My analysis, though arriving at similar conclusions about what the music communicates, is much more superficial and perhaps even simplistic. When it comes to talking about this theme at work in the film, Lehman provides a preliminary short summary of the narrative—what happens in the film sequence—and then turns again to the musicological analysis of the score without many references to what happens visually. About the musical closure of the 'Map Room' sequence, he says:

> The exaggeratedly definitive 'functional' cadence to C# minor that finishes the section (and establishes the concluding tonic of the cue) stands out amidst the chromaticism. The cadence, which begins at m. 27, is itself a reinterpretation of the cadence of the more neutral version of the theme presented in example 1. The thunderous underlining of G#2–C# 3—and E5–D#5–C# is so rhetorically overstated that one suspects Williams is intentionally overcompensating for the radical *underdetermination* of tonal trajectory during the passage's bulk. (Lehman 2012a, p. 185)

This is what I wrote about the same sequence:

> [A]n upward chord progression follows Jones turning his head toward the entrance of the room....When Jones inserts the pole, the Ark motif starts over, played forte by the full orchestra, with a vocalizing female choir rising from the orchestral texture and coming to the fore in the second reprise of the theme....An orchestral crescendo of harmonic progressions resolves to the tonic when the sun hits the medallion and a beam illuminates the burial spot. (Audissino 2014, pp. 171–172)

Evidently, we see things from different angles: the music theorist Lehman explains the 'exaggeratedly definitive' cadence in terms of musical construction—film music is analysed on the score. For me, the interest is to explain that cadence in terms of audio-visual coupling: the final chord of the cadence happens exactly in synch with the sun rays hitting the medallion and thus indicating where the Ark is to be found, with a burst of bright light. So, to me, the cadence is so 'exaggeratedly definitive' because the music follows the visuals very tightly, and this obtrusive musical gesture is functional both to eloquently mark the success of the mission—finding where the Ark is located—and to duplicate musically the burst of light that we see visually. The flow of the music and the final cadence closely interacts with such cinematic devices as editing, lighting, and camerawork.

Within the Music Studies perspective, there are also some instances that are not so much musicological analysis as speculations in music theory/philosophy. These are characterised by taking film music or a particular film score as a pretext to talk about music in general. Nicholas Cook's 'Representing Beethoven' takes the BBC TV film *Eroica* (2003, dir. Cellan Jones) as a starting point to discuss how Beethoven is represented in films (Cook 2007), while Peter Franklin's 'The Boy on the Train, or Bad Symphonies and Good Movies' uses the *Star Wars* music to offer a wider reflection on nineteenth-century symphonic music (Franklin 2007). A classical example of using film music to talk about music in general is the T.W. Adorno and Hanns Eisler book *Composing for the Films*, which examined the then-contemporary Hollywood music of the 1930s and 1940s in order not so much to write about what it was like and how it functioned, as to prescribe how it should be—with the particular scope of promoting the use of modernistic music (Adorno and Eisler 2007). Their reflections are somehow invalidated by a basic flaw running throughout the whole text: their misunderstanding of and ideological bias against cinema.[5] Indeed, Adorno and Eisler's study stems from a larger political agenda aiming at condemning Mass Culture and the Culture Industry. Cinema is seen as one of the most dangerous and deceitful manifestations of the Culture Industry, bearing all the marks of its conservative agenda. According to them, cinema is not art. Film music is seen as an even more devious servant of these nefarious cinematic commodities: 'All music in the motion picture is under the sign of utility, rather than lyric expressiveness. Aside from the fact that lyric-poetic inspiration cannot be expected of the composer for the cinema, this kind of inspiration would contradict the embellishing and subordinate function that industrial practice still enforces on the composer' (Adorno and Eisler 2007, p. 4).

The Adorno/Eisler example, since it is concerned both in stating what film music should be and in addressing the 'Big Picture'—Mass Culture— besides film music, also overlaps with another category of film–music analysis, which can be called 'Culturalist.' The aim here is to use film music as a pretext to talk about extra-musical issues such as gender, race, ethnicity, post-colonialism, ideological discourses, subject positioning, and the like. One example is Anahid Kassabian's *Hearing Film*, whose interest is in the cultural use of film music in tracing the dynamics of group identification—composed film score favours 'assimilating identification,' while compilations of songs an 'affiliating identification (Kassabian 2001). Another instance of similarly agenda-driven analysis is Kay Dickinson's *Off Key*, which focusses on examples of 'bad' music in films—such as the Elvis vehicle *Harum Scarum* (1965, dir. Nelson)—as a sign of the times (Dickinson 2008, pp. 3–12). The representation of gender and race through music in particular is a recurring topic. Robynn Stilwell reads the music of *Closet Land* (1991, dir. Bharadwaj) through the lens of feminist studies (Stilwell 2001), while Gary C. Thomas's 'Men at the Keyboard' takes as a pretext the diegetic piano music being played in *The Rope* (1948, dir. Hitchcock) and *Five Easy Pieces* (1970, dir. Rafelson) to discuss masculinity and Michel Foucault's concept of 'heterotopia' (Thomas 2007). Kathryn Kalinak's 'Disciplining Josephine Baker' blends post-colonial and feminist studies to examine 'how gender and race become encoded in film, and, in a large sense, how representations of race and gender circulate through culture' (Kalinak 2000, p. 317). A key representative of this perspective is the film scholar Richard Dyer. Amongst his many interests—spanning from Italian genre cinema to pastiche, to stardom, to race and gender representation— is film music, and he has provided many contributions (notably, a monograph on Nino Rota, one on songs and musicals, and an article on Disco music).[6] Yet, his interest in film music is not per se but subordinated to an overarching culturalist concern: film music is studied as a manifestation of some ideological discourse or as one of the tools of representation. Culturalist analysis sees the music in a given film as something of interest because (and often only if) it can be read as a manifestation of larger cultural phenomena. It is an overlapping category that embraces both Film Studies (Kassabian, Dickinson, Kalinak, and Dyer) and Music Studies (Stilwell, and Thomas). For film scholars wishing to handle film music, culturalist analysis is a convenient way to dodge the problem of musicological analysis. Since the interest here is in the cultural phenomena and ideological messages constructed by the film and the music—the 'content'—close musicological analysis, which is traditionally formalistic (Neumeyer and Buhler 2001, pp. 17–18), can be avoided.

Film Music in Film Studies

Film scholars address music as one of the constituent elements of the film 'text.' Or they simply ignore music altogether and give total pre-eminence to the visuals. Our perception of the world is multimodal (Bertelson and De Gelder 2004), but neuro-psychologically the vision is the dominant sense in humans (Colavita 1974; Colavita and Weisberg 1979;

Posner et al. 1976), which led to a cultural visual bias.[7] Film scholars, for a long time, have addressed film as a predominantly visual medium, hence downplaying or totally neglecting the role of music and sound. Early film theorists—such as Hugo Münsterberg (1916)—focussed their attention on cinema as a visual art form. Ricciotto Canudo defined cinema as a 'plastic art in motion' (Canudo 1988), linking it to the visual arts and thus legitimising the visual bias—which was quite appropriate at the time, given that there were no sound elements on the filmstrip but just images. Yet, with the coming of sound—when a soundtrack was added next to the visual track on the filmstrip, thus undeniably becoming part of the film medium/artefact—the visual-biassed trend continued, fuelled by such theoreticians as Rudolf Arnheim, who decried sound cinema as a mortification of the true cinematic art (Arnheim 1957, p. 154). And Andre Bazin—to name one whose realism-based idea of cinema is the opposite of Arnheim's—hardly mentions sound elements in his 1940/1950s writings. And when he discusses the 'mummy complex' (the desire to crystallise and preserve one person's semblance from ageing and death) as the underlying motivation behind art in general, he compares cinema with paintings and sculptures, again highlighting cinema's visual component (Bazin 2005, p. 9). The visual bias provided a perfect excuse to ignore film music. And those few who approached music did so by devising analytical categories that are deeply influenced by the visual bias.

Consider the traditional terminological pairs 'parallelism/counter point' and 'comment/accompaniment.' When music is emotionally and formally linked to the images—for example, a bucolic landscape accompanied by pastoral music—that would be an instance of 'parallelism' or 'synchronism.' When music is in contrast—a bucolic landscape with industrial-rock music, let us say—that would be 'counterpoint, or 'asynchronism.'[8] Classical examples can be found in some of Rene Clair's films—in *The Million* (1931) a number of people are fighting in an opera house to get hold of a winning lottery ticket kept in a coat pocket, and the noisy sound of a football match is ironically dubbed over the visuals—and in the first Soviet sound films—the finale of *Deserter* (1933, dir. Pudovkin), where the violent repression and the defeat of the demonstrators is scored with a triumphant March.[9] These two terms—parallelism and counterpoint—are controversial both from a terminological point of view and from a theoretical one. First of all, counterpoint in music does not mean a struggle between two melodies that have nothing to do with each other. Counterpoint is the interweaving of two melodic lines having two distinct characters but being in harmonic and rhythmic fusion. Using 'counterpoint' to say that music and visuals are in sharp contrast is not quite correct—pace Eisenstein.[10] From a theoretical point of view, Kathryn Kalinak criticises these terms precisely because they are connected to the long-standing and still active 'visual bias' of film studies: 'Sound was divided according to its function in relation to the image: either parallel or in counterpoint to the visual image. Such nomenclature assumes that meaning is contained in the visual image and that sound can only reinforce or alter what is already there' (Kalinak 1992, p. 24).

Similarly, the comment/accompaniment category implies that music is a subsidiary element of the visuals, not really operating on the same level: the key level is the visual, music can add its own comment or simply provide a sort of accompanying background. In both cases, no real interaction and mutual influence is implied. But the comment/accompaniment pair has also engendered an analytical prejudice. Consider the term 'comment.' The agent that offers a commentary on something is typically external to the event/object that s/he is commenting—think of the sportscaster and a football match, or a Dante scholar commenting on the *Divina Commedia*. The first implication is that 'comment' encourages thinking of music as something not internal to the film. Moreover, for a comment to be interesting, it is important that said comment should add something to the commented event. If we had a voice-over commentary in a documentary that merely described what we are already and clearly seeing in the visuals—'You can see here the ants carrying seeds into their nest'—we would judge said comment pointless and redundant. That would not even be a comment proper but a voice *accompanying* what we are seeing. We expect a comment to explain and to disclose meanings— for example, why those ants are doing what they are doing. Thinking of music as a comment leads to think that music is noteworthy only when it does something foregrounded and meaningful.

This comment/accompaniment division has some discriminatory impact on where the analytical focus is directed, with instances of film music automatically dismissed or celebrated according to which category they belong to. Bernard Herrmann is often singled out as one of the best film composers ever, even praised as the 'Beethoven of Film Music.'[11] Herrmann is famous not so much for his melodic flair as for his penchant for character psychology and narrative subtleties.

For him, music has to add to the images what is not visible: 'Whatever music can do in a film is something mystical. The camera can only do so much; the actors can only do so much; the director can only do so much. But the music can tell you what people are thinking and feeling, and that is the real function of music' (in Thomas 1991, p. 177). Similarly, Ennio Morricone is considered a prominent master of film scoring, whose music is not a background simply accompanying the action but 'foreground music' (Leinberger 2004, p. 18). Indeed, Morricone strongly rejects music that simply replicates the visuals: 'I think that music should be present when the action stops and crystallises;…when…there are thoughts and introspection, not when the action has its own narrative dynamic' (in Miceli 1982, p. 319). Coincidentally, when John Williams is criticised, his detractors typically resort to the allegedly illustrative and duplicative nature of his music: 'plastering movies with bits of what we know, rather than revealing an unseen dimension' (Lebrecht 2002, online). Herrmann's and Morricone's music—in their estimators' view—adds something subtle to the film and hence is superior: it is a comment. Williams's—in his detractors' view—is just a superficial decoration adding nothing meaningful: it is an accompaniment. The comment/accompaniment and counterpoint/parallelism distinctions have come to be improperly charged with an automatic value judgement. They originated from theoreticians[12] and were soon spread through practitioners who were professedly against the new sound technology and advocated 'audiovisual counterpoint' or 'asynchronism' as the only way to save film art from becoming 'talkies' or 'photographed theatre.'[13] Consequently, sound or music that was not asynchronous/in counterpoint with the images was seen as detrimental to film art. And the Adorno/Eisler book *Composing for the Films*, with his unsparing critique of Hollywood music, also had much influence in reinforcing the prejudice against accompaniment music—for example, the typical Hollywood leitmotiv[14] associated with a character is compared to a 'musical lackey, who announces his master with an important air even though the eminent personage is clearly recognizable to everyone' (Adorno and Eisler 2007, p. 3).

A new wave of film scholarship aiming to treat film as an audiovisual unit was launched at the beginning of the 1980s and blossomed in the 1990s. Early contributors were Michel Chion and Rick Altman,[15] with an agenda striving to overturn the traditional 'visual bias' of film scholarship. As one of the audio elements of films, film music has become an important element in the audiovisual paradigm. Therefore, film scholars had to come up with an approach to the study of music in films and some theoretical/analytical tools to deal with it. Musicological approaches have been generally eschewed that might be too focussed on film music as 'music'—that is, 'discuss[ing] music *for* films...instead of analyzing music *in* films' (Altman 2000, p. 340)—and that might demand too specialistic competences from film scholars not possessing an adequate musical education. From a Film Studies perspective, music is a sound element to be addressed as it appears within the film. Film scholars adopted tools already in use in Film Studies that had been imported from literary semiotics and narratology, on the one hand, and Lacanian psychoanalysis corrected with Althusserian ideology, on the other, both pillars of the then-dominant paradigm of post-structuralism—also called 'Screen Theory,' because it was principally disseminated through the British journal *Screen*.

Semiotics is interested in signs and in what they communicate. Film semiotics adapted tools that had been created for textual analysis of literary works, that is, texts whose basic material is verbal language. Although the post-structuralist semiotics moved away from linguistics—as attested by Christian Metz's move to Lacanian Psychoanalysis (Metz 1986)—its approach still shows such derivation and such focus, mainly as to the predominant interest in 'message reading.' When applied to film—whose material is a combination of images and sound in which, in a strict sense, such linguistic analytical categories would be fitting only to intertitles and the verbal content of dialogue—some limitations arise. One is that semiotics works with signs (something that refers to something else or, in C.S. Peirce's words, 'anything which is so determined by something else, called its Object, and so determines an effect upon a person' [Peirce 1998, p. 478]) and codes (sets of conventions used to interpret sign systems and to communicate meanings). Each means of communication has its own signs and codes, and consequently there are semiotic studies of music (Tarasti 1994), theatre (Fischer-Lichte 1992), art (O'Toole 1994), comic books (Saraceni 2003), cinema (Metz 1974), and so on. Therefore, when it comes to music in films, there is the tendency to approach the task with a 'multi-code' mindset, that is, to think of cinema as one code system and of music as another code system, the two of them interacting in some way. This approach promotes a 'separatist' conception of images and music and perpetrates those old parallelism/counterpoint and accompaniment/comment pairs, which are still around in the present day, possibly because, from the 1970s onwards, they have somewhat received a renewed theoretical validation from this 'multi-code mindset.' Indeed, in all these traditional pairs an idea was already subtended that music and film were two separate entities—two sign systems—working on two separate levels, sometimes working in tandem, sometimes struggling against each other. When music is 'parallel' or 'accompanies' the musical semiotic system simply replicates the filmic semiotic system—that is, music is in a 'slave' position to the visuals' 'master' position—and, as in the old days, the risk is to prejudicially consider all the film/music interactions that fall within the parallelism/accompaniment category as less interesting or even not interesting at all. The greater (and often sole) importance given to communication and messages also makes semiotics naturally in favour of 'comment and counterpoint' over 'accompaniment and parallelism.' Parallel or accompanying music has mostly a formal/structural function rather than a communicative one: Mickey-Mousing does not communicate much. Alternatively, because the music does not fight against the images but is subservient to them, such cases of 'parallelism/accompaniment' might be considered interesting only as long as they are 'read' as communicating some sort of ideological manipulation. For example, the analysis would deconstruct how the music is accommodatingly complicit with the ideological tenets of society represented through the apparatus of mainstream cinema, whose aim is to promote conformism and repress counter-readings and critical thinking.[16]

This drive to 'interpret' the film derives from the post-structuralist fusion of the linguistic-based Semiotics with Althusserian Marxism and Lacanian Psychoanalysis, which was a good marriage because Lacan redesigned the Freudian models integrating elements from linguistics—the psyche works as a language and the use of language is a powerful manifestation of the psyche. Textual analysis already had per se a penchant for interpreting texts, that is, unearthing their less obvious meanings. Similarly Psychoanalysis—whether Freudian or Lacanian—is interested in interpreting the psyche's contents through its external manifestations—dreams being the most obvious case. To the interpreting concern of Semiotics, Psychoanalysis added its own concern for interpretation. The output was a theoretical framework in which the film-viewing experience was described as uncannily similar to dreaming or to a hypnotic status, which renders the viewer particularly vulnerable, acritical, and passive. Such situation is perfect to pour into the viewer's mind any ideological indoctrination without him or her noticing that. Two founding texts of the academic study of film music, Claudia Gorbman's *Unheard Melodies* and Caryl Flinn's *Strains of Utopia*, stem from this background. Gorbman adopts Lacanian Psychoanalysis to study why film music is so effective despite its inaudibility: it is so precisely because viewers typically do not pay attention to music that music is allowed to bypass their critical awareness and connect directly to the viewers' unconscious. Film music is like the 'canned music' played in elevators and supermarkets. Its function is to soothe the consumers/viewers and to make them less problematic social elements; if they think less, they are supposed to buy more—in both senses of the term. Music is like an anaesthetic that lowers the listener's critical threshold (Gorbman 1987, pp. 5–7 and 57–64). Flinn explains the success of classical-styled Romantic Hollywood music in terms of its ability of evoking a sense of nostalgia and of triggering reassuring regressions. This 'out-fashioned' music has a soothing effect on listeners since it evokes a 'romantic' past, happier times in which people (supposedly) lived a simpler life in more cohesive communities, as opposed to the fragmentation, individualism, and complexity of contemporary society: music creates a false consciousness that keeps hidden the dominant capitalist ideology at work in Hollywood (Flinn 1992, pp. 70–90). By baring the film's hidden ideological constructs, psychoanalytic film analysis aims to make the viewer aware of the unconscious processes at work and of the ideological manipulation s/he is undergoing during film viewing.

Besides the multi-code problem of semiotics and the 'hermeneutic impulse' (Bordwell 1996, p. 24) of psychoanalysis, there is a shared issue in their adoption of a 'communications model.' In such model, the key interest is in the message being communicated—the 'content'—and less in the material and structural way in which this message is carried—the form. The film form is seen like a box that carries a content—'the message'—and the analyst opens the box, takes the content out, and throws the box away.[17] In a communications model, film is seen primarily as a vehicle for messages. Coming to film music, primary attention is, again, given to those instances of musical comments or 'audiovisual counterpoints' that bring a message, while such formal agency of music as, say, building the rhythm of a scene or emphasising with fitting orchestral colour and timbres the chiaroscuro or the colour patterns of the cinematography are given secondary attention, if any at all. Music that comments is music that communicates some meaning, it is 'high-grade' film music;

music that accompanies is not really communicating anything: it is 'low-grade' film music.

In a communications model, with the first focus of interest fixed on the message, the second focus is on the sender of the message—with the receiver mostly seen as the passive final destination of the communication chain on which the message impacts. In communications, if someone sends a message, her/his motivations for sending it and the explicit and implicit points that s/he places in the message are quite central, and I need to know who the sender of the message is to fully interpret the implicit points and the connotations. If I receive the following message: 'Today Betsy was milked again by little Scottie', I need to know who the sender is. If the sender is Joe the Farmer and I know he owns cows and has a little nephew called Scottie who enjoys lending a helpful hand, then the message means that Betsy the cow was milked by the helpful Scottie once more, and consequently, I form a positive idea of this little Scottie person. If the message was sent by Joe the Disenchanted Grandpa saying that his little grandson Scottie came to meet the grandparents only to get, as usual, money from grandma Betsy, then my idea of little Scottie is much different: an opportunistic little brat. Note that also in Pragmatics, which devotes much attention to the practical use and contextual interpretation of communication exchanges, there is a basic orientation towards the sender: for example, John Austin's locutory, illocutory, and perlocutory acts can be defined as such not in relation to the receiver's but in relation to the sender's intention (Austin 1975). Semiotics came with the basic principle of analysing texts without resorting to biographical data or psychological profiling of the real author: everything useful for the analysis is to be found in the text itself. Yet, in order to fully assess and interpret the meanings of a text in a communications model, it is essential to construct a sender from whom this text has been transmitted. There is no communication without a sender. A 'narrator' and an 'implied author' are needed who can be constructed out of the textual cues themselves. We may either have no idea of who the author in flesh and blood of a given narrative was—we may find an old book by a nameless author—or, even if the author is known, the real person might have different beliefs and proclivities than the ones that emerge as the author from the reading of the book. In any case, the semiotic analysis is still possible because we have the text, and that is all we need. In Literary Studies, to build this hierarchy that descends from the real author (the person in flesh and blood), to the implied author (the system of values, beliefs, and judgements that are ascribable to the author from cues in the text) to the narrator or more narrators, in case of smaller narratives within the larger narrative (the voice/s that tell/s the story) is rather straightforward. Linguistics is of help: for example, deictics clearly indicate the location of the narrator within the story ('here' rather than 'there'), pronouns give an indication of who is sending the message and whom the message is sent to ('I am talking to you' rather than 'She is talking to us') and verb tenses of what the time-line is on which the various moments of the communication take place ('I am told that he received the gift from a man who had received it from a stranger with the promise that he would give it to someone else one day'). These operations are a bit more difficult when imported into Film Studies because there are no such clear-cut linguistic indicators in films: for example, Francesco Casetti's attempts (Casetti 1999), after Benveniste's Theory of Enunciation, to find the cinematic equivalents of 'I', 'You', 'She/He' in, respectively, the subjective point-of-view shot, in the direct interpellation to the viewer, and in the objective shot does not sound much convincing.[18]

The communications model and its need of a sender may have determined the adoption in film–music studies of the terminological pair 'diegetic/non-diegetic,' adapted from literary narratology and introduced by Claudia Gorbman.[19] Diegetic music is the ambiance music that comes from some source within the narrative world and can be heard by the characters—for example, we see a dance orchestra play and we hear a fox trot, to which the characters dance. Non-diegetic music is the 'comment/accompaniment' music that is external to the film's world and cannot be heard by the characters—if Chrissie at the beginning of *Jaws* had heard the menacing shark motif, she would have rushed back to the shore. And 'metadiegetic' (or 'internal diegetic') is the music that comes from a character's psyche. Again, the precise application of these terms is easier in Literary Studies, as the linguistic indicators are of much help, which is not the case in films.[20] However, this diegetic/non-diegetic pair seems to be the basic analytical category to study the interaction of music and film. For example, it has a central and significant role in James Buhler's account:

> Musicals especially often render a strict binary opposition between diegetic and non-diegetic music moot by means of an audio dissolve from source accompaniment, typically a piano, to background orchestral accompaniment....Rick Altman suggests that such audio dissolves mark a

> transition from the real to the ideal realm….The *Ol' Man River* sequence from the 1951 version of *Showboat* makes especially effective use of an audio dissolve….While Joe sings the tune at an oppressively slow, dirge-like tempo, the camera remains fixed on him as wisps of white fog floats by…. Unlike the stage show, where the black community gathers around Joe as he sings, and they join him after his first chorus, the black community of the 1951 film is pushed to the margins….Thus, his performance in the film does not receive the confirmation of a diegetic community as it does in the show. Instead, it is followed by an audio dissolve to a non-diegetic orchestra and wordless choir….The musical effect of the film, therefore, is highly ambivalent, because the community has been displaced to the transcendent and universalising non-diegetic register: for the mythic community thus engendered remains that—not real, not yet actual. The film mirrors society: where society pushes the black community to the side, so too does the film. (Buhler 2001, pp. 42–43)

As expected, an approach based on a communications model tends to guide the attention to prominent film/music moments where the music offers a comment and therefore there is some 'message' whose meaning can be interpreted—'The film mirrors society.' These prominent moments are often those in which music moves from the diegetic to the non-diegetic level. To stress how meaningful these moments are, the concept of 'Fantastical Gap' has been coined to designate such diegetic/non-diegetic dialectics and that transitional intermediate area between the diegetic and non-diegetic (Stilwell 2007). The terms itself suggests that this trespassing of the music is seen as a privileged locus for interpretation, because something almost magical happens—*fantastical*—something of great valence, and hence of great significance (More on this in Chap. 7).

The theoretical debate over the diegetic/non diegetic positioning has been widespread and lively. Recent contributions are Giorgio Biancorosso's discussion of the unexpected shift from one level to the other as an 'epistemological joke,' similar to the ambiguous or 'multistable images' studied by the psychology of perception (Biancorosso 2009); Daniel Yacavone's philosophical distinction between a diegetic world (that inhabited by the characters) and a film world (the overall film system) (Yacavone 2012); Jerrold Levinson, who adds a further term, 'quasi-diegetic' (meaning music that is diegetic but has some unrealistic incongruity, such as no room reverberation) and creates a subdivision of non-diegetic music coming from the 'narrator' (for example, the standard Hollywood score) and non-diegetic music coming from the 'implied film-maker' (for example, the use of music in Godard's films) (Levinson 1996). On the one hand, David Neumeyer has defended the use of these terms as they are, and he embeds them into a theoretical proposal aimed at clarifying their usage (Neumeyer 2009, 27). On the other hand, Ben Winters has criticised the use of these terms as inexact and 'straightjacketing' and has argued that the so-called non-diegetic music is, on the contrary, something that belongs to the diegesis (Winters 2010, p. 229). Sergio Miceli proposed to drop the diegesis-related terminology and rename the three 'internal level' (formerly 'diegetic'), 'external level' (formerly 'non-diegetic'), and 'mediated level' (formerly 'metadiegetic') (Miceli 2011). Aaron Hunter employs the term 'trans-diegetic' to refer to the music that moves from the one level to the other and vice versa—something similar to Stilwell's 'Fantastical Gap' (Hunter 2012). This debate seems to be more philosophically focussed on the ontology of film music—what realm the music belongs to and where it comes from—rather than analytically focussed on what the reasons are for such a trespassing, what the function of the music is.

To summarise the positions we have surveyed so far, music scholars are mostly interested in the micro-analysis (detailed musicological score analysis), in connecting the overall design of the score to the film narrative (not differently from how they would analyse the musical dramaturgy of an opera score), or they take film music as a launching pad for talking about music in general. Film scholars—but also music scholars willing to analyse music with Film Studies tools—have adopted a theoretical framework blending semiotics and psychoanalysis, which has, I think, a series of limitations. It comes with a multi-code mindset, which leads to thinking about film and music as two separate and competing entities; this causes a bias for counterpoint and against parallelism. It stems from a communications model that favours content interpretation over analysis sensu stricto, and, again, this favours counterpoint over parallelism; a communications model also makes the interest stronger for 'where music comes from?' rather than 'what does music do in the film?' and this leads the debate to concentrate on the diegetic/non-diegetic placement of music. The import of a set of psychic mechanisms from psychoanalysis—such as the suturing effect, primary and secondary identification, illusionistic effect of the cinematic apparatus and so on—posits a viewer that is but a passive subject responding in predictable and mechanical ways: a deconstructionist hermeneutics aimed at unmasking the deceitful ideological messages is thus favoured. The semio-psychoanalitic framework in general gives particular salience to the film/music moments where music comments, while it underestimates or neglects those moments where the music 'simply' accompanies. In the next chapter I survey some more recent attempts at bridging the gap between Music Studies and Film Studies and at eradicating the separatist conception.

Notes

1. Named after the late-nineteenth-century theorist Hugo Riemann, it was developed by Lewin (1987). For an introduction, see Cohn (1998). It should be noted that such strongly formalistic and textual-analysis-oriented approaches as the Schenkerian and the Neo-Riemannian do not represent the majority of contemporary Music Studies.
2. See, for example, Murphy (2014) and Lehman (2012b). In his study of chordal progressions, Schneller prefers a more tonal-oriented approach called 'Modal Interchange' (Schneller 2013).
3. Actually, this is encouraging for everyone, because obtaining the access to the full film scores for analysis is not as easy as going to a library and asking for the score to, say, *Parsifal*; it can indeed be quite daunting to find out where the materials are and how and from whom one should get the permission to access them, and to verify if the retrieved materials are indeed the original ones. On this, see Wright (1989) and Winters (2007a).
4. *The Journal of Film Music Online*, http://www.equinoxpub.com/journals/index.php/JFM. Accessed on 2 December 2016.
5. A sharp critique of Adorno and Eisler's book is in Miceli (2009, pp. 536–537).
6. Dyer (1979, 2010, 2012).
7. On film music and cultural biasses based on the visual dominance, see Kalinak (1992, pp. 20–39).
8. On the origin of the term, see Kalinak (1992, pp. 20–29).
9. Audio/visual counterpoint in early sound films, Soviet ones in particular, is discussed and exemplified in Thompson (1980).
10. The same criticism of Eisenstein's use of the term 'counterpoint' can be found in Chion (1994, pp. 36–37), who suggests replacing it with 'audiovisual dissonance.' A critique of Eisenstein's theory of audiovisual counterpoint and 'vertical montage' is offered in Cook (1998, pp. 57–97).
11. See Neumeyer et al. (2000, p. 21). The privileged consideration that Herrmann has long enjoyed is examined in Rosar (2003): '[He was the

object of the] first dissertation devoted to a film composer....It could almost be said that Herrmann studies emerged as a field of academic inquiry prior to film music studies as a whole' (p. 145).
12. The 'parallelism/counterpoint' and 'comment/accompaniment' pairs can be traced back to the late 1920s, most notably in the famous 'Statement' on sound: Eisenstein et al. (1994). This binary separation was then further elaborated by Arnheim (1957, p. 209), Balázs (1970, p. 236) and Kracauer (1965, pp. 139–142).
13. On the resistance against the 'talkies,' see Wierzbicki (2009, pp. 96–101).
14. The use of leitmotiv in cinema has been criticised on the grounds of its being inadequate for the film medium (Adorno and Eisler 2007, pp. 2–3) and because the film–music 'leitmotiv' is not the Wagnerian leitmotiv sensu stricto (Miceli 2009, pp. 667–670). It has been proposed that 'condensed leitmotiv' would be a better term for film music (Brown 1994, pp. 97–118).
15. The journal issue *Yale French Studies* 60: Cinema/Sound, edited by Rick Altman, was devoted to film sound and brought attention to the need of seeing cinema as an audiovisual art (Altman 1980). The focus on film sound was established by Weis and Belton (1985) and then consolidated by Chion (1994) and Altman (1992). The study of film as not a visual-based but as an audiovisual medium seems now to be well established, carried on, for example, by Chion (2009), Beck and Grajeda (2008) and Donnelly (2005, 2014).
16. See, for example, Anahid Kassabian's reading of Hollywood music as 'assimilating' (Kassabian 2001, pp. 2–3) or Heather Laing's feminist approach (Laing 2007), or Neil Lerner's interpretation of *Close Encounters of the Third Kind* and *Star Wars* as authoritarian and masculinist scores (Lerner 2004).
17. For example, the term 'style' is defined as an ineffable and even 'unidentifiable' concept by the semiologist Christian Metz (1995, p. 183).
18. Casetti too seems to have abandoned this line of research and has turned to Culturalism, as he stated during the conference 'Il lavoro sul film. La Post-Analisi' at the University of Turin, Italy, in December 2003—see Carluccio and Villa (2005). Indeed, his latest books deal with cinema, culture, and society (Casetti 2008, 2015). The pitfalls of adapting the enunciation theory to films are detailed in Bordwell (1985, pp. 21–26). Yet, a revival of Casetti and Metz's cinematic Theory of Enunciation under the framework of Cognitive Psychology was attempted in Buckland (2000).
19. The terms intradiegetic, extradiegetic, and metadiegetic are inherited from Genette (1972), in which they are used to define the location of the narrating voice in relation to the narrative world, thus permitting to identify a nesting that is helpful to the narratological analysis. So, an

intradiegetic narrator would be the voice of some character telling the story from within the narrative world (e.g., Philip Marlowe in a Raymond Chandler's novel); an extradiegetic narrator would be the often omniscient narratorial voice placed outside of the narrative world (e.g., the narrating voice in the Lord of the Rings books); and the metadiegetic narrator would be one character telling a story within the main narrative, in which story he acts as a extradiegetic narrator (e.g., the Mr Mulliner character in P.G. Woodehouse's *Mr Mulliner Speaking* [1929]). The application of Genette's categories to film music is discussed in Gorbman (1987, pp. 20–26), who modified them into 'diegetic' and 'non-diegetic'.
20. 'The idea of assigning different music to different narrative levels clearly results from a tendency to see cinema in overtly literary narrative terms.… Yet while Genette's description of these discrete levels is entirely convincing when we are faced with the epistolary narrative of a novel, it is far less obviously applicable to most narrative cinema' (Winters 2010, pp. 22–26).

References

Abbate, Carolyn, and Roger Parker. 2012. *A History of Opera: The Last Four Hundred Years*. London: Allen Lane.

Adorno, Theodor W., and Hanns Eisler. 2007 [1947]. *Composing for the Films*. London and New York: Continuum.

Altman, Rick (ed.). 1980. *Yale French Studies* 60.

Altman, Rick (ed.). 1992. *Sound Theory. Sound Practice*. London and New York: Routledge.

Altman, Rick. 2000. Inventing the Cinema Soundtrack. Hollywood's Multiplane Sound System. In *Music and Cinema*, ed. James Buhler, Caryl Flinn, and David Neumeyer, 339–359. Hanover, NH: Wesleyan University Press.

Arnheim, Rudolf. 1957. *Film as Art*. Berkeley, CA: University of California Press.

Audissino, Emilio. 2014. *John Williams's Film Music. 'Jaws,' 'Star Wars,' 'Raiders of the Lost Ark,' and the Return of the Classical Hollywood Music Style*. Madison, WI: University of Wisconsin Press.

Austin, John L. 1975. *How to Do Things with Words*, ed. J.O. Urmson and Marina Sbisà. Cambridge, MA: Harvard University Press.

Balázs, Béla. 1970 [1945]. *Theory of the Film: Character and Growth of a New Art*, trans. Edith Bone. New York: Dover.

Bazin, André. 2005. *What is Cinema?* vol. 1, trans. and ed. Hugh Gray. Berkeley, CA: University of California Press.

Beck, Jay, and Tony Grajeda (eds.). 2008. *Lowering the Boom: Critical Studies in Film Sound*. Champaign, IL: University of Illinois Press.

Bertelson, Paul, and Béatrice De Gelder. 2004. The Psychology of Multimodal Perception. In *Crossmodal Space and Crossmodal Attention*, ed. Charles Spence and Jon Driver, 141–178. Oxford: Oxford University Press.

Biancorosso, Giorgio. 2009. The Harpist in the Closet: Film Music as Epistemological Joke. *Music and the Moving Image* 2 (3): 11–33.

Bordwell, David. 1985. *Narration in the Fiction Film*. Madison, WI: University of Wisconsin Press.

Bordwell, David. 1996. Contemporary Film Studies and the Vicissitudes of Grand Theory. In *Post-Theory. Reconstructing Film Studies*, ed. David Bordwell and Nöel Carroll, 3–36. Madison, WI: University of Wisconsin Press.

Brown, Royal S. 1994. *Overtones and Undertones. Reading Film Music*. Berkeley, CA: University of California Press.

Buckland, Warren. 2000. *The Cognitive Semiotics of Film*. Cambridge and London: Cambridge University Press.

Buhler, James. 2000. Star Wars, Music, and Myth. In *Music and Cinema*, ed. James Buhler, Caryl Flinn, and David Neumeyer, 33–57. Hanover, NH: Wesleyan University Press.

Buhler, James. 2001. Analytical and Interpretive Approaches to Film Music (II): Analysing Interactions of Music and Film. In *Film Music. Critical Approaches*, ed. K.J. Donnelly, 39–61. New York: Continuum International Publishing.

Canudo, Ricciotto. 1988. The Birth of a Sixth Art [1911]. In *French Film Theory and Criticism: A History/Anthology, Vol. I: 1907–1929*, ed. Richard Abel, 58–65. Princeton, NJ: Princeton University Press.

Carluccio, Giulia, and Federica Villa (eds.). 2005. *La post-analisi. Intorno e oltre l'analisi del film*. Turin: Edizioni Kaplan.

Casetti, Francesco. 1999 [1986]. *Inside the Gaze: The Fiction Film and Its Spectator*, trans. Charles O' Brien and Nell Andrew. Bloomington, IN: Indiana University Press.

Casetti, Francesco. 2008. *Eye of the Century: Film, Experience, Modernity*, trans. Erin Larkin and Jennifer Pranolo. New York: Columbia University Press.

Casetti, Francesco. 2015. *The Lumière Galaxy: Seven Key Words for the Cinema to Come*. New York: Columbia University Press.

Chion, Michel. 1994 [1990]. *Audio-Vision. Sound on Screen*, trans. Claudia Gorbmam. New York: Columbia University Press.

Chion, Michel. 2009. *Film: A Sound Art*, trans. Claudia Gorbman. New York: Columbia University Press.

Cohn, Richard. 1998. Introduction to Neo-Riemannian Theory: A Survey and a Historical Perspective. *Journal of Music Theory* 42 (2): 167–180.

Colavita, Francis B. 1974. Human Sensory Dominance. *Perception & Psychophysics* 16 (2): 409–412.

Colavita, Francis B., and Daniel Weisberg. 1979. A Further Investigation of Visual Dominance. *Perception & Psychophysics* 25 (4): 345–347.

Cook, Nicholas. 1998. *Analysing Musical Multimedia*. Oxford: Clarendon Press.

Cook, Nicholas. 2007. Representing Beethoven. Romance and Sonata Form in Simon Cellan Jones's *Eroica*. In *Beyond the Soundtrack. Representing Music in Cinema*, ed. Daniel Goldmark, Lawrence Kramer, and Richard Leppert, 27–47. Berkeley: University of California Press.

Dickinson, Kay. 2008. *Off Key. When Film and Music Won't Work Together*. Oxford and New York: Oxford University Press.

Donnelly, K.J. 2005. *The Spectre of Sound: Music in Film and Television*. London: BFI.

Donnelly, K.J. 2014. *Occult Aesthetics: Synchronization in Sound Film*. Oxford and New York: Oxford University Press.

Dyer, Richard. 1979. In Defense of Disco. *Gay Left* 8 (Summer): 20–23.

Dyer, Richard. 2010. *Nino Rota. Music, Film and Feeling*. Basingstoke and London: Palgrave MacMillan/BFI.

Dyer, Richard. 2012. *In the Space of a Song: The Uses of Song in Film*, rev. ed. Abingdon and New York: Routledge.

Eisenstein, Sergei M., Vsevolod I. Pudovkin, and Grigori V. Alexandrov. 1994 [1928]. A Statement, trans. Jay Leyda. In *The Film Factory: Russian and Soviet Cinema in Documents 1896–1939*, new ed., ed. Ian Christie and Richard Taylor, 234–235. London and New York: Routledge, new ed.

Fischer-Lichte, Erika. 1992. *The Semiotics of Theater*. Bloomington, IN: Indiana University Press.

Flinn, Caryl. 1992. *Strains of Utopia. Gender, Nostalgia, and Hollywood Music*. Princeton, NJ: Princeton University Press.

Franklin, Peter. 2007. The Boy on the Train, or Bad Symphonies and Good Movies. In *Beyond the Soundtrack. Representing Music in Cinema*, ed. Daniel Goldmark, Lawrence Kramer, and Richard Leppert, 13–26. Berkeley, Los Angeles and London: University of California Press.

Genette, Gérard. 1972. *Figures III*. Paris: Seuil.

Gorbman, Claudia. 1987. *Unheard Melodies. Narrative Film Music*. London and Bloomington: BFI/Indiana University Press.

Hunter, Aaron. 2012. When is the Now in the Here and There? Trans-Diegetic Music in Hal Ashby's *Coming Home*. *Alphaville: Journal of Film and Screen Media* 3 (Summer). Online http://www.alphavillejournal.com/Issue%203/HTML/ArticleHunter.html. Accessed 12 Apr 2017.

Kalinak, Kathryn. 1992. *Settling the Score. Music and the Classical Hollywood Film*. Madison, WI: University of Wisconsin Press.

Kalinak, Kathryn. 2000. Disciplining Josephine Baker. Gender, Race, and the Limits of Disciplinarity. In *Music and Cinema*, ed. James Buhler, Caryl Flinn, and David Neumeyer, 316–335. Hanover, NH: Wesleyan University Press.

Kassabian, Anahid. 2001. *Hearing Film: Tracking Identification in Contemporary Hollywood Film Music*. New York and London: Routledge.
Kracauer, Siegfried. 1965. *Theory of Film: The Redemption of Physical Reality*. New York: Oxford University Press.
Laing, Heather. 2007. *The Gendered Score: Music in 1940s Melodrama and the Woman's Film*. Aldershot: Ashgate.
Lebrecht, Norman. 2002. John Williams—The Magpie Maestro. *La Scena Musicale*, 20 (November). Online www.scena.org/columns/lebrecht/021120-NL-williams.html. Accessed 10 Jan 2017.
Lehman, Frank. 2012a. Music Theory Through the Lens of Film. *Journal of Film Music* 5 (1–2): 179–198.
Lehman, Frank. 2012b. Reading Tonality Through Film: Transformational Hermeneutics and the Music of Hollywood. PhD dissertation, Harvard University, Cambridge.
Leinberger, Charles. 2004. *Ennio Morricone's the Good, the Bad and the Ugly, a Film Score Guide*. Lanham, MD: Scarecrow.
Lerner, Neil. 2004. Nostalgia, Masculinist Discourse and Authoritarianism in John Williams' Scores for *Star Wars* and *Close Encounters of the Third Kind*. In *Off the Planet. Music, Sound and Science Fiction Cinema*, ed. Philip Hayward, 96–108. Eastleigh: John Libbey Publishing.
Levinson, Jerrold. 1996. Film Music and Narrative Agency. In *Post-theory. Reconstructing Film Studies*, ed. David Bordwell and Nöel Carroll, 248–282. Madison, WI: University of Wisconsin Press.
Lewin, David. 1987. *Generalized Musical Intervals and Transformations*. New Haven, CT: Yale University Press.
Metz, Christian. 1974 [1968]. *Film Language: A Semiotics of the Cinema*, trans. Michael Taylor. Chicago, IL: University of Chicago Press.
Metz, Christian. 1986 [1977]. *The Imaginary Signifier. Psychoanalysis and the Cinema*, trans. Celia Britton, Annwyl Williams, Ben Brewster, and Alfred Guzzetti. Bloomington and Indianapolis, IN: Indiana University Press, reprint ed.
Metz, Christian. 1995 [1991]. *L'enunciazione impersonale o il luogo del film*, trans. Augusto Sainati. Naples: ESI.
Miceli, Sergio. 1982. *La musica nel film. Arte e artigianato*. Fiesole: Discanto.
Miceli, Sergio. 2009. *Musica per film. Storia, Estetica, Analisi, Tipologie*. Lucca and Milan: LIM-Ricordi.
Miceli, Sergio. 2011. Miceli's Method of Internal, External, and Mediated Levels: Elements for the Definition of a Film-Musical Dramaturgy, trans. Gillian B. Anderson, with the assistance of Lidia Bagnoli. *Music and the Moving Image* 4 (2): 1–29.

Moormann, Peter. 2012. Composing with Types and Flexible Modules: John Williams' Two-Note Ostinato for *Jaws* and its Use in Film-Music History. *Journal of Film Music* 5 (1–2): 165–168.

Münsterberg, Hugo. 1916. *The Photoplay. A Psychological Study*. New York and London: Appleton.

Murphy, Scott. 2014. Transformational Theory and the Analysis of Film Music. In *The Oxford Handbook of Film Music Studies*, ed. David Neumeyer and James Buhler, 471–499. Oxford and New York: Oxford University Press.

Nattiez, Jean Jacques. 1990. *Music and Discourse. Toward a Semiology of Music*, trans. Carolyn Abbate. Princeton, NJ: Princeton University Press.

Neumeyer, David. 1998. Tonal Design and Narrative in Film Music: Bernard Herrmann's *A Portrait of Hitch* and *The Trouble With Harry*. *Indiana Theory Review* 19 (1–2): 87–123.

Neumeyer, David. 2009. Diegetic/Nondiegetic: A Theoretical Model. *Music and the Moving Image* 2 (1): 26–39.

Neumeyer, David, and James Buhler. 2001. Analytical and Interpretive Approaches to Film Music (I): Analysing the Music. In *Film Music. Critical Approaches*, ed. K.J. Donnelly, 16–38. New York: Continuum International Publishing.

Neumeyer, David, James Buhler, and Caryl Flinn. 2000. Introduction. In *Music and Cinema*, ed. James Buhler, Caryl Flinn, and David Neumeyer, 1–30. Hanover, NH: Wesleyan University Press.

O'Toole, Michael. 1994. *The Language of Displayed Art*. Cranbury, NJ: Associated University Presses.

Peirce, Charles S. 1998. *The Essential Peirce*, vol. 2, ed. The Peirce Edition Project. Bloomington, IN: Indiana University Press.

Posner, Michael I., Mary J. Nissen, and Raymond M. Klein. 1976. Visual Dominance: An Information-Processing Account of Its Origins and Significance. *Psychological Review* 83 (2): 157–171.

Rosar, William H. 2003. Bernard Herrmann: The Beethoven of Film Music? *Journal of Film Music* 1 (2/3): 121–150.

Saraceni, Mario. 2003. *The Language of Comics*. New York: Routledge.

Schneller, Tom. 2013. Modal Interchange and Semantic Resonance in Themes by John Williams. *Journal of Film Music* 6 (1): 49–74.

Stilwell, Robynn J. 2001. Sound and Empathy: Subjectivity, Gender and the Cinematic Soundscape. In *Film Music. Critical Approaches*, ed. K.J. Donnelly, 167–187. New York: Continuum International Publishing.

Stilwell, Robynn J. 2007. The Fantastical Gap Between Diegetic and Nondiegetic. In *Beyond the Soundtrack. Representing Music in Cinema*, ed. Daniel Goldmark, Lawrence Kramer, and Richard Leppert, 184–203. Berkeley, Los Angeles and London: University of California Press.

Tagg, Philip. 2012. *Music's Meanings: A Modern Musicology for Non-Musos*. New York and Huddersfield: Mass Media Music Scholars' Press.

Tagg, Philip, and Bob Clarida. 2003. *Ten Little Tunes. Towards a Musicology of the Mass Media*. New York and Montreal: The Mass Media Musicologists' Press.

Tarasti, Eero. 1994. *A Theory of Musical Semiotics*. Bloomington, IN: Indiana University Press.

Thomas, Gary C. 2007. Men at the Keyboard: Liminal Spaces and the Heterotopian Function of Music. In *Beyond the Soundtrack. Representing Music in Cinema*, ed. Daniel Goldmark, Lawrence Kramer, and Richard Leppert, 277–292. Berkeley, Los Angeles and London: University of California Press.

Thomas, Tony. 1991. *Film Score. The Art and Craft of Movie Music*. Burbank, CA: Riverwood.

Thompson, Kristin. 1980. Early Sound Counterpoint. *Yale French Studies* 60: 115–140.

Weis, Elisabeth, and John Belton (eds.). 1985. *Film Sound: Theory and Practice*. New York: Columbia University Press.

Wierzbicki, James. 2009. *Film Music. A History*. Abingdon and New York: Routledge.

Winters, Ben. 2007a. Catching Dreams: Editing Film Scores for Publication. *Journal of the Royal Musical Association* 132 (1): 115–140.

Winters, Ben. 2007b. *Erich Wolfgang Korngold's the Adventures of Robin Hood. A Film Score Guide*. Lanham, MD: Scarecrow.

Winters, Ben. 2010. The Non-Diegetic Fallacy: Film, Music, and Narrative Space. *Music & Letters* 91 (2): 224–244.

Wright, H. Stephen. 1989. The Materials of Film Music: Their Nature and Accessibility. In *Film Music 1*, ed. Clifford McCarty. New York and London: Garland Publishing.

Yacavone, Daniel. 2012. Spaces, Gaps, and Levels: From the Diegetic to the Aesthetic in Film Theory. *Music, Sound and the Moving Image* 6 (1): 21–37.

CHAPTER 3

Recent Attempts to Bridge the Gap and Overcome a Separatist Conception

As we have seen, there are two preconceptions that influence the analysis of music in films. The first is a 'separatist conception' of the audiovisual artefacts: music and visuals are thought of as two distinct entities, with the visual medium being the dominant. This has contributed to the creation of a disciplinary gap. Music Studies have traditionally treated music as a stand-alone object to be analysed in relation to the notes written on the score rather than the sounds present in the film. Film Studies have given precedence to the visuals and mostly neglected the presence of the music in the film. The second preconception is the generally adopted 'communications model' that causes interpretation to be emphasised over general analysis. Attention is pointed to those instances in which the music communicates some 'content' to be interpreted, to the detriment of those other instances in which the music 'merely' performs some formal task.

Proposals to Overcome the Separatism

The separatist conception has been fought for more than two decades now, with scholars operating within the 'audiovisual' paradigm advocating a change of perspective. Kathryn Kalinak, in 1992, stated:

> A conceptual model in which music and image share power in shaping perception has a number of important implications for the study of film music as well as the study of film itself. Among them is the necessity of

confronting a reliance upon terminology that perpetuates, wittingly and sometimes unwittingly, an earlier paradigm. (Kalinak 1992, p. 30)

The study of music in films needed new perspectives and new, possibly non-separatist, terminology. An important step forward was the 1998 book by the musicologist Nicholas Cook, a study of the interactions of music with the other media seeking 'to extend the boundaries of music theory to encompass…words and moving images' (Cook 1998, p. vi). First of all, it aimed to discard the long-standing prejudice that had been favouring 'absolute music' or 'music alone' (autonomous art music written for concert performances, like Beethoven's symphonies) against 'applied music' (music written to complement some other non-music medium, the theatre, ballet, cinema, etc.), 'to challenge the very coherence of the concept of absolute music….Outside the imagination of aestheticians and analysts, music never *is* alone' (Cook 1998, p. 265). This is a much welcome attitude, as the basic requirement to study film music rigorously is to be free from the prejudice that film music is a necessarily inferior type of music, but also because thinking of music as something that is 'never alone' is a way to expand the medium's boundaries and proceed, seemingly, towards a non-separatist conception of music and the other media it encounters. Distinguishing between the concept of 'meaning' and that of 'effect' (Cook 1998, p. 4), Cook also seems to be taking into account a model that is broader in scope than the communications model: 'Multimedia lies in the *perceived* interaction of media' (Cook 1998, p. 33). The media involved in the multimedia product are like the two terms of a metaphor, similar but producing a new result when metaphorically associated: 'The metaphor model…invokes similarity not as an end, but as a means. Meaning now inheres not in similarity, but in the difference that similarity articulates by virtue of the transfer of attributes' (Cook 1998, pp. 80–81). Cook also provides an analytical tool that can be practically applied, the 'similarity/difference test' (are the two media communicating the same thing or not?), which brings three kinds of results. If the two are indeed similar, there is a relationship based on 'conformance'; if they differ, there can be either a state of 'complementation' stemming from the two elements being contrary to each other (an 'undifferentiated difference,' in Cook's words) or a state of 'contest' deriving from the two elements being in contradiction (a 'collision or confrontation between the opposed terms') (Cook 1998, pp. 98–102). In the case of film music, the three effects of these three interactions would be, respectively, one of 'amplification' (basically, the case of the so-called 'parallel' music, as in Mickey-Mousing, in which music closely mirrors what happens on-screen); 'projection,' in which music adds something new to the visuals, 'the extension of meaning into a new domain, but without the collision of signification that defines contest' (as an example, Cook points to Bernard Herrmann's music communicating the characters' inner feeling, and thus projection would identify with those types of accompaniment music subtler than Mickey-Mousing); 'dominance,' in which music antagonises, resists, and struggles against the meaning presented by the visuals (this can be assimilated to the so-called 'audiovisual counterpoint'). This proposal discarded the rigid dualism of parallel/counterpoint in favour of a three-zone spectrum. Also, the metaphor model, with its implication of the reciprocal transformation of the two terms involved, jettisons the visual bias and its separatist approach: 'Music—like any other filmic element—participates in the *construction* of cinematic characters, not their reproduction, just as it participates in the construction, not the reproduction, of all cinematic effects' (Cook 1998, p. 86).

Since Cook's study offers a viable method to study the interaction of music with other media, why not use it for film music? Because it offers a limited applicability for films. Its broader interest is in multimedia products more than in films and it is, again, fundamentally concerned with 'meaning.' Cook's interest is for 'readings' and deconstruction: 'Music is the discourse that passes itself off as nature; it participates in the construction of meaning, but disguises its meaning as effect. Here is the source of its singular efficacy as a hidden persuader' (Cook 1998, p. 21). This view is likely, once again, to favour 'counterpoint' over 'parallel' music because the former is the one that produces some meaning. 'Conformance' (synchronism, 'parallelism'), says Cook, 'is not of multimedia but of 'juxtapositional hybrid art-forms' (Cook 1998, p. 106). For Cook, 'Contest' (asynchronism, 'counterpoint') is the relationship that characterises the truly multimedia products: '[E]ach medium strives to deconstruct the other, and so create space for itself.... Conformance begins with originary meaning, whether located within one medium or diffused between all; contest, on the other hand, ends in meaning' (Cook 1998, pp. 103–106). The use of the term 'contest' also reintroduces some separatism. Instead of thinking of music and visuals as two interrelated elements of a unified whole—producing effects of audiovisual harmony (conformance) or disharmony (contest)—'contest' envisages two separate elements fighting 'for the same terrain.' In a non-separatist conception, music and visual *build together* that terrain. As is often the case, a separatist conception is accompanied by a communications model, and Cook's study is no exception, despite some premises that, at first, may have led us to think otherwise. The very fact that it is about 'multi*media*' is already telling:

> The basic idea of a medium…is that it is *just* a medium, *a channel of communication* [emphasis mine], and as such transparent.…[M]y argument in this book is predicated on the assumption that media such as music, texts, and moving pictures do not just *communicate meaning* [emphasis mine], but participate actively in its construction. They *mediate* it, in other words. (Cook 1998, p. 261)

As in any approach based on a communications model, a central interest is in 'messages' and 'meanings,' which implies a predominance of interpretation. One example that Cook provides is revealing as to how the focus on 'contest' and the 'rush to interpretation' (Middleton 1990, p. 220) may prevaricate historically/practically informed analysis. In a dialogue scene between the Marlon Brando and the Eva Marie Saint characters in *On the Waterfront* (1954, dir. Kazan), Leonard Bernstein's music is too texturally thick for a dialogue scene and we can hear that it was noticeably dialled down at the audio-mixing stage to make room for the actors' lines. This had already been pointed out by Roy Prendergast, who had provided a straightforward, technical explanation: unfamiliar with the film medium, Bernstein approached the task as if he were writing for the stage or the concert hall, not taking into account the need to make room for the dialogue (Prendergast 1977, pp. 130–132). Instead, Cook 'reads' in this anomaly an episode of 'contest': 'music and words are fighting for the same terrain, and the words establish their dominance only by brute force (literary *ex machina*) [by having the music dialled down at the mixing table]. By contrast, conventional underscore music is specifically composed to complement the words' (Cook 1998, p. 141). This sounds like over-interpretation. I am more inclined to explain this anomaly in terms of Bernstein's inexperience, not as a deliberate act of contest. Moreover, there are other documented cases of concert composers lacking film experience whose film music was similarly too imposing—for example, Aaron Copland's score for *Of Mice and Men* (1939, dir. Milestone).[1]

Another influential theorist against separatism, and one of the most active proponents of the new audiovisual paradigm, has been Michel Chion—he called Film a 'Sound Art.' His neologism 'synchresis'—a crasis of synchronism and synthesis—is 'the spontaneous and irresistible weld produced between a particular auditory phenomenon and visual phenomenon when they occur at the same time' (Chion 1994, p. 63). Synchresis aptly conveys the non-separatist idea that sound and image are fused into a single entity through their synchronisation. Another proposal has come from Rick Altman, the 'mise-en-bande' diagram, a notational method for audiovisual analysis that encompasses all the sound and visual elements (Altman 2000). More recently, the film scholar K.J. Donnelly has contributed a book-length study on the aesthetics of audio-visual synchronisation, stressing the equal importance of sound and visuals, and employing Gestalt Theory to account for the holistic perception of audiovisual products (Donnelly 2014). As the powers of film editing are traditionally explained with the 'Kuleshov Effect,' Donnelly explains the powers of audiovisual synchronisation with the 'McGurk Effect' and the 'Ventriloquist Effect' (Donnelly 2014, pp. 17–24). The latter explains the brain's tendency to find a visual anchorage to sound, to the point of even synchronising a sound to a visual source that is not really producing that sound—as in the case of ventriloquists (Choe et al. 1975). Says Donnelly, 'When images and sound relations are ambiguous, sound compels the perceiver to try to make sense of elements by integrating sound and vision into a single event....Consequently, when presented with images and sounds that might possibly be construed as the same source, we assume it is so' (Donnelly 2014, p. 26). The 'Ventriloquist Effect' supports the idea that, in film viewing, we anchor the visual and the aural together, perceiving an interconnected whole. One step further, the 'McGurk Effect' describes the brain's tendency to create, from the fusion of one visual and one aural stimulus, a percept that is different from the two stimuli taken separately. In the original 1976 experiment, the silent video of a person's lips articulating the sound /ga/ was synchronised with the sound of a voice saying /ba/, which produced /da/ as a resulting percept (McGurk and MacDonald 1976). Donnelly concludes: 'The McGurk Effect...demonstrates the interaction of sound and image stimuli in perception and cognition. Rather than being totally separate channels, our vision is able to affect our hearing, suggesting that the senses are never fully autonomous when used in combination' (Donnelly 2014, p. 25). The 'McGurk Effect' offers strong evidence to encourage us to consider sound and visuals at the same level in films, as it demonstrates that our perception of the world itself is interconnectedly audiovisual.

An attempt to bridge the gap between the two disciplines is the 2015 monograph by the music scholar Danijela Kulezic-Wilson on the musicality of film, an investigation of the long-standing analogy between film and music dating back to the 1920s French Impressionist cinema.[2] This study distances itself from the 'usual historical, semiotic, musicological or cultural approaches' (Kulezic-Wilson 2015, p. 4), embracing instead phenomenology, cognitive psychology and Gestalt theory—in particular, Cooper and Meyer's study on grouping and perception of rhythms (Cooper and Meyer 1960). In its musical and yet film-oriented approach, this is a valuable contribution to supersede the separatist conception: 'a shift from the habitual segregation of the visual ad sonic aspects of film towards a practice which recognizes their interdependence in realizing film's musicality.' (Kulezic-Wilson 2015, p. 5). Similarly, from a film scholar's perspective, Lea Jacobs has scrutinised rhythm in the production and post-production practices of early sound cinema, showing how discussions of tempo, pacing, and rhythm and the integration and synchronisation of sound and visuals were central even in those formative years of cinema as an audio-visual art (Jacobs 2014). On the other side, the musicologist David Neumeyer, developing Chion's work, has not focussed on the musicality of films but on the 'vococentric' nature of narrative cinema, proposing a method to study the role of music in the hierarchical system of the soundtrack dominated by dialogue (Neumeyer 2015).

Instead of focussing on the corroboration of the audiovisual nature of cinema and superseding a separatist conception, other recent proposals have directly tackled the gap between music studies and film studies. To do so, they have offered a linking non-musicological theoretical framework, and hence handy for both departments. Dominique Nasta starts from a non-separatist perspective, advocating an approach that does not see films as something principally visual (Nasta 1991, p. 43). Then, she proposes to study sound and music in films employing Peirce's Semiotics and Grice's Pragmatics—with references to Wittgenstein's philosophy of language too. Her proposal has offered innovative points (for example, the use of Peircian's Semiotics instead of the more common Saussurian), but it is much too focussed—from the very title of the book—on the 'meaning in film' and on interpretation over analysis, which continues to favour those moment in which music 'communicate' some 'content.' We are still in the 'communications model', which tends to slip into a separatist conception even with those who admittedly adhere to the non-separatist audiovisual paradigm—indeed, Nasta still uses the old term 'counterpoint.' (Nasta 1991, pp. 73–77). More recently, Guido Heldt proposed an approach to the analysis of film music titled *Music and Levels of Narration in Film. Steps across the Border* (Heldt 2013) and based on Edward Branigan's film narratology (Branigan 1992). The book presents itself as a detailed account of all the possible positions that music can have within the diegetic/non-diegetic spectrum. This proposal still endorses a communications model; it is not about 'What is the function of the music?' but 'Where is the music coming from?' Therefore, it offers very sharp analytical instruments that nevertheless have a limited employability: the interpretation of film music, within a semiotics/narratology framework, in those moments in which it crosses the narrative borders between one level of the diegesis and the other.

Another limit that can often be found in many proposals is the adoption of some 'Grand Theory' around which the approaches are shaped and to which the practical applications always strive to conform. Instead of analysing what the film at hand is and selecting adequate analytical tools suitable to that specific film (bottom-up route), the risk of the 'Grand Theory' approach is that of moving along a top-down route; theory comes first and then a film is selected that conforms to the specific theory. If Hollywood is dominated by a patriarchal system expressed through the power of the Gaze and all the stories are about the Oedipal complex, then analysing a film means to focus on the Gaze dynamics that will certainly betray the patriarchal systems underneath and to look for the traces of Oedipus in the narrative.[3] Surely, there are films that ostensibly call for the application of psychoanalytical tools: *Psycho* (1960, dir. Hitchcock) is one that clearly asks for Oedipal interpretations, and *Mulholland Drive* (2000, dir. Lynch) is one whose obscure narrative can be clarified through the Freudian dream-work theory. But one thing is to select a theory as an analytical/interpretive tool when the film calls for it (bottom-up route) and another is to elect one as the dominating theoretical framework to be applied to everything (top-down route). With the latter, the result is to force some meanings onto the film, or to overemphasise secondary meanings to the detriment of more relevant ones.

As Kristin Thompson points out: 'The films we use as examples are those appropriate to the method, with the result that our approach becomes perpetually self-confirming' (Thompson 1988, p. 4). The proposal of the musicologist Gregg Redner is a good case study of such a Grand Theory approach. He moves from observations similar to mine about the gap between the music scholars' and the film scholars' approaches:

> The drawback [of the musicological approach] is that the score is treated much as any other musical composition might be. It is analysed for its musical value with little possibility of relating the musical findings to the mise-en-scene of the film....The problem with [the film studies] approach is that the emphasis relies too heavily on the area of film theory....What often results from this are discussions of where the music imitates the mise-en-scene or where it does not. (Redner 2011, pp. 4–5)

His solution is to adopt elements of Gilles Deleuze's philosophy to build a bridge between film theory and music theory: 'The result of this will be to demonstrate that the score participates in the *construction of meaning* [emphasis mine] in a way which is much deeper than it is currently thought to do' (Redner 2011, pp. 17–20).

Besides the fact that 'meaning' (interpretation) is again favoured over analysis, the first problem here is that Redner keeps referring to the films in terms of 'mise-en-scene.' There are occurrences in the parts quoted previously, and many more scattered throughout the book, notably on p. 4: 'possibility of relating the musical findings to the mise-en-scene of the film'; 'little of it gives us any real idea of what is actually happening when the music enters into the mise-en-scene'; 'the actual interaction between score and mise-en-scene.' 'Mise-en-scene' seems to be thought as a synonym of film style, which it is not. Mise-en-scene is just one of the film's many stylistic devices.[4] It is a *profilmic* element, and an element that one finds in opera and theatre as well. The properly *filmic* elements that one finds in films—editing being the most specific—are not mentioned in Redner's proposal.[5] Once again, this is a music scholar's approach in which film music is seen as a sort of updated version of opera/theatre music and treated mainly as regards story-telling and staging. Secondly, and most importantly, to bring in Gilles Deleuze means to replace the old Saussure-Lacan-Althusser-Barthes paradigm with a new paradigm; it may change the conceptual terms but keeps the very same risk of a Grand Theory approach. The analysis—actually an interpretation or a 'reading'—is mostly a way to use films in order to prove that the Grand Theory is valid. Indeed, Redner does not propose a set of universal tools but selects one different Deleuzian concept to interpret each one of the films in his sample—or rather, he selects one suitable film to illustrate each Deleuzian concept. 'Nomadology' is applied to *East of Eden* (1955, dir. Kazan)—whose musical contrast between tonality and atonality, incidentally, could be perfectly addressed without mobilising Deleuze—but is not applied to *Three Colors: Blue* (1993, dir. Kieslowski), for which another one is brought in: 'Becoming.'

The Grand-Theory approach remains a strong option, in the form of more recent (for Film Studies) paradigms. For example, Benjamin Nagari has proposed an approach to the analysis of music in films that uses Jung's analytical psychology, a welcome and interesting addition to counter the Freud/Lacan predominance, but still more top-down (or theory-driven, if you prefer) than bottom-up (or film-driven), more interested in Jung than in analysing films per se—indeed, it is published in a series called 'Research in Analytical Psychology and Jungian Studies' (Nagari 2016). Despite the more recent adoption of paradigms like Phenomenology, Deleuzian Philosophy, and Analytical Psychology, the 1970s post-structuralist paradigm has still much currency. An example is Elsie Walker's monograph *Understanding Sound Tracks through Film Theory* (Walker 2015). A film scholar, she proposes to revisit film theories by applying them to the study of the sound elements in film. Her pool of theories is based on the 1970s classics (Psychoanalysis, Critical Theory, ideological Deconstructionism) updated with more recent Cultural Studies and Queer Theory approaches. In Walker's survey of Film Theory—and in her idea of film analysis—there is not even a passing trace of formalism or poetics, that is, there is no consideration at all for those approaches that are more concerned with aesthetics and form rather than cultural/ideological significance and meaning. Consequently, Walker's position is likely, once again, to see cinema primarily as a means of communication, to think of analysis primarily as an interpretation, and to favour music that passes some notable 'content' to be interpreted, deciphered, or critically debunked.

Communications Model Vs. Perception Model

If the problem with some of these recent proposals aimed at bridging the gap between film and music studies is that they still rely too much on a communications model and on a top-down, theory-driven approach, another is the persistence of the separatist conception. This still exerts some influence even on those authors operating within the 'audiovisual paradigm,' for example, in Chion's concept of anempathetic music:

> On the one hand, music can directly express its participation in the feeling of the scene, by taking on the scene's rhythm, tone, and phrasing.... In this case we can speak of *empathetic music*....On the other hand, music can also exhibit conspicuous indifference to the situation, by progressing in a steady, undaunted and ineluctable manner....I call this second kind of music *anempathetic*. (Chion 1994, p. 8)

The implied idea is that there is some sort of entity that emits the music, and that said entity is empathetically indifferent to what it is happening on-screen; once again, music is seen as a sort of separated system that, in this case, refuses to align with what is happening on-screen. Also, the fact that the music is said to be 'anempathetic' subtends a personification of the music, which brings back some sort of implied author from communications-model narratology. In this respect, 'anempathetic music' is not much dissimilar from 'audiovisual counterpoint': there is a music track that contrasts with what is happening visually (I shall reprise the discussion over 'anemapthetic music' in Chap. 7). Terminology is also important, and to secure a really audiovisual, non-separatist approach, we should also eschew terminology that might hint to a separatist conception: 'When *tremolo* strings are heard, the music is not *reinforcing* the suspence of the scene; it is a part of the process that creates it,' as Kathryn Kalinak points out (Kalinak 1992, p. 31). Much of this separatist terminology, I think, comes from the influence of the communications model—for example, its need for a narrator.

The imprint of the communications model may also be the cause of the long-standing problems surrounding the diegetic/non-diegetic categories. The underlying fixation on where the music comes from is a consequence of the attention being focussed on the sender of the musical message. As we have seen, the diegetic/non-diegetic placement of the music is one of the most debated concepts in the film-music field, a problematic one and accused by many of restricting the possibilities of analysis down to predetermined paths.[6] The diatribe about where the music comes from also reinforces a separatist conception. The focus on the placement and movement of the music from one diegetic level to the other presupposes that music is seen again as an entity separate from the film that enters and exits the diegetic visual dimension.[7] A non-separatist conception should see the film as an integrated system of elements (say, a soup) and the analysis as something similar to a chemical analysis: we break down the single substance to its single ingredients (tomatoes, salt, oil, etc.). Music is an internal element, one of the ingredients blended together to make a film: camerawork, lighting, editing, acting, set design, and so forth. To carry on with this (perhaps not too scholarly) simile, the separatist perspective sees music as an external element, a fly in the soup: something that does not really belong to the film substance, that does not blend in, that just happens to float on the surface more or less deeply. Ben Winters has been particularly active in advocating a new conceptualisation of the role and position of the music within the narrative, trying to break with the now-sclerotised diegetic/non-diegetic pair: '[The] possible desire for clandestine-modernist respectability for the [young] discipline [of film-music studies] should not straightjacket us into accepting Gorbman's model as the only option' (Winters 2012, p. 52). Employing Carolyn Abbate's study on the musical narrativity in opera (Abbate 1991) and Daniel Frampton's film Phenomenology (Frampton 2006), Winters argues for a different perspective, distinguishing between 'diegetic' (music within the narrative that also characters can hear), 'extra-diegetic' (limited to the music accompanying the end credits or a montage), and, most importantly, renaming the old 'non-diegetic' type 'intra-diegetic', thus stressing that music too is part of the narrative and not coming from outside (Winters 2010, p. 243). Even if music is not heard by the characters—the typical test in the old model to ascertain whether some piece of music is diegetic or non-diegetic—it nevertheless emanates from the settings and situations of the diegesis, the narrative world. This leads Winters to a reevaluation of 'wallpaper music'—a once derogatory term for that sort of music that is merely as decorative as wallpaper—'utilised to define the shape and character of a narrative space' (Winters 2012, p. 40).

> [Music] is *the product of narration not the producer of narrative*. As such, just as the wallpaper in a film scene can be seen as a product of narration, and might lend itself to characterising the nature and feeling of the space in which the action takes place, but itself does not narrate, so might we hear music (scoring as well as source music). (Winters 2012, pp. 42–43)

He provides the example of *The Best Years of Our Lives* (1946, dir. Wyler), in which the terse Americana music by Hugo Friedhofer can be seen as a part of the story world as the houses and landscape are, it 'has a particular Coplandesque musical flavour...that is as at least as important an articulation of American identity as any visual information Fred, Al, and Homer see' (Winters 2012, p. 47).

In a further exploration of this model, Winters also envisions that the renamed 'intra-diegetic' music is so much part of the narrative world as to influence the characters' feelings and actions: In *Saving Private Ryan* (1998, dir. Spielberg):

> Captain Miller suffers equally by engaging with the film's intra-diegetic music. By that I mean that he seems to respond to the presence of underscoring—that his emotional crisis triggers the presence of music in the narrative space of the film and is, in turn, fed by it in a kind of self-destructive feedback loop....In the scene where he breaks down and weeps, for example, we hear low clarinets and strings, and it is only by pulling himself together that he silences the music seemingly emanating involuntarily from him. (Winters 2010, p. 241)

Winters's is a refreshing perspective, one that allows us to get rid of too rigid Grand Theory-like a model—Gorbman's. It also affirmatively embraces a non-separatist conception: 'Music and image are an audio-visual unity to which violence is done when theoretically separated,' he states (Winters 2012, p. 51). It offers a way to bridge the gap between Music and Film Studies, as at the centre of Winter's model is the fusion of a Music Studies theory, Abbate's, and one from Film Studies, Frampton's. It discards a communications model—rejecting the narratological categories imported from literary studies—in favour of a phenomenological model that pays closer attention to the perceptual, sensuous, and emotional dynamics of the film. While acknowledging the originality and applicability of Winter's proposal, there are two points that makes it a bit problematic to me. The first is the idea of 'intra-diegetic' music emanating from the characters and, more importantly, characters reacting to the 'intra-diegetic' music. This seems to be much too influenced by Opera Studies to be applied to films, as this is not the way film music is practically built into films. (As a film scholar with a film-maker's background, I always strive to keep a firm eye on the technical and concrete practices of film-making.) In opera, characters do react to and emanate the 'intra-diegetic' music[8]: they speak by singing, and they are part of the musical texture; moreover, music is not only intra-diegetic (it is there with the characters) but also physically there with the singers (there's a live orchestra playing in the pit). In films there is no music on set during the shoots with the actors, except for old silent-cinema routines and rare cases in the sound cinema.[9] Secondly, I find the phenomenological framework here adopted a potential risk as it may lead to the adoption of a new Grand Theory, thus straight-jacketing the analytical practice once again. Frampton's 'Filmosophy' and his postulated 'Filmmind' that is responsible for the creation of all of what we see and hear on the screen sounds to me like an unnecessary and a bit mystic anthropomorphisation of a technical process, an exercise in philosophical conceptualisation that seeks to impose on the films a certain model, Phenomenology. The 'Filmmind' sounds too much like the phenomenological rechristening of the 'narrator' from narratology. And why postulate this 'Filmmind' and not use 'film-maker' (to stay closer to the film practice) or 'narration,' which I find a more elegant and concrete way to get rid of the external narrator of the communications model? Because, since Film Phenomenology posits that films have a body (Sobchack 1992, pp. 194–259), then they must possess a 'Filmmind' too. But this move seems like another top-down 'Film Theory'—Theory tells me how films are, therefore films must be that way—not a bottom-up 'theory about film', to use Noël Carroll's differentiation (Carroll 1988, p. 232).

A way to solve this diegetic/non-diegetic dilemma not by advancing new theories but by considering film practice is offered by Jeff Smith: 'Why…do we as film scholars readily suggest that the manipulation of music's aural fidelity necessarily suggests a shift from diegetic to nondiegetic?' (Smith 2009, p. 7). While most of the recent accounts have focussed their concerns on ontological scrutiny of the dimensions of existence of the music in and out of the narrative—Where is the music?—Smith shifts the attention to the film itself—What does the music do in the film? Smith takes aim at the 'Fantastical Gap' and proposes that those situations in which we hear some music in the film that at first we judge to be non-diegetic and then is revealed to be diegetic are to be explained not in 'abstract' terms of an ontological shift of music's status but in 'concrete' terms of aesthetic manipulation of the filmic materials: 'Whereas Stilwell attributes the ambiguity of the music's status to its place within the fantastical gap, I submit that its spatial ambiguity is the product of the film's narration' (Smith 2009, p. 22). It is not so much a matter of ontological pondering (philosophical interpretation of the film) as one of attention to the expressive use of the film's devices (analysis of the film):

> At the start of the scene [in *Zodiac* (2007, dir. Fincher)], the music ['Hurdy Gurdy Man'] is quite clearly motivated within the diegesis….When the Zodiac killer begins shooting, however, the music suddenly swells in volume in a manner that departs from any sort of realistic motivation for the sound….The sudden change in volume might encourage some critics to read the music shifting from diegetic to nondiegetic. Alternatively, some critics may simply locate the music in the so-called fantastical gap….In my view, 'Hurdy Gurdy man' remains anchored within the diegesis throughout the scene, but departs from conventions of aural fidelity in order to heighten the expressive qualities of the music during the murder itself.… Considered in this way, the nonrealistic treatment of diegetic music is merely comparable to other kinds of expressive devices in the cinema, such as the use of slow motion in action or fight scenes. (Smith 2009, pp. 7–14)

Replacing the 'Fantastical Gap' with narration's manipulation of the 'expressive devices in the cinema' is a move from the separatist to the non-separatist conception because it is a way to see music as one of the expressive techniques at the film-maker's disposal, instead of considering it an external entity coming from somewhere outside. It is also a move from an idea of film as a means of communication—where the message, its sender, and the narratological location of said sender are the central concern—to one of film as an art—where the aesthetic effects of a film are the central concern. In Bordwell's words: 'If I want you to feel sad about what's onscreen, I can insert sad music. Where does this music come from? I can motivate it by locating it in the story world, or I can simply add it as sourceless (nondiegetic) accompaniment. As far as the experience is concerned, its provenance is less important than the effect of triggering a sad feeling in you' (Bordwell 2008, p. 125).

To prevent the analysis of music in films from privileging the moments in which music communicates something over those in which it 'merely' performs a formal function, we should replace the communications model with a *perception model*. And to avoid films—and the music in them—being only 'interpreted' and used to illustrate general theories instead of being 'analysed' in the fullest sense of the term, no theory should be exclusively and a priori adopted that has more general and broader interest than film: 'What is coming after Theory is not another Theory but theor*ies* and the activity of *theorizing*. A theory of film defines a problem within the domain of cinema (defined nondogmatically) and sets out to solve it through logical reflection, empirical research, or a combination of both' (Bordwell and Carroll 1996, p. xiv).

To fight the separatist conception, film is to be thought as a *system*, built of equally important, interconnected, and reciprocally influenced elements analysed in terms of the overall form they construct, and in which music is to be considered one of such constituting internal elements. In his critique of Seymour Chatman's communications model narratology, David Bordwell employs a fitting musical example:

> Chatman suggests that thinking of the narrator can be helpful in certain problematic cases, as when we try to track unreliable narration. When the image track contradicts the soundtrack, as in *Badlands* (1973), we have 'a conflict between two mutually contradictory components of the cinematic narrator.' Again, however, what have we gained by postulating this extra agent and then saying that two 'components' of it clash? Why not simply say that we encounter an organized disparity of image and sound?' (Bordwell 2008, p. 129)

From this and other Bordwell quotes, it will probably be quite clear at this point that the approach I deem most fitting to address and solve the difficulties I have exposed in this and in the previous chapter is Neoformalism.

Neoformalism sees films as artworks more than means of communication, and it is based on a perception model. This does not mean that art does not communicate at all and has no meaning:

> A stress upon perception might be thought to militate against meaning. Yet the crucial assumption is that in art, meaning depends upon perception. The art work does not exist simply to transmit a message; if it did, there would be no difference between art and ordinary informational discourse. Art is primarily an engagement of ourselves with materials and forms....Instead of simply reading the films, we must consider the very terms of readability which they propose. (Bordwell 1981, p. 7)

Neoformalism has a strong concern for form: 'Film scholars have tended to spend most of their time figuring out what films mean. For the neoformalist, however, this is just part of a much broader task of figuring out how films work' (Thomson-Jones 2011, p. 140). It has at its centre the idea of a formal system built by interconnected devices, one of which is music. Contrary to Film Phenomenology, with which it does share a number of points—such as the perception model and the active role of the viewer—Neoformalism does not employ an 'extra-cinematic' theory. In her presentation of Film Phenomenology, Vivian Sobchack states:

> From a phenomenological perspective, cinema becomes a philosophical exemplar of 'intentionality,' making manifest the directed and irreducible correlation of subjective consciousness (evidenced by the camera's projected and thus visible choice-making movements of attention) and its objects (whether 'real' or 'imaginary'). Furthermore, through editing, the cinema also demonstrate acts of reflection that organize and express the tacit meaning of its own and the world's explicit conjunction and movement. In effect, the cinema both enacts and dramatizes the intentional correlation as an actively lived structure through which meaning is constituted as such. (Sobchack 2011, pp. 436–437)

The stress on the way in which the technical processes of cinema are said to enact the experiential mechanisms posited by Phenomenology seems a replacement of the old 'ideological cinema apparatus' with a 'phenomenological cinema apparatus.' In both cases, cinema is of interest not in itself but because its techniques provide a good illustration of how the relation works between the individual and society/world according to the theory. Film Phenomenology is liable to become another Grand Theory, studying films not so much for an interest in films but for an interest in Phenomenology, to which films happen to be apt 'philosophical exemplar.' Indeed, the phenomenological philosopher Maurice Merleau-Ponty showed a keen interest for cinema because it was a 'phenomenological art, "peculiarly suited to make manifest the union of mind and body, mind and world, and the expression of one in the other"' (in Sobchack 2011, p. 439). Neoformalism does not hold any such theory to validate through cinema and by which to provide answers to broader socio-political questions: 'Although these are important questions, the neoformalists may not feel the need to answer them, since they are not defending a theory of art but merely a functional mode of film analysis' (Thomson-Jones 2011, p. 136). Indeed, Neoformalism is not a *theory*, and even less so a Grand Theory aiming at interpreting other socio/cultural/psychic/ideological phenomena besides film. It is not even meant to be a method as an *approach* to film analysis (Thompson 1988, p. 9). In the next chapter, I present the basic tenets of this approach and show how it can be used to analyse music in films.

Notes

1. See Wierzbicki (2009, p. 155).
2. See, for example, Bordwell (1980).
3. A Criticism of the Grand Theories is in Bordwell (1996).
4. Bordwell and Thompson (2010) lists 'mise-en-scene', 'cinematography', 'editing', and 'sound' as the constitutive elements of film style (pp. 118–311).
5. 'Filmic' and 'profilmic' are two terms introduced by the 'Association française pour la recherche filmologique' gravitating around the journal Revue internationale de Filmologie (1947–1961) and aiming at studying cinema on more scientific basis. 'Profilmic' is any event that is before a camera and captured by it (e.g., an actor); 'filmic' is every element that is created by the capturing of profilmic elements (e.g., the close-up of one actor) or by the elaboration of the shots (e.g., an editing match between two shots) through the means of the cinematic technique.
6. For example, see Kassabian (2001, p. 42). Ben Winters states that 'branding music with the label "non-diegetic" threatens to separate it from the space of the narrative, denying it an active role in shaping the course of onscreen events, and unduly restricting our reading of film....Music's description in film as "non-diegetic" is both overly reliant on the concept's narratological meaning, and representative of an unwillingness to recognize film's inherent "unreality"' (Winters 2010, p. 224).
7. Although there can be non-diegetic images that do not exist in the narrative world—like the mechanic peacock in *October* (1928, dir. Eisenstein)—the vast majority of images in mainstream cinema are diegetic.
8. I keep the term 'intra-diegetic' to indicate music that has not a physical source in the narrative world of the opera, as opposed to 'diegetic' music, that is those cases in which the characters play some musical instrument on stage, like Lindoro's serenade 'Se il mio nome saper voi bramate' in Rossini's *The Barber of Seville* (1816).
9. In the silent cinema, music was often played on-set to put actors in the right mood, but only in very rare instances—like Fritz Lang's *Metropolis* (1927)—the music played on-set was the same music that viewers would later hear during the projections, thus making Winters's model untenable in practical terms, as actors reacted to one piece of music on-set and to another piece of music on-screen. An example of the survival of these routines in sound cinema is *Once upon a Time in the West* (1968, dir. Leone), in which Morricone's music was played on-set during some scenes.

References

Abbate, Carolyn. 1991. *Unsung Voices: Opera and Musical Narrative in the Nineteenth Century*. Princeton, NJ: Princeton University Press.
Altman, Rick. 2000. Inventing the Cinema Soundtrack. Hollywood's Multiplane Sound System. In *Music and Cinema*, ed. James Buhler, Caryl Flinn, and David Neumeyer, 339–359. Hanover, NH: Wesleyan University Press.
Bordwell, David. 1980. The Musical Analogy. *Yale French Studies* 60: 141–156.
Bordwell, David. 1981. *The Films of Carl-Theodor Dreyer*. Berkeley and Los Angeles: University of California Press.
Bordwell, David. 1996. Contemporary Film Studies and the Vicissitudes of Grand Theory. In *Post-Theory. Reconstructing Film Studies*, ed. David Bordwell and Nöel Carroll, 3–36. Madison, WI: University of Wisconsin Press.
Bordwell, David. 2008. *Poetics of Cinema*. New York and London: Routledge.
Bordwell, David, and Kristin Thompson. 2010. *Film Art. An Introduction*, 9th ed. New York: McGraw and Hill.
Bordwell, David, and Noël Carroll. 1996. Introduction. In *Post-Theory. Reconstructing Film Studies*, ed. David Bordwell and Noël Carroll, xiii–xvii. Madison, WI: University of Wisconsin Press.
Branigan, Edward. 1992. *Narrative Comprehension and Film*. New York: Routledge.
Carroll, Noël. 1988. *Mystifying Movies: Fads and Fallacies in Contemporary Film Theory*. New York: Columbia University Press.
Chion, Michel. 1994. *Audio-Vision. Sound on Screen* [1990], trans. Claudia Gorbmam. New York: Columbia University Press.
Choe, Chong S., Robert B. Welch, Robb M. Gilford and James F. Juola. 1975. The "Ventriloquist Effect": Visual Dominance or Response Bias? *Perception & Psychophysics* 18 (1): 55–60.
Cook, Nicholas. 1998. *Analysing Musical Multimedia*. Oxford: Clarendon Press.
Cooper, Grosvenor, and Leonard B. Meyer. 1960. *The Rhythmic Structure of Music*. Chicago: University of Chicago Press.
Donnelly, K.J. 2014. *Occult Aesthetics: Synchronization in Sound Film*. Oxford and New York: Oxford University Press.
Frampton, Daniel. 2006. *Filmosophy*. Chichester and New York: Wallflower-Columbia University Press.
Heldt, Guido. 2013. *Music and Levels of Narration in Film. Steps Across the Border*. Bristol: Intellect.
Jacobs, Lea. 2014. *Film Rhythm after Sound: Technology, Music, and Performance*. Berkeley, CA: University of California Press.
Kalinak, Kathryn. 1992. *Settling the Score. Music and the Classical Hollywood Film*. Madison, WI: University of Wisconsin Press.

Kassabian, Anahid. 2001. *Hearing Film: Tracking Identification in Contemporary Hollywood Film Music.* New York and London: Routledge.
Kulezic-Wilson, Danijela. 2015. *The Musicality of Narrative Film.* Basingstoke: Palgrave MacMillan.
McGurk, Harry, and John MacDonald. 1976. Hearing Lips and Seeing Voices. *Nature* 264 (December): 746–748.
Middleton, Richard. 1990. *Studying Popular Music.* Buckingham: Open University Press.
Nagari, Benjamin. 2016. *Analytical Psychology and Music in Film.* Hove and New York: Routledge.
Nasta, Dominique. 1991. *Meaning in Film: Relevant Structures in Soundtrack and Narrative.* Berne and Berlin: Peter Lang.
Neumeyer, David. 2015. *Meaning and Interpretation of Music in Cinema.* Bloomington and Indianapolis: Indiana University Press.
Prendergast, Roy M. 1977. *Film Music: A Neglected Art: A Critical Study of Music in Films.* New York: W. W. Norton.
Redner, Gregg. 2011. *Deleuze and Film Music. Building a Methodological Bridge Between Film Theory and Music.* Bristol: Intellect.
Smith, Jeff. 2009. Bridging the Gap: Reconsidering the Border Between Diegetic and Nondiegetic Music. *Music and the Moving Image* 2 (1): 1–25.
Sobchack, Vivian. 1992. *The Address of the Eye: A Phenomenology of Film Experience.* Princeton, NJ: Princeton University Press.
Sobchack, Vivian. 2011. Phenomenology. In *The Routledge Companion to Philosophy ad Film*, ed. Paisley Livingston and Carl Plantinga, 435–445. Abingdon and New York: Routledge.
Thompson, Kristin. 1988. *Breaking the Glass Armor: Neoformalist Film Analysis.* Princeton, NJ: Princeton University Press.
Thomson-Jones, Katherine. 2011. Formalism. In *The Routledge Companion to Philosophy and Film*, ed. Paisley Livingston and Carl Plantinga, 131–141. Abingdon and New York: Routledge.
Walker, Elsie. 2015. *Understanding Sound Tracks Through Film Theory.* Oxford and New York: Oxford University Press.
Wierzbicki, James. 2009. *Film Music: A History.* Abingdon and New York: Routledge.
Winters, Ben. 2010. The Non-Diegetic Fallacy: Film, Music, and Narrative Space. *Music & Letters* 91 (2): 224–244.
Winters, Ben. 2012. Musical Wallpaper? Towards an Appreciation of Non-narrating Music in Film. *Music Sound and the Moving Image* 6 (1): 39–54.

PART II

Pars Construens

CHAPTER 4

The Neoformalist Proposal

Kristin Thompson explains: 'Neoformalism as an approach does offer a series of broad assumptions about how artworks are constructed and how they operate in cueing audience responses. But neoformalism does not prescribe *how* these assumptions are embodied in individual films. Rather, the basic assumptions can be used to construct a method specific to the problems raised by each film' (Thompson 1988a, p. 6). The problems that have been raised throughout this study are how to talk about music in films from a film scholar's perspective and how to take into account the broadest gamut of roles that music can have, both the 'meaning-carrying' and the formal ones. I am convinced that the assumptions of Neoformalism can be used to construct a method that is a convincing solution.

NEOFORMALISM: AN INTRODUCTION

Neoformalism was launched at the University of Wisconsin-Madison in the second half of the 1970s. The names associated with this methodological framework are those of Kristin Thompson and David Bordwell, but only Thompson calls herself a Neoformalist, Bordwell being more precisely identified as a cognitive film theorist and a film poetician.[1] The development of the Neoformalist approach has been carried out in a number of books and articles,[2] but the first outcome was *Film Art. An Introduction*, the first edition dating 1979.[3]

The now classic textbook was one of the first attempts to reconcile film theory with film practice, blending together the 'film grammar' manuals—whose audience was those interested in the practical mechanics of film-making—and film theory treatises, aimed at film scholars and theorists and handling films in a more abstract way. *Film Art* moves from the claim that films are artworks constructed in such a way as to produce certain aesthetic effects and elicit specific responses in the viewers. To analyse any artwork, the basic requirement is (should be) a knowledge of the norms and conventions governing that particular art, and also some understanding of its technique. Therefore, *Film Art* begins by explaining the mechanics of cinema—for example, illustrating how a film camera and a projector work—and then, drawing from Russian Formalism,[4] Noël Burch's studies in film style and form (Burch 1973), and Ernst Gombrich art theories (Gombrich 1961), it proposes a way to deal with films that put form at its centre: 'Artworks arouse and gratify our human craving for form. Artists design their works—they give them form—so that we can have a structured experience. For this reason, form is of central importance in any artwork, regardless of its medium' (Bordwell and Thompson 2010, p. 56). From Gombrich they adopted a constructivist view based on the psychology of perception, thus turning the viewer into an active pole of the spectatorial experience, contrary to the first semiotics that saw her/him as an arrival point in a somewhat automated communicational chain, or to the second semiotics influenced by Lacan and Althusser that saw the viewer as a passive and mostly oblivious target for the ideological manipulation of the film. From Burch they inherited an attention to the concrete practicalities of film-making, which was a way to bring the attention more on the form in a period of time where the interpretation of the 'content' was the main concern. Indeed, Neoformalism was a reaction against the Grand Theory-led methods circulating in the Film Studies circles. It aimed at bringing films as artworks back as the central concern of analysis, and 'analysis'—reduced to a synonym of 'interpretation' in 1970s—was also brought back to its proper meaning: 'Neoformalism does not do "readings" of films. For one thing, films are not written texts and do not need to be read. For another, "reading" had come to equal "interpretation" and,…for the neoformalist, interpretation is only one part of analysis' (Thompson 1988a, p. 34, n. 25).

The very distinction between form and content is cast into a different light:

Very often people think of 'form' as the opposite of 'content.' This implies that a poem or a musical piece or a film is like a jug. An external shape, the jug, *contains* something that could just as easily be held in a cup or a pail. Under this assumption, form becomes less important than whatever it's presumed to contain. We don't accept this assumption. If form is the total system that the viewer attributes to the film, there is no inside or outside. Every component *functions as part of the overall pattern* that engages the viewer. So we'll treat as formal elements many things that some people consider content. From our standpoint, subject matter and abstract ideas all enter into the total system of the artwork. (Bordwell and Thompson 2010, p. 58)

This rejection of the form/content split is one of the strongest borrowings from Russian Formalism, which was further taken as a model for the book that launched the term 'Neoformalism' itself: Kristin Thompson's *Eisenstein's Ivan the Terrible: A Neoformalist Analysis*. Thompson adapted the literary theories of the Russian Formalist School—mainly Yury Tynyanov, Viktor Shklovsky, and Boris Eichenbaum—to the study of film, followed in the same year 1981 by David Bordwell, who imported the same concepts to analyse the films of Carl-Theodor Dreyer (Bordwell 1981). The Russian Formalists had themselves developed a 'Poetika Kino' based on the principles they used for literary criticism, but Thompson felt Russian Formalism as such could not be imported to film studies. A 'new formalism' was needed because the Russian Formalism as a movement is now discontinued but, more importantly, because the Russian Formalism was designed for literary study and, when dealing with cinema, it saw it as a language: 'The current study makes no assumptions that film is a kind of language. One the whole, then, the Formalists' writings on cinema are of little use in this analysis' (Thompson 1981, p. 31).

Unlike the two leading school of literary criticism at the time of Thompson's writing, New Criticism and (Post)Structuralism, both committed to a communications model, Russian Formalism rejected it: 'For them, the poet was not trying to communicate meaning…; instead, he or she uses language in a distinctive way to create a new perceptual experience for the reader.…[Russian Formalists] didn't see the poet as a communicator of ideas that grow into artworks but as a skilled artisan in a special field (Thompson 1981, pp. 11–12). Russian Formalism was based on a perception model: 'The fundamental assumption is that art is an affair of perception, and as such it presents the perceiver with problems of unity and disunity' (Bordwell 1981, p. 3). The rejection of a communications model can at first be mistaken for the endorsement of a purely aesthetic/contemplative model, 'formalistically' disconnected from any social concern and usefulness, and as such has been seen by some critics of Neoformalism and before that by some critics of the Russian Formalists as well—Joseph Stalin included. This is a misunderstanding, as Russian Formalism and Neoformalism posit that art has an indispensable 'recreative' function in society:

> Russian Formalists [distinguished] between practical, everyday perception and specifically aesthetic, non-practical perception....Art is set apart from the everyday world, in which we use our perception for practical ends.... Films and other artworks, on the contrary, plunge us into a non-practical, playful type of interaction. They renew our perceptions and other mental processes because they hold no immediate practical implications for us.... This is not to say that films have no effect on us. As with all artworks, they are of vital importance in our lives. The nature of practical perception means that our faculties become dulled by the repetitive and habitual activities inherent in much of daily life. Thus art, by renewing our perceptions and thoughts, may be said to act as a sort of mental exercise, parallel to the way sport is an exercise for the body. (Thompson 1988a, pp. 8–9)

The practical perception is quick and aimed at extracting the piece of information we need. A traffic light, in the context of the everyday experience, has the function of alerting us as to whether we can proceed or not. The communications model is operating here, as the traffic light is designed to send a message through colour signs. We perceive the green colour and go on, we perceive the red and we halt; perception here is the gateway for the reception and interpretation of a message. And, as Shklovsky says, 'as perception becomes habitual, it becomes automatic' (in Thompson 1988a, p. 10). Probably, we do not perceive the traffic light in itself as an object any more, but just its lights, because *that* is the important piece of information that we, for habitualisation, automatically pick up. And Shklovsky continues: 'Habitualization devours work, clothes, furniture, one's wife, and the fear of war....And Art exists that one may recover the sensation of life; it exists to make one feel things, to make the stone *stony*' (Thompson 1988a, p. 10). In an aesthetic dimension, I can see the traffic light in itself again, I can turn my eye on how it is shaped, on the rectangular form of its main body in which the three circles of its 'eyes' intersect; on the shininess of the material it is made of; perhaps on the scratches and faded spots that the prolonged exposure to weather conditions has produced; I can appreciate the visual contrast between the primary colours red and green, and the choice of orange/yellow as a 'smoother' between the more 'soothing' colour green and the more 'aggressive' colour red. Using a more famous example, an urinal has a crude, very concrete purpose in the everyday life; if placed in a museum, it enters the aesthetic dimension, becomes *The Fountain*, and its practical function ceases to be—hopefully. The purpose of art is to make us see the world around us with different eyes, finding aspects of it that, in the hectic perceptual modalities of everyday life, we are likely to bypass and miss. What art does is 'defamiliarise' the world for us, making its perception 'roughened' so that habitualisation and automatisms are removed and we can appreciate it anew.

By aesthetically transforming the 'materials' of the world, cinema operates such defamiliarisation. A comedy film can pinpoint for us, through exaggeration and satire, the ridiculous essence of many of our daily routines—think of Chaplin's *Modern Times* (1936); a horror film can cast an ominous new light on everyday objects—you may not look at a puppet with the same eyes after watching *Dead Silence* (2007, dir. Wan) or cemeteries after watching *Night of the Living Dead* (1968, dir. Romero); you might not think of the war refugees issue with the same detachment after watching *Hotel Rwanda* (2004, dir. George). Film-makers, and artists in general, break 'the glass armor of familiarity' (Shklovsky 1973). On the other side, the job of the film critic and analyst is that of helping the viewer connect to those films whose form may be too 'roughened' and more difficult than the average, or, on the other hand, to defamiliarise those mainstream or conventional films that viewers have become accustomed to watch in a habitualised mode. Thompson explains:

> The works that we single out as most original and that are taken to be the most valuable tend to be those that either defamiliarize reality more strongly or defamiliarize the conventions established by previous art works—or a combination of the two. Yet if we single out an ordinary film and submit it to the same scrutiny that we afford more original works, its automatized elements can shed their familiarity and become intriguing. (Thompson 1988a, p. 11)

A central task for the critic is that of reconstructing the original 'background' for those classics that used to be non-conventional in their times—think of *Citizen Kane* (1941, dir. Welles)—but have been so canonised and their innovations have in the meantime been so normalised as to have come themselves to be covered in that 'glass armour.'

Cinema is a story-telling-based medium. Hence, some narratological model is required of how viewers make sense of the narrative being told by films. The narratological model employed by Neoformalism is articulated in Bordwell's *Narration in the Fiction Film*. It jettisons many of the established approaches—for example, Benveniste's Theory of Enunciation—and makes a strong case against the communications model altogether.[5] Hence, we dispense ourselves with the need to trace implied authors or narrators:

> The narrator…is an unnecessary and misleading personification of the narrative dynamics of a film….At many moments, each novel's narrator comes forward and projects a certain attitude toward the action represented. But in cinema, a speaker's 'voice' is seldom so explicit….For ordinary audiences, the relevant agent or agents are the filmmakers, commonly known as *they*….Very few viewers would take, say, a bit of actor's business or pattern of lighting as having its source in an intermediary, a cinematic narrator, rather than in either 'the film itself' or the creative individuals on the set.[6] (Bordwell 2008, pp. 122–123)

This reversal of perspective is possible precisely because attention is shifted from the sender to the receiver, the viewer: with a perception-oriented model he who is sending the message is not so important anymore; the viewer's activity and how the formal qualities of the film interact with her/him is the central concern. To account for the viewer's activity, Constructivism and Cognitivism replace Psychoanalysis. Psychoanalysis sees the viewer mainly as a passive recipient of the film's ideological message, guided by irrational drives. Cognitivism sees the viewer as an active constructor of the film's form and meaning, applying rational procedures. The cognitive aesthetician Noël Carroll thus argues against the use of Psychoanalysis:

> We must recall that psychoanalytic theory is designed to explain the *irra*tional….So to mobilize psychoanalysis, we must show that the phenomena or behavior in question are irrational rather than rational. At the very least, one problem with Metz, Baudry, and their epigones is that they have not bothered to show that such things as the cinematic apparatus or cinematic representation are irrational or that our interactions with them as viewers

are irrational….The notion that representation per se is irrational, given the way humans are built and the way they communicate, is absurd. The practice of representation, like that of bridge building, is a *normal* part of human life. (Carroll 1988, pp. 50–52)

The film-viewing experience is seen as rational and based on natural perceptual and cognitive mechanisms and assumptions—'contingent universals'—that all human beings share: 'The process of film spectatorship are best understood as rationally motivated attempts to make visual or narrative sense out of the textual materials; and…these processes of making sense are not dissimilar to those we deploy in our everyday life experience' (Stam 2000, p. 237). A film presents a set of perceptual cues that the viewer actively organises and completes through inferences and hypotheses, combining bottom-up inductive moves (from the empirical data provided by the film) and top-down deductive moves (from previous knowledge and mental schemata). Watching a film, the viewer applies mental 'prototype schemata' (I see a dog on-screen, and I recognise it as a dog because I have the dog prototype stored in my mind), 'template schemata' (I can foresee how a romantic comedy is going to end because I have had previous experience of its typical format), and 'procedural schemata' (through repeated exposures to film viewing, I have developed the skill to make sense of the use of a dissolve as opposed to a fade-out/fade-in, or to understand cross-cutting) (Bordwell 1985, pp. 34–36).The text that recapped and presented Neoformalism in its more complete form was Thompson's *Breaking the Glass Armor: Neoformalist Film Analysis*. While Thompson called Neoformalism a 'method' in *Eisenstein's Ivan the Terrible* (Thompson 1981, p. 8) developed to analyse a specific film, she called it an 'approach' in *Breaking the Glass Armor* (Thompson 1988a, p. 6) to stress its adaptability and flexibility—it is tested on eleven films from different times, film schools, and statuses—and perhaps also to reduce the risk that it might be taken too dogmatically.

The new approach soon met criticism, often the fruit of misunderstanding. For example, in his critique Berys Gault conflates Neoformalism (not a *theory* but a *functionalist approach* to film analysis) with Cognitivism (a theory) under the label of 'Constructivism' and exaggerates the constructivist aspects of Neoformalism: 'There is a genuine role for audiences to make meaning, but this role varies in scope from film to film and is limited within a detectivist framework [*the framework Gault opposes to Constructivism*]. Such a limited construction, precisely because of its limits, is incompatible with the neoformalist view that meanings are always made.' (Gault 2010, p. 179). Neoformalism may say that meanings are made but that does not mean that they are *made up*, preposterously invented at the viewer's capricious discretion. They are made from precise cues given in the film, and the making of meaning is guided, limited within the boundaries set by the artwork and its historical background. Much of the misunderstandings and consequent critique come, I gather, from the way the past Grand Theory has biassed film scholars to think about their discipline: the study of film must rest on some broad theory that can address not only films but also society at large. A critique by the Marxist film scholar Nick Browne is telling:

> If formalism is to claim recognition and standing as a critical system or as a general method, which offers more than coincidental or occasionally useful critical application, it must prove itself by being able to offer broad and coherent models of explanation for a range of problems of history, ideology, and spectatorship now formulated within this field....The analyses are excellent within the framework set out, yet the theoretical scope of the essay remains constrained by formalist reduction. (Browne 1982, pp. 83, 88)

The previous passage precisely shows how a Grand Theory-biassed mindset can miss the key point: Neoformalism does not want to be a theory of film—and even less so a 'Grand Theory of everything'—but a way to analyse film; to offer 'useful critical application' is exactly all it wants. There is a preconception that Film Studies must be necessarily committed to broad socio-cultural commentaries and interpretations. Some film scholars may indeed find such socio-cultural mission 'compelling', but cannot there be room in the discipline for scholars who wish to give relevance to the aesthetic analysis too? After all, we are dealing with an *art* form.

Neoformalism has been typically chastised over three main points: (1) its alleged ahistoricism; (2) its socio-political disengagement; and (3) the pure logical and disembodied nature of the viewer it posits. The weakest point of criticism is ahistoricism, which easily crumbles if the Neoformalist concept of 'background' is carefully considered. The Russian Formalists already pointed out that 'every work depends on its relations to other systems: nonpoetic language, other artworks, aspects of the everyday world. These external systems were referred to as *backgrounds*....The background allows the Formalist to deal with history'

(Thompson 1981, p. 12). Neoformalism does not see the aesthetic objects it studies as detached from history and society—aethernal *ars gratia artis* entities. On the contrary, they are the products of specific socio-cultural and historical contexts, made according to specific and historical artistic conventions, norms and industrials routines, and made sense of by the viewers according to their experience of the real world and the other artworks of their time: 'Our most frequent and typical experiences form our perceptual norms, and idiosyncratic, defamiliarizing experiences stand out in contrast....The film's adherence to and departure from its background norms are the subjects of the analyst's work.... Neoformalist analysis depends upon an understanding of historical contexts' (Thompson 1988a, p. 21).[7] The functions and motivations of the devices that shape the film's overall form can be only understood within its historical context of production and reception. Also, both Bordwell and Thompson are notable film historians with a track records of remarkable historiographical studies: it would be odd that they might find history irrelevant when they analyse films.

Another stronger accusation, similarly cascading from the supposed *ars-gratia-artis* orientation of Neoformalism, is the rejection of socio-political engagement, which the critics automatically infer from the priority that Neoformalism gives to form over 'content.' The study of how a film is constructed (analysis of form) is of no use for society and for political struggle, while unearthing the film's hidden messages and idealogical manipulation (interpretation of content) is an active political stance. Bordwell says, 'Many scholars would object to my position on the grounds that is inhibits progressive political thinking' (Bordwell 2008, p. 75). The impression is that in this case Neoformalism is not so much criticised on the grounds of its more or less effective applicability as on political grounds. It has been accused of authoritarianism and of silencing pluralism, imposing itself as 'totalizing' (Lehman 1997).[8] Robert Stam goes as far as implying that Cognitivism (and by relation, Neoformalism) can almost be a manifestation of fascism, or at least complacency: 'Cognitivism shows a touching faith in reason (after Auschwitz) and science (after Hiroshima). It keeps its faith with science, even though "science" had not so recently "proved" black, Jewish, and Native American inferiority' (Stam 2000, p. 241). Noël Carroll ponders on these political prejudices:

> Proponents of the Theory let on that the Theory grew out of the student movement and out of a resistance to oppression everywhere. Consequently, from their point of view, criticism of the Theory virtually represents a clear and present danger to the very Revolution itself. Anyone who opposes the Theory, for whatever reason, is politically suspect—probably a ruling class, neoconservative, homophobic misogynist.... Speaking from a personal experience, I can recall more than one occasion when, as a result of my criticism of the Theory, people told me that they were surprised by my conversion to neoconservatism, despite no discernible changes in my real-world political views....In film studies, rival theories to the Theory are rejected out of hand as politically pernicious. One very popular gambit...is to argue that competing views are 'formalist.'... To call an alternative theory formalist is, in other words, a way of saying that the alternative theory is politically incorrect....In general, it seems counterposed to the 'political.'...Film scholars...seem so anxious about the issue of formalism because of their convictions that we find ourselves in a moment of political crisis, in which an understanding of the operation of ideology is paramount. In such circumstances, a concern with forms and structures strikes them as being as frivolous as Nero fiddling while Rome burned. (Carroll 1996, pp. 45–49)

This accusation, political prejudices aside, stems from a misconception. Neoformalism *does not* reject interpretation altogether. It states that it is one part of the analysis and not the only activity:

> The stress on perception, it is claimed, treats the viewer as the isolated individual, locked in rapt apprehension of the art work. How, then, can Formalist theory situate an art work socially?...Marxist aesthetic theory points out that ideology is often transformed through the 'relatively autonomous' processes of art. Art is related to ideology but cannot be reduced to it, and an account of the relation must include the particular aesthetic dynamics of the work. Here Formalism can be of use. (Bordwell 1981, pp. 7–8)

Neoformalism is suitable to tackle ideological films, such as Godard's,[9] or revealing and interpreting the connotations and ideologies of mainstream films.[10]

The one criticism that has more grounds than others charges Neoformalism and its constructivist narratology with positing an abstract and disembodied viewer whose main activity is a logic-driven inferential reconstruction of the cause/effect chain. 'The spectator is a complicated entity, in terms of desire, fantasies, wishes, fears,' said Ann Kaplan,

'Bordwell thinks of the film viewer as a computer, a neutered cyborg. He doesn't care about its gender or its emotions or its race. He cares only if it picks up the right cinematic cues' (in Quart 2000, p. 41). This may be a pertinent criticism. Like the viewer postulated by Psychoanalysis—a passive and hypnotised recipient of all the ideological messages—the one posited by Bordwell's Constructivism is similarly predetermined by the film's cues and has equally predictable reactions. Bordwell himself has admitted that he had previously 'slighted' the affective and individual aspects of the viewing experience (Bordwell 2008, p. 51), recognising now their importance and also introducing a third level of viewer activity, 'appropriation,' in addition to 'perception' and 'comprehension' (Bordwell 2008, p. 46).[11] Appropriation takes into account such issues as race, gender, class, and the uses that viewers make of the films in their personal sphere and socio-cultural contexts:

> Films are appropriated by individuals and communities for all manner of purposes. People employ favorite films for mood management, watching *Die Hard* to pump themselves up or *Sleepless in Seattle* to have a good cry. Bloggers may use films to flaunt their taste or strike a posture, whereas academics interpret films to validate a theory. Social groups appropriate films to a multitude of ends, treating some as praiseworthy representations of political positions and castigating others as harmful....Accordingly, much of what interests cultural critics are acts of appropriation.' (Bordwell 2008, pp. 48–49)

This self-criticism itself and the fact that Bordwell's Neoformalism-based poetics produced an offspring of scholars studying those aspects that Bordwell had neglected—for example, sound and emotions[12]—show that Neoformalism is an approach open to integrations and corrections.

Neoformalist Film Analysis

Film-making starts by taking *materials* from the real world and transforming them into an aesthetic experience. Materials may comprise a real-life event, a historical character, a sunset, an ideology, any concrete, conceptual, or imaginary element that can be the basis for artistic creation: 'For the artist, the external world is not the content of a picture, but the material for the picture' (Viktor Shklovsky in Thompson 1981, p. 24). These materials are transformed into an artwork through their being structured into a *formal system*, which is the overall film's form.

The concept of 'system' means that it is the result of an *interplay of different elements*. Such elements, the smallest unit of the film's formal system, are called *devices*.

Devices are all those basic elements of a technical, narrative, or thematic nature that combine to shape a film's overall form. For example, a piece of dialogue is a narrative device, and so are characters; the suggestion of a certain view of the world or a political idea—'friendship and love are more important than money' or 'the 1980s was a conservative decade'—is a thematic device; *plan sequence*, cross-cutting, low-key lighting, music are all technical (stylistic) devices. Devices can be seen as organised into three levels: the *stylistic* level, the *narrative* level, and the *thematic* level.

Style is defined as 'the use of the specific techniques of the medium in a significant and systematic way' (Bordwell 1997, p. 4), and the study of the stylistic level consists in observing how the cinematic techniques are applied to create a film's *space* (the representation of the three dimensions and off-screen space), *time* (the chronological or non-chronological order of the narrative events), and the '*abstract play among the non-narrative spatial, temporal, and visual aspects of film*—the graphic, sonic, and rhythmic qualities of the image and sound tracks' (Thompson 1988a, p. 43). The stylistic devices fall into four technical categories: (1) *mise-en-scène* (the appearance, placement, blocking, movements of the profilmic elements on the set, such as actors, props, set decorations and furniture, costumes, make-up and hairdos, lighting, etc.); (2) *cinematography* (camerawork, type of lenses, type of film-stock, type of framing, slow motion/fast motion, focus and depth of field, etc.); (3) *editing* (the process of putting one shot in relation to the others in graphical, rhythmic, spatial, and temporal terms, using cross-cutting, continuity editing/jump cuts, dissolve/fades, montage sequences, non-diegetic inserts, etc.); and (4) *sound* (dialogue, sound effects and music elaborated through sound editing, filtering, mixing, overlapping, volume control, fades and dissolves, etc.).[13]

The *narrative level* is about story-telling, it concerns how the narrative events are made accessible, ordered, and related to each other. What is presented by the film is only a selection of the most salient and meaningful events; the narrative itself is always wider both in terms of time and space. Imagine a dialogue scene where the protagonist is asked to pay a visit to an old aunt. Cut. In the next scene we see him sitting in a démodé living room chatting and having tea with an elderly lady. It is clear to us that the lady must be the aforementioned aunt and that, if he is there with her, the protagonist has evidently obliged to the request. Yet, what the film offers us is just two segments of the narrative; omitted are the scenes where the protagonist leaves his house, travels to his aunt's home, knocks at the door, and is received and offered a seat and tea in the living room. The omitted stages would not have added anything because we are able to fill in the blanks and logically connect the two salient segments. The constructive activity of the viewer is not only at work in basic instances as the one I have presented—where we do the connecting operation almost automatically, given how ostensibly simple the connection is—but in more complex forms as well, in which we may even struggle to grasp the logical connection or chronological order of the events. Think of the circular narrative level of *Pulp Fiction* (1994, dir. Tarantino), the ambiguous chronology of *Memento* (2000, dir. Nolan), the reversed timeline of *Irreversible* (2002, dir. Noé), or the oneiric illogical structure of *Lost Highway* (1997, dir. Lynch). To engage our perception in new ways, the artwork may purposely make the form 'roughened' by scattering the narrative events out of their logical order or by withdrawing some, thus making our comprehension of the narrative less automatised. What is presented in the film is called *syuzhet* (sometimes also called 'plot'). From that set of narrative events we reconstruct, through inferences and logical cause/effect criteria, the bigger picture, the whole narrative, which is called *fabula* (or 'story') (Bordwell 1985, pp. 49–50).

Speaking of narratives, here comes the question: Who is the narrator? Neoformalism calls 'narrator' only a character within the narrative that tells a story: for example, Walter Neff is the narrator in *Double Indemnity* (1944, dir. Wilder), as he tells his story, which we see in flashback with his voice-over explanations, to a dictation machine. The syuzhet is presented by *narration*, 'the process by which the film prompts the viewer to construct the ongoing fabula on the basis of syuzhet organization and stylistic patterning' (Bordwell 2008, p. 98). Narration forms the narrative by interweaving three dimensions: *narrative logic* (mainly cause/effect), *time*, and *space* (Bordwell 1985, pp. 51–53). Narration is neither an entity liable to be taken as a personification, as is the 'implied author,' nor an external entity that produces the film, as the narrator is in enunciation theory.

> At the start of *Jerry Maguire*, the hero's voice introduces us to his lifestyle and his personal crisis, and then his voice vanishes, never to return. To whom was he speaking? The question is as irrelevant as the physics of

light sabers. The film doesn't need to anchor his discourse in a full-fledged communication situation because it recruits part of the communication template to get information out to us. Communicative logic can go hang; all that the narration cares about is cueing us to make the right inferences. (Bordwell 2008, p. 99)

Narration can be seen like a record of the artistic choices that were made to produce the film and its effects, which an analyst extracts and reconstructs while studying a film. It is a unified and unifying process internal to the formal system and does not require postulated intermediaries: 'Who produces the narrational process? The filmmakers' (Bordwell 2008, p. 123).

The *thematic level* is the one that encompasses the meanings of the film. There are four types of meaning: referential, explicit, implicit, and symptomatic.[14] In the *referential* meaning we recognise in the film elements from the real world and from the historical context of the film's period of fictional time or also of the film's period of production time. A film may open with an establishing shot of the House of Parliament to tell us that it is set in London, but if we don't recognise the Big Ben tower or ignore that such building is in London, the referential meaning is lost to us. If I am not aware of the Pearl Harbour attack, much of the comic paranoia in *1941* (1979, dir. Spielberg) may seem unjustified. The *explicit meaning* can be identified with the semantics of the fabula as reconstructed by the viewer: it is the reply one may give to the question, 'What is the film about?' Grasping the explicit meaning means grasping the characters' feeling, motivations, desires, the cause/effect chain connecting the events, the correct temporal order, and its obvious meanings—for example, in *Gentlemen Prefer Blondes* (1953, dir. Hawks) one of the explicit meanings is that blondes are dumber or at least more absent-minded than brunettes, and that both categories of women are greedy for jewellery. In some films the explicit meaning is not explicit at all, being rendered difficult to emerge other than in sketchy lines, for example in David Lynch's films or in Surrealist cinema—What is the explicit meaning of *Inland Empire* (2006) or of *The Seashell and the Clergyman* (1928, dir. Dullac)? The *implicit meaning* can be identified as the 'message,' the 'lesson' that the film-maker wants to teach us, the ideology or set of values that the film consciously supports. The implicit meaning inscribed in the finale of *Scarface* (1932, dir. Hawks), for example, is that gangsterism, though it might seem exciting at first sight, leads to self-destruction and despair, and that mobsters are nothing but vile cowards. Finally, the *symptomatic meaning* is like the film's unconscious, the ideological product of its time, the real socio-political position of the film-maker and/or the film industry, despite the one apparently presented as the film's implicit meaning, or it can even be the unconscious thoughts and desires of the film-maker—Hitchcock's sadist fantasies involving icy blondes. Symptomatic meaning is the one that Critical Theory and Psychoanalysis typically set to uncover. For example, in the American Civil War film *Gone with the Wind* (1939, dir. Fleming), the issue of slavery and racism is neutralised by showing black 'employees' that are perfectly happy to be with their white 'employers': this is a symptom of the still unresolved and unreconciled socio-political context at the time of the film production.

Referential and explicit meanings fall within the domain of *comprehension*; implicit and symptomatic meanings within that of *interpretation*. Consider *The Green Berets* (1968, dir. Wayne). When the viewer recognises the Vietnamese locales and the references to the war between the USA and the Viet Cong, s/he has comprehended the film's referential meaning; when s/he understands that the narrative is about a group of selected American soldiers on a special mission who heroically and selflessly defend a military base from vicious and deceitful enemies, s/he has comprehended the explicit meaning; when s/he gets that the film, by exposing the cruelty of the Vietnamese guerrilla and exalting the disinterested heroism of American soldiers, means to endorse the American intervention in the Vietnam War as something necessary and good, then s/he has interpreted the film's implicit meaning; when s/he digs deeper into the ideological simplifications, the racist stereotyping and the rhetoric and biased tone of the dialogue—and comes to the conclusion that the film is a piece of right-wing propaganda bending the facts to support American intervention—s/he has deconstructed the film's symptomatic meaning. The referential and explicit meanings are also called *denotative meanings*, the implicit and symptomatic *connotative meanings*. Denotative meanings can be directly comprehended if one possesses the required skills—for example, some geographical/historical knowledge of the time and place the film is set in, and general skills to follow and understand storytelling, plus specific skills to follow cinematic storytelling. Connotative meanings are indirect and require an interpretive effort. While implicit meanings are generally more openly inscribed in the film—because they are something that film narration meant to pass onto us—symptomatic meanings require a higher degree of interpretation, a work of critical deconstruction, because they are 'hidden messages' that the narration did not intentionally/consciously mean to communicate. Given this higher degree of interpretation and this more covert and 'collateral' nature of symptomatic meanings, films may be over-interpreted; symptomatic meanings are assigned to them that may not really be in the film as in the interpreter's eye, or—with films that are ideologically in line with the 'reader'—they might be ignored, with interpretation lingering on the political implicit meanings only. Says Bordwell,

> I am particularly interested in the strategy, common in post-1960s film interpretation, of finding that whereas some films must be read symptomatically in order to reveal their grasp of social contradictions (is *Gaslight* an example?), other films, such as *Salo* have already achieved that grasp, are not read symptomatically, and are instead treated as implicitly delineating the social contradictions. But surely *Salo* could also be read symptomatically, by someone with another conception of strategically adjusted contradictions. (Bordwell 1993, p. 104)

Since implicit meanings, though interpreted, are more securely linkable to the film itself, in this study I favour the interpretation of implicit meanings over that of symptomatic ones.[15]

Film's overall formal system is built out of the interaction amongst the narrative, the thematic, and the stylistic levels.[16] For example, on a narrative level I might need to let the viewer know that a certain amount of time (filled with irrelevant actions) has passed between the two actions that are important for the narrative. Through the use of, say, a dissolve, the stylistic level implements this. The interaction amongst these levels is coordinated by some *dominant*, an hegemonic principle of formal organisation that regulates the work of the devices, the interactions of systems, and their combination into a whole: 'the dominant determines which devices and functions will come forward as important defamiliarizing traits, and which will be less important. The dominant will pervade the work, governing and linking small-scale devices to large-scale ones' (Thompson 1988a, p. 43). For example, in classical Hollywood cinema 'clear storytelling' is a dominant that bends all the other devices and levels to its service—the classical Hollywood style is often referred to as 'invisible' because the stylistic level must not attract attention to itself but be subordinated to the narrative level. It is particularly important to find out the dominant in case of complex films, as the dominant can shed light on the organisation of the formal system and be the key to comprehend and interpret the film—for example, if *Mulholland Drive* (2000, dir. Lynch) is analysed by keeping in mind that the Freudian mechanisms of dream-work are the film's dominant, the film's construction appears much clearer. In studying this interplay of the levels, particular attention is to be paid to the *function* and *motivation* of the devices.

Function is 'the interrelationship of each element with every other in a…work and with the whole…system' (Yury Tynyanov in Thompson 1988a, p. 15). Each device, like a cog, works in some way within the formal system, and the analysis has to retrieve what this function is. A function can operate according to or in violation of the norms and conventions. For example, in the classical Hollywood cinema there was an institutionalised difference between a dissolve and a fade out/fade in, the former device having the function of signalling that a brief period of time had lapsed, the latter signalling a longer one. In the car journey sequence in Godard's *Breathless* (1960) jump cuts have this function, they are used to compress the duration of the journey in alternative to the smoother temporal-ellipsis devices of classical cinema, such as dissolves. A device can have more than one function: for example, the jump cuts also mean to subvert the polished style associated with the *cinéma de papa*—the literary-based 'cinema of the fathers' that the 'Young Turks' of the French *Nouvelle Vague* deplored—and create visual jolts that undermine the classical 'invisibility' of continuity editing. Neoformalism does not list all the functions that a device can have; it is up to the analyst to detect what function a device is performing in a given situation.

Since the film is an artwork put together intentionally and rationally, each device has a *motivation* for being in its place. Motivation is 'the reason the work suggests for the presence of any given device.…[It] prompts us to decide what could justify the inclusion of the device; motivation, then, operates as an interaction between the work's structures and the spectator's activity' (Thompson 1988a, p. 16). There are four types of motivation. When a device is in the film because it is essential to build either the causal, temporal, or spatial system of the narrative—in short, when it makes the narrative progress—that is called *compositional motivation*. When a device is in the film because its presence is plausible according to our experience of how things are in the real world, that is called *realistic motivation*. When a device is in the film because its presence is expected/required according to the conventions of a given genre, that is called *transtextual motivation*. At the opposite side of the spectrum from the realistic motivation, when a device has no other motivation than its inclusion for some purely aesthetic or idiosyncratic effect on the film-maker's part, that is called *artistic motivation* (Thompson 1988a, pp. 16–20). The presence in any hospital narrative of doctors and nurses hectically moving around is motivated realistically; that is the work force and the work pace in real hospitals. Compositional motivation can be seen in the set-up/pay-off technique: one element is introduced in the story (set-up) that will receive an explanation or produce a result (pay-off) later in the narrative (Field 1998, pp. 269–286). In *The Apartment* (1960, dir. Wilder) the insurance clerk C.C. Baxter is trying to climb the corporate ladder by letting his managers use his apartment as a pied-à-terre for their adulterous rendezvous. He is finally promoted to an executive position as a reward for allowing the 'big boss' and his mistress to use the apartment. Baxter is in love with Fran, the 'elevator girl,' and thinks the feeling might be reciprocal. One morning Baxter hands back to his boss a cracked pocket mirror that was left in the apartment by the boss's mistress (set-up). Later in the film, Baxter is proudly showing his new office to his beloved Fran, and also sports a bowler hat to impress her. She hands him a pocket mirror so that he can admire himself in that headgear. The moment Baxter recognises the cracked pocket mirror he realises that his boss's mistress is Fran (pay-off). The presence of the pocket mirror is motivated compositionally. In virtually every horror film, in particular in those with a supernatural subject matter, the climax takes place at night, and mostly in a stormy one: this is motivated transtextually, as it is a long-standing convention, dating at least back to the Gothic novel tradition, that such tales are set in such atmospheric surroundings—'It was a dark and stormy night.' The saturated soundtracks of Federico Fellini's and Robert Altman's films—where dialogue is made at times difficult to follow because of the overlapping lines, interfering voices, music, and noises—are motivated artistically; they are the fruit of the directors' authorial marks.[17] As with the function, a device can have more than one motivation. For example, the aforementioned jump cuts in *A bout de souffle* can be motivated both compositionally—they are there to tell us that some time has lapsed between one shot and the other—and artistically—their choice as devices to perform that ellipsis function, instead of the classical dissolves, are part of Godard's poetics. The best instances of compositional motivation at first hide their set-up/pay-off structure behind some realistic motivation. In the episode 'Phoenix' of *Breaking Bad* (2008–2013, prod. Gilligan)[18] there is a seemingly casual scene in which the series' protagonist, the soon-to-be drug kingpin Walter White, is shown carefully settling his newborn baby in the cradle. His over-solicitous sister-in-law is giving him advice, and he demonstrates that he knows that infants must be put on their side, instead of belly up, so they will not choke in case they have some regurgitation in their sleep. Since the protagonist has just had a new baby, this piece of dialogue seems realistically motivated by the parenting situation. Later in the episode, Walter happens to be in the same room when Jane, the heroin addict who has tried to blackmail him, turns belly up during her comatose sleep and starts choking on her regurgitation. From the previous scene, we know that Walter perfectly understands what is happening to Jane and he could turn her on the side to stop the choking. But, after a brief hesitation, he decides to watch her die instead, thus solving his blackmailing problem. The seemingly realistically motivated cradle scene is now revealed as compositionally motivated too.

Neoformalism and Music in Films

In the Neoformalist framework, since the interest is not in communication but in perception, the analysis is encouraged to tackle those instances in which music does not pass any message at all—for example, the interplay between the music's orchestral colours and the colour palette of the costumes and the light design, or between music's timbre and the timbre of the actors' voice, or between the pace of the music and the pace of editing. In a Neoformalist analysis, 'accompaniment' and 'synchronous' music is not a lesser musical intervention than 'comment' or 'asynchronous' music. 'Everything in a film has a formal function' (Bordwell 1981, p. 5), music included, and this may 'only' consist in building the editing pace in a chase sequence or casting a unifying thread over a montage sequence. Such an example is Thompson's analysis of the formal contribution of Prokofiev's music in *Ivan the Terrible—Part I* (1945, dir. Eisenstein). As regards the jolting configuration of the dance piece in the banquet scene, she points out:

> Editing creates the dance by interweaving these overtones and dominants in a rhythmic relation to the music. A conventional choreographer would probably find this disturbing, for one cannot really watch the dancers or determine what the whole dance is like with the actions cut into bits....Eisenstein...makes music, color, movement, and editing equal in

importance: none—not even the dancers' bodies—takes precedence. As a result, *Ivan*'s dance is dependent on the fusion of these several 'voices' acting in conjunction with each other. (Thompson 1981, p. 244)

There is no privilege given to music when it provides meanings compared to when it performs some other formal function.

What is the difference between this Neoformalist approach and others? First of all, since music is treated as one of the interdependent filmic devices—something at the same level with editing, acting, lighting, and so on—it is treated as something internal to the system. This favours a non-separatist conception. Others have already pointed out the importance of considering the interaction of music with visuals, of course, and in a seemingly non-separatist fashion, for example, Cook. But Cook, as we have seen, implies that analysis *equals* interpretation: 'The role of analysis...is to oppose such sedimented patterns of perception, testing easy, "within-the-grain" interpretations against other possible readings' (Cook 1998, p. 133). If the first part of Cook's statement— 'oppose such sedimented patterns of perception'—seems to echo the formalist concept of defamiliarisation and thus seems to find roots in a perception model, the second part makes it clear that perception is not interesting per se. For Cook, the interest is in finding new 'readings' to oppose to the obvious interpretations: we are still in a communications model. Unlike Cook, Neoformalism is as interested in 'conformance' as it is in 'contest,' and it is particularly suitable to handle those generally underestimated instances in which music is in 'conformance' and 'parallel.' Neoformalism is suitable to account for any kind of musical agency, and in any kind of film: 'Because playfully entertaining films can engage our perceptions as complexly as can films dealing with serious, difficult themes, neoformalism does not distinguish between 'high' and 'low' art in films' (Thompson 1988a, p. 9).

What method does Neoformalism suggest to tackle music? There have been many proposals, more or less prescriptive, to cope with the analysis of music in films, from strongly theory-based ones—for example, Winters's of Redner's—to procedural ones that lay out the steps that the analysis should take—such is Ronald Sadoff's 'Eclectic Methodology' (Sadoff 2012), or Neumeyer's Chion-inspired four-stage method.[19] Given that Neoformalism is 'a functional mode of film analysis' (Thomson-Jones 2011, p. 136), its application to film music results in a function-based method. The Neoformalist method I propose does not prescribe a series of analytical stages but suggests where and how to look; the analysis starts having in mind what functions music can perform in films. A function-based method is not new. At various times, many scholars have compiled lists of possible functions that music can have in films, from Raymond Spottiswoode in 1935 (Spottiswoode 1962, pp. 192–193), to T.W. Adorno and Hanns Eisler in 1947 (Adorno and Eisler 2007, pp. 13–20), Aaron Copland in 1949,[20] up to the eleven-function systematisation of Zofia Lissa (1965),[21] Claudia Gorbman's four functions of Hollywood music,[22] and more recently Annabel J. Cohen's three main functions from the viewpoint of Cognitive Psychology,[23] and David Neumeyer's five functional macro-areas.[24] Typically, these inventories take the move from an observation of the diverse actions of music in the films and try to distillate and list all the possible functions. Such catalogues are useful reference points and the recurrence of functions from one to the other—for example, Copland's 'building a sense of continuity' is reprised by Gorbman—confirms most of these abstractions as accurate. The risk is that, for the sake of completion, the number of itemised functions in the list might grow to such an extent that the catalogue becomes too cumbersome to be employed for practical analytical uses. For example, the inventory by the semiotician Cristina Cano amounts to more than thirty items subdivided into functions and sub-functions (Cano 2002). Inventories like Cano's are good on paper as they give a detailed overview of the many potentialities of film music, but they are quite impractical for analytical purposes. The analyst who wished to employ Cano's functions would have to constantly keep the list in front of her/him because keeping in mind all those functions would be a rather daunting task, and the constant list-checking would end up drawing attention away from the film. Another risk is that of naming categories that look fine on paper but prove to be slippery when concretely applied to analysis—Gorbman's functions of 'unity' seems at times to overlap with that of 'continuity.' The more numerous and fine-grained the classifications, the more indistinct the boundaries tend to become between one function and the other, and hence the more difficult it may be to discern which function is performed at a particular moment in the film—Is one instance a 'transitive function' or perhaps a 'demarcating narrative function?' (Cano 2002, p. 188).

A function-based method that aims at being comfortable for practical analytical applications should have a limited set of functions—so that they can be comfortably mastered by memory—and should name them in accordance with some criterion that is itself easy to remember. Music can do a number of things in a film; a list of functions compiled from films can end up being quite extended. Hence, we should not start from the film. We should start from the viewer. In films, music helps the viewer comprehend and interpret what s/he is watching and hearing. And the viewer's activity involves three levels: perceptive (we see and hear things in films); emotive (we respond affectively to what we experience); cognitive (we comprehend and interpret what we experience). Hence, the method focusses on how music functions in these three areas. I call this Neoformalist method 'Film/Music Analysis' to mark the strong audio-visual interrelation subtended to it—it is not a musical analysis of 'film music' but a filmic analysis of how film and music interact to produce an interconnected audiovisual system. Although music is treated here as a filmic device, music is *music* after all. Even if tackled from a film scholar's perspective, some basic grasp and knowledge of the musical art is needed. Some theoretical grounds are also needed to explain how music can fuse with the visuals. The next chapter provides such grounding.

Notes

1. For this reason, Thompson is the main reference in my work. Her approach adopts the framework of cognitivism (as opposed to psychoanalysis), but it is mainly employed as a tool for film analysis and historiography, while in Bordwell the development and defence of a cognitivist film theory is more central; see, for example, Bordwell (1989a, 1990, 2011).
2. The main texts I will be referring to are Thompson (1981, 1988a). I also use other works by Bordwell (see previous note) that, although not Neoformalist nominally, nevertheless have theoretically expanded specific aspects of the Neoformalist approach, in particular by stressing the importance of Cognitivism as the theoretical framework. The narrative level is studied in Bordwell (1985); the stylistic level in Bordwell (1997); the thematic level in Bordwell (1989b). The book that best encompasses Bordwell's entire work is Bordwell (2008). It must be noted that the analytical philosopher Noël Carroll has theoretical positions similar to Bordwell—in his defence of Cognitivism against psychoanalysis, most notably in Carroll (1988)—and the two have co-edited Bordwell and Carroll (1996), which stirred much heated debate for its bold attack of the Grand Theory 'doctrines.' A brief history of Formalism and Neoformalism is (from a critical point of view) Salvaggio (1981)

and (from a sympathetic point of view) Blewitt (1997). More neutral accounts are Christie (1998), Thomson-Jones (2011), Rushton and Bettison (2010, pp. 132–135).
3. Now in its 13th edition: Bordwell et al. (2016). Their first adaptation of Russian Formalism is Thompson and Bordwell (1976).
4. See Bann and Bowlt (1973), Erlich (1980), Lemon and Reis (1965).
5. Bordwell has further developed his narratology in Bordwell (2008, pp. 85–133).
6. A criticism of Bordwell's narratology and a defence of the communications model and the narrator are in Chatman (1990, pp. 126–129) in particular.
7. Of course, Neoformalism is a 'textual-centred' approach to film; it is not Reception Studies or Audience Research. If only these audience-context-centred approaches are considered really connected to history, then Neoformalism is ahistorical, but it is not more ahistorical than other approaches and methods (Psychoanalysis, Critical Theory, Semiotics, etc.).
8. Bordwell's reply and defence is Bordwell (1998).
9. See Thompson (1988b, c).
10. See Bordwell and Thompson (2010, pp. 64–65).
11. 'Perception' is how the viewer receives and elaborates the audiovisual stimuli that the film passes onto her/him, and 'Comprehension' is how s/he reconstructs the narrative cues into a narrative that makes sense to her/him.
12. For example, M. Smith (1995) and Plantinga and Smith (1999) as regards emotions; J. Smith (1996, 1999) as regards film music.
13. In Thompson (1981), five categories are listed: mise-en-scene; sound; camera/frame; editing; optical effects. I have adopted the four-item list offered in Bordwell and Thompson (2010) because optical effects are part of cinematography.
14. On interpretation and the different types of meaning, see Bordwell (1989b, pp. 8–9).
15. That is why, although Bordwell points out that the 'units of implicit meaning are commonly called "themes"' (Bordwell 1989b, p. 9), I have called 'thematic level' the formal level that accommodate all the types of meanings. I take the thematic level to be the one in which the analyst focusses when he aims to interpret the film, and in interpretation I give priority to 'themes,' to implicit meanings (see Chap. 8).
16. Of all the levels we have considered, the stylist level is the one that has to do with the film's specificity as an art medium; while the narrative and thematic levels can be found also in literature and theatre and maybe in painting, the stylistic level of an art-from has to do to the specific techniques of that art-form. I have mentioned in the 'Introduction' that Film Studies may be taken less seriously than other disciplines—say,

musicology—because they do not have a strong discipline-specific method but tend to use tools imported from other departments of the Humanities. One solution would be for film scholars to focus more on the analysis of the stylistic level, which is often neglected in favour of the more general narrative and thematic levels.
17. On artistic motivation-based films—parametric form—see Bordwell (1985, pp. 274–310) and Thompson (1988a, pp. 19–20, 247–250).
18. Season 2, Episode 2, aired on 24 May 2009.
19. The four stages are: Itemize; Characterize; Locate Synch Points; Compare Sound and Image (Neumeyer 2015, p. 51).
20. Copland (1949) was issued on 6 November 1949 in *The New York Times Magazine* and later re-published in Thomas (1991, pp. 10–17). Copland's list is also discussed in Prendergast (1977, pp. 201–214) and Cooke (2010, pp. 317–326).
21. Lissa's functions are also cited and discussed in Miceli (2009, pp. 549–551).
22. Gorbman's functions are: '(1) Signifier of emotion: Soundtrack music may set specific moods and emphasize particular emotions suggested in the narrative [...], but first and foremost, it is a signifier of emotion itself. (2) Narrative cueing: (a) referential/narrative: music gives referential and narrative cues, e.g., indicating point of view, supplying formal demarcations, and establishing setting and characters; (b) connotative: music 'interprets' and 'illustrates' narrative events. (3) Continuity: music provides formal and rhythmic continuity—between shots, in transitions between scenes, by filling 'gaps'. (4) Unity: via repetition and variation of musical material and instrumentation, music aids in the construction of formal and narrative unity' (Gorbman 1987, p. 73).
23. Cohen's functions are: Music interprets the visuals and adds meaning; Music helps the memory; Music creates the suspension of disbelief (Cohen 2000, pp. 360–377).
24. Neumeyer has indicated three ways in which music often work: referentially, expressively, and motivically, and has identified five functional macro-areas or 'binaries' ('Principle,' 'Method,' 'Space,' 'Time,' 'Agency'), each articulated into two sub-functions, one of which is the time-honed 'counterpoint' (Neumeyer 2015, p. 11, 63).

References

Adorno, Theodor W., and Hanns Eisler. 2007 [1947]. *Composing for the Films*. London and New York: Continuum.
Bann, Stephen, and John E. Bowlt (eds.). 1973. *Russian Formalism*. New York: Harper and Row.

Blewitt, John. 1997. A Neo-Formalist Approach to Film Aesthetics and Education. *Journal of Aesthetic Education* 31 (2): 91–96.
Bordwell, David. 1981. *The Films of Carl-Theodor Dreyer*. Berkeley and Los Angeles: University of California Press.
Bordwell, David. 1985. *Narration in the Fiction Film*. Madison, WI: University of Wisconsin Press.
Bordwell, David. 1989a. A Case for Cognitivism. *Iris* 9 (Spring): 11–40.
Bordwell, David. 1989b. *Making Meaning. Inference and Rhetoric in the Interpretation of Cinema*. Cambridge, MA: Harvard University Press.
Bordwell, David. 1990. A Case for Cognitivism: Further Reflections. *Iris* 11 (Summer): 107–112.
Bordwell, David. 1993. Film Interpretation Revisited. *Film Criticism* 17 (2–3): 93–119.
Bordwell, David. 1997. *On the History of Film Style*. Cambridge, MA: Harvard University Press.
Bordwell, David. 1998. Preaching Pluralism: Pluralism, Truth, and Scholarly Inquiry in Film Studies. *Cinema Journal* 37 (2): 84–90.
Bordwell, David. 2008. *Poetics of Cinema*. New York: Routledge.
Bordwell, David. 2011. Cognitive Theory. In *The Routledge Companion to Philosophy and Film*, ed. Paisley Livingston and Carl Plantinga, 356–367. Abingdon and New York: Routledge.
Bordwell, David, and Kristin Thompson. 2010. *Film Art: An Introduction*, 9th ed. New York: McGraw-Hill.
Bordwell, David, and Nöel Carroll (eds.). 1996. *Post-Theory. Reconstructing Film Studies*. Madison, WI: University of Wisconsin Press.
Bordwell, David, Kristin Thompson, and Jeff Smith. 2016. *Film Art: An Introduction*, 13th ed. New York: McGraw-Hill.
Browne, Nick. 1982. The Formalist's Dreyer. The Films of Carl-Theodor Dreyer by David Bordwell. Review. *October* 23 (Winter): 80–88.
Burch, Noël. 1973. *Theory of Film Practice*, trans. Helen R. Lane. New York: Praeger.
Cano, Cristina. 2002. *La musica nel cinema. Musica, immagine, racconto*. Rome: Gremese.
Carroll, Noël. 1988. *Mystifying Movies: Fads and Fallacies in Contemporary Film Theory*. New York: Columbia University Press.
Carroll, Noël. 1996. Prospects for Film Theory: A Personal Assessment. In *Post-theory. Reconstructing Film Studies*, ed. David Bordwell and Noël Carroll, 37–68. Madison, WI: University of Wisconsin Press.
Chatman, Seymour. 1990. *Coming to Terms: The Rhetoric of Narrative in Fiction and Film*. Ithaca, NY: Cornell University Press.

Christie, Ian. 1998. Formalism and Neoformalism. In *The Oxford Guide to Film Studies*, ed. John Hill and Pamela Church Gibson, 58–64. Oxford: Oxford University Press.

Cohen, Annabel. 2000. Film Music: Perspectives from Cognitive Psychology. In *Music and Cinema*, ed. James Buhler, Caryl Flinn, and David Neumeyer, 360–377. Hanover, NH: Wesleyan University Press.

Cook, Nicholas. 1998. *Analysing Musical Multimedia*. Oxford: Clarendon Press.

Cooke, Mervyn (ed.). 2010. *The Hollywood Film Music Reader*. Oxford-New York: Oxford University Press.

Copland, Aaron. 1949. Tip to Moviegoers: Take Off Those Ear-muffs. *New York Times Magazine*, 6: 28–32.

Erlich, Victor. 1980. *Russian Formalism. History—Doctrine*, 4th ed. The Hague, Paris and New York: Mouton.

Field, Syd. 1998. *The Screenwriter's Problem Solver: How to Recognize, Identify, and Define Screenwriting Problems*. New York: Dell Publishing.

Gault, Berys. 2010. *A Philosophy of Cinematic Art*. Cambridge: Cambridge University Press.

Gombrich, Ernst H. 1961. *Art and Illusion: A Study in the Psychology of Pictorial Representation*. Princeton, NJ: Princeton University Press.

Gorbman, Claudia. 1987. *Unheard Melodies. Narrative Film Music*. London and Bloomington: BFI/Indiana University Press.

Lehman, Peter. 1997. Pluralism Versus the Correct Position. *Cinema Journal* 36 (2): 114–119.

Lemon, Lee T., and Marion J. Reis (eds.). 1965. *Russian Formalism Criticism: Four Essays*. Lincoln, NE: University of Nebraska Press.

Lissa, Zofia. 1965. *Ästhetik der Filmmusik*. Berlin: Henschelverlag.

Miceli, Sergio. 2009. *Musica Per Film. Storia, Estetica, Analisi, Tipologie*. Lucca and Milan: LIM-Ricordi.

Neumeyer, David. 2015. *Meaning and Interpretation of Music in Cinema*. Bloomington and Indianapolis: Indiana University Press.

Plantinga, Carl, and Greg M. Smith (eds.). 1999. *Passionate Views. Film, Cognition, and Emotion*. Baltimore, MD: Johns Hopkins University Press.

Prendergast, Roy M. 1977. *Film Music: A Neglected Art: A Critical Study of Music in Films*. New York: W. W. Norton.

Quart, Alissa. 2000. David Bordwell Blows the Whistle on Film Studies. *Lingua Franca* 10 (March): 36–43.

Rushton, Richard, and Gary Bettison. 2010. *What Is Film Theory? An Introduction to Contemporary Debates*. Maidenhead: McGraw-Hill/Open University Press.

Sadoff, Ronald. 2012. An Eclectic Methodology for Analyzing Film Music. *Music and the Moving Image* 5 (2): 70–86.

Salvalaggio, Jerry L. 1981. The Emergence of a New School of Criticism: Neo-Formalism. *Journal of the University Film Association* 33 (4): 45–52.

Shklovsky, Victor. 1973 [1914]. The Resurrection of the Word. In *Russian Formalism: A Collection of Articles and Texts in Translation*, trans. and ed. Stephen Bann and John E. Bowlt, 41–47. Edinburgh: Scottish Academic Press.

Smith, Jeff. 1996. Unheard Melodies? A Critique of Psychoanalytic Theories of Film Music. In *Post-theory. Reconstructing Film Studies*, ed. David Bordwell and Nöel Carroll, 230–247. Madison, WI: University of Wisconsin Press.

Smith, Jeff. 1999. Movie Music as Moving Music: Emotion, Cognition, and the Film Score. In *Passionate Views. Film, Cognition, and Emotion*, ed. Carl Plantinga and Greg M. Smith, 146–167. Baltimore, MD: Johns Hopkins University Press.

Smith, Murray. 1995. *Engaging Characters: Fiction, Emotion, and the Cinema*. Oxford: Clarendon Press.

Spottiswoode, Raymond. 1962 [1935]. *A Grammar of the Film: An Analysis of Film Technique*. Berkeley, CA: University of California Press.

Stam, Robert. 2000. *Film Theory: An Introduction*. Malden, MA: Blackwell.

Thomas, Tony. 1991. *Film Score: The Art and Craft of Movie Music*. Burbank, CA: Riverwood.

Thompson, Kristin, and David Bordwell. 1976. Space and Narrative in the Films of Ozu. *Screen* 17 (2): 41–73.

Thompson, Kristin. 1981. *Eisenstein's Ivan the Terrible: A Neoformalist Analysis*. Princeton, NJ: Princeton University Press.

Thompson, Kristin. 1988a. *Breaking the Glass Armor. Neoformalist Film Analysis*. Princeton, NJ: Princeton University Press.

Thompson, Kristin. 1988b. Godard's Unknown Country: *Sauve qui peut (la vie)*. In *Breaking the Glass Armor. Neoformalist Film Analysis*, 263–288. Princeton, NJ: Princeton University Press.

Thompson, Kristin. 1988c. Sawing through the Bough: *Tout va bien* as a Brechtian Film. In *Breaking the Glass Armor. Neoformalist Film Analysis*, 110–131. Princeton, NJ: Princeton University Press.

Thomson-Jones, Katherine. 2011. Formalism. In *The Routledge Companion to Philosophy and Film*, ed. Paisley Livingston and Carl Plantinga, 131–141. Abingdon and New York: Routledge.

CHAPTER 5

Film/Music Analysis I: Music, Gestalt, and Audiovisual Isomorphism

In the previous chapter I proposed Neoformalism as a fruitful approach to treat music as a cinematic device. But before examining *what* music can do in films, we should first understand *how* music can do that. Here, I trace in big strokes the musical theories that I find appropriate as a framework for my method. Those (forgiving) music scholars that are reading this will hopefully be tolerant as to the sketchy nature of the following overview and the outdated status of some of the scholarship I cite.[1]

MUSIC AS MUSIC

Given my interest in a perception model and in the viewer activities, I have borrowed concepts from 'Psychomusicology'—named after one of the discipline's most notable journals—or, more generally, 'Psychology of Music.' Psychology of music studies how music is made sense of by the listener, how the discreet sound stimuli that we perceive are elaborated by our mind into the organised and meaningful phenomenon that we call music, and, vice versa, how music is composed so that the single sound stimuli will meaningfully combine when heard by human ears and processed by the brain. It is a rich, complex field that has now a long history and a variety of contributions from different perspectives—from Carl Seashore's Psychoacoustics (Seashore 1967) to Leonard B. Meyer's Gestalt Psychology (Meyer 1956) to John Sloboda's Cognitive Psychology (Sloboda 1999).[2] There is no space here to delve into the matter satisfactorily. Suffice it to say that I follow the general psycho-musicological framework launched by Leonard B. Meyer's studies and further developed, within the framework of Cognitive Psychology, by Eugene Narmour (Narmour 1990) and, more recently, by David Huron (Huron 2006). According to this thread, the structures that realise emotion and meaning in a piece of music are not to be look for only in the musical text itself—as methods of musical analysis such as Schenker's did—but as a result of the encounter between the compositional processes within a piece of music ('implications') and the processes of the listener's mind, in particular her/his expectations. Expectations are formulated from our previous knowledge and experience of the musical conventions of a given style and period, and also on innate structures of our sensory and cognitive systems that music engages at different levels. For example, tonal music sounds more easy to the ear not only because our cultural familiarity with and extended exposure to the tonal system offers us more reference points to make predictions and advance expectations—which is not the case with the more recently developed and thus more unpredictable non-tonal music. Tonal music sounds 'easier' also because it is based on the natural series of harmonics that constitutes each sound, and thus has more 'innate' psychoacoustic grounding (Sloboda 1999, pp. 5, 197, 235).

The emotional and semantic effects of music are the result of the encounter of certain structures of the music and certain processes of the mind. For example, music generates emotional/affective[3] responses by 'playing' with our expectations. If a melody develops in such a way as to lead me to anticipate a perfect cadence as a closure but then pauses on the fifth grade (typically the penultimate stage before a harmonic closure) without resolving on the tonic (the harmonic closure), the emotional effect is likely to be dysphoric, one of frustration of one's expectation. On the contrary if the piece builds up to a satisfying closure that confirms the expectations, the effect is euphoric—because music conforms to the 'Law of Good Continuation' (Meyer 1956, pp. 83–127), there is a 'realization of the hypothesis' (Narmour 1990, pp. 4–5), or a 'prediction response' is generated (Huron 2006, pp. 12–13). Atonal music may produce a sense of anxiety precisely because the lack of tonal reference points causes us to feel disoriented and unable to make hypothesis about what is going to happen (Meyer 1956, p. 35, 158). Similarly, the tension and even exasperation that the statical repetition of ostinatos may induce are the effect of 'tension responses' (Huron 2006, pp. 9–12) or of the 'Principle of saturation' (Meyer 1956, p. 135), as music is stuck on the same passage and does not progress; we expect music to change but it does not, and the tension generated by the waiting for a change cannot be released but is frustratingly fed over and over.

The meaning of a piece of music is also the result of its encounter with our mental faculties; a piece of music makes sense to us if we see a pattern in it. Most people can connect with Beethoven's *Fifth Symphony* (1808) and other tonal works, they can follow the musical flow and perceive it as meaningful. They recognise an agitated if not tragic meaning in it because music moves along a logical path, sets implications (a harmonic pattern that points towards a tonal resolution) that are realised (the tonal resolution is reached) or deferred (creating a sense of struggle, of a difficult journey in the achieving of its destination). A musical path—or even some narrative—is detectable in some measure also by musically illiterate listeners; they can simply recognise that the piece 'makes sense' in that patterns and an overall developmental form are noticeable—Meyer calls this 'embodied meaning.' On the other hand, musical laypersons may find aleatoric or avant-garde music (such as John Cage's or Luciano Berio's) 'meaningless' because no trajectory or pattern at all is easily discernible. Tonal music sounds more meaningful because it is 'teleological,' it has a clear orientation towards a point of arrival (Meyer 1967, p. 72).

But a piece of music can also have a 'designative meaning' that is more specific than the general 'making sense' of the 'embodied meaning': it can translate extra-musical entities into music.[4] Music may possess a heroic ethos or communicate humorous inflections. Explains Meyer: 'Ethos is the result of a combination of factors. Register and sonority, tempo and dynamics are obviously crucial. Had the same pitch-time relationship been presented in a high register, at a fast tempo, and with *forte* dynamics, character would have been very different' (Meyer 1973, p. 243).The ethos or character of a piece of music is given by musical structures that resemble attitudes, shapes, or gestures from our real-life experience. Music can also express more specifically designative meaning by utilising tropes that are culturally charged with some meaning. For example, the sound of the oboe communicates bucolic images because it is traditionally associated—in painting, poetry, and music—with pastoral tunes and imagery.[5]

Specific meaning and connotations in music are the result of cultural stratifications. And besides the emotional response induced by the confirmation or frustration of our anticipations and expectations, specific emotions/moods can also be evoked within a specific culture because music reproduces the moods and gestures of certain emotional situations—'designative emotional behaviour' (Meyer 1956, p. 266). 'Bereavement' in the Western culture is associated with weeping, sobbing, slow movements, a sense of loss, depressed tone and pace of speech; consequently funeral music is traditionally characterised by slow tempi, stern and plain rhythm, restrained dynamics, sobbing melodic lines, and minor mode, which is less 'tonal' than major mode and thus more distressing (Meyer 1956, pp. 256–272). Meyer reminds us that:

> A competent listener perceives and responds to music with his total being. As tonal stimuli, filtered and processed by a selective auditory nervous system, are related to one another by the patterning proclivities and habits of the human mind, every facet of behaviour—physiological and psychological, motor and mental—becomes attuned to and congruent with the process and structure of musical events. Through such empathetic identification, music is quite literally *felt*, and it can be felt without the mediation of extramusical concepts or images....Because human experience is not compartmentalized into musical and nonmusical, aesthetic and nonaesthetic, the ethos of a musical event will often seem similar to and suggest some aspect of the extramusical world. The musical event is felt to be sad or joyful, restrained or exuberant, calm or agitated, and the like. And such characteristic states of being may in turn be associated with more specific circumstances and ideas: a summer evening's calm, the gaiety and bustle of a social gathering. Moreover, when it explicitly imitates extramusical sounds—as in birdcalls, wind and thunder, and the like—or is established as part of the tradition of Western musical iconography, a musical pattern may denote quite specific kinds of events, actions, and ideas in the extramusical world. (Meyer 1973, pp. 242–243)

But who is this 'competent listener?' Luckily, one is not required to master musicological analysis and music theory to be one: 'Just as one can ride a bicycle without knowing how a bicycle really works, so experienced listeners can respond sensitively to music without knowing anything about what makes music work: without knowing about the theory or history of music' (Meyer 1973, p. 15).

The first reason why I have chosen Meyer's studies is that they are not totally focussed on in-depth musicological analysis. Other more recent theorists have proposed approaches that dispense from such musicological requirements—Kivy (1981), for example. True, but I have three other reasons to prefer Meyer. Firstly, Meyer's studies were amongst the first to link musical meaning to the listener's psychological activities. Meyer is a classic. For a study like mine that aims to borrow concepts from one field that are fitting to investigate aspects in another field (film analysis) rather than innovate a field (psychology of music), the choice of such a renowned and a well-tested theory seemed a sensible one. Secondly, Meyer's views—particularly in *Music, the Arts, and Idea*—are very close to that of Neoformalism, making his most fitting theory to provide complementary musico/analytical tools to a Neoformalist approach to film music.[6]

The Neoformalists' take on film-viewing is much similar to Meyer's on music-listening. For example, Meyer discusses the demise of the content/form dichotomy, linking this dichotomy to an old way of conceptualising that was influenced by the Cartesian mind/body dualism: 'just as the mind-body dichotomy has come to seem less and less tenable, so differentiation of *materials* and *form* from *subject matter* and *meaning* has come to seem less and less convincing' (Meyer 1967, p. 210). As a consequence, he argues for a concentration upon the analysis of forms and 'means' instead of interpretation of 'contents' and, as the formalists/neoformalists, he sees content as part of the form: 'content is [not] necessarily irrelevant or unimportant, but…the *what* and the *why* of content are seen as inseparable from the *how* of structure and process—from the craft by which content is communicated' (Meyer 1967, p. 223). As the formalists, Meyer is interested in art as craftsmanship (Meyer 1967, p. 223), and he sees the perception of art as based on cross-cultural universal structures of the human mind—the 'fundamental constant' of human perception—which bears similarities with Bordwell's 'contingent universals' (Bordwell 2008, p. 61). The following Meyer passage about the dichotomy between content and form/materials sounds as if it were taken from some Bordwell/Carroll critique of the Grand Theory:

> [S]ome artists and critics still preserve the dichotomy, stressing the primal importance of content, whether manifest or symbolic, as against materials and form. Significantly, these are most often men who use—'interpret'—works of art to support, or exhibit the relevance of, some extra-aesthetic theory or dogma: for instance, the Freudians or the Marxists. The need to label and stereotype through the interpretation of subject matter, however, is by no means confined to those committed to an orthodoxy. Whenever a work of art seems strange or eludes easy understanding, there is a temptation to discover that the work represents or symbolizes the artist's beliefs about decadence, war, religion, sex, and so forth. Much contemporary art has, without warrant, been subjected to this sort of blatant and flatulent criticism. (Meyer 1967, p. 212)[7]

And in turn, this Bordwell passage resembles Meyer's theory: 'When we bet on a hypothesis, especially under the pressure of time, confirmation can carry an emotional kick;...The mixture of anticipation, fulfillment, and blocked or retarded or twisted consequences can exercise great emotional power' (Bordwell 1985, pp. 39–40), and also 'From beginning to end, our involvement with a work of art depends largely on expectations' (Bordwell and Thompson 2010, p. 59). Most important, both Meyer and Neoformalism see the search for unity, completeness, and stability as the primary goal in any perceptual experience, both in the real world and in the aesthetic realm: Meyer says, 'The human mind, striving on stability and completeness, "expects" structural gaps to be filled in' (Meyer 1967, p. 7), and Bordwell somewhat echoes, 'Th[e] effort toward meaning involves an effort toward unity. Comprehending a narrative requires assigning it some coherence....The organism enjoys creating unity' (Bordwell 1985, pp. 34–39). This innate craving for unity and stability leads to the third reason why I have selected Meyer's *passé* theory; it is based on Gestalt Psychology, which to me is the best theoretical framework to support a function-based method of film/music analysis within the Neoformalist approach.

MUSIC AND GESTALT QUALITIES

A theory of mental activity developed in the first part of the twentieth century,[8] Gestalt Psychology studies how the human mind—in terms of perception, behaviour, recalling, association, and thinking—has a natural tendency to organise the external stimuli into an experiential whole, and to pursue perceptual stability, balance, and completeness. Interestingly for our study here, all started from music. In 1890, the philosopher and psychologist Christian von Ehrenfels noticed that a melody cannot really be defined as the sum of the parts—the tones—it is made of: 'Is a melody (i) a mere sum of elements, or (ii) something novel in relation to this sum, something that certainly goes hand in hand with but is distinguishable from the sum of elements?' (von Ehrenfels 1988, p. 83). If hypothesis 'i' (the most common at that time) were true, a melody in the scale of C transposed to the scale of C# (which shares not a single tone with the scale of C) would not be recognisable at all. On the contrary, the melody can still be perfectly recognised as the same even if made of completely different tones. A melody is a relational structure of rhythmic distribution and frequency difference; what we perceive as characteristic of a particular melody is its structure, not the single elements.

Ehrenfels called this relational structure amongst elements that transcends the elements themselves 'Gestalt Quality.'[9] The word 'Gestalt'—often translated as 'form' or 'shape'—is actually better rendered as 'configuration,'[10] which refers to a 'form' but also to a dynamic process of organisation and a relation amongst the parts of a system. Any melody has a specific and identifying Gestalt, and rhythm is one of the Gestalt qualities that contribute to the organisation of the Gestalt.[11] It was from Ehrenfels's investigation of the Gestalt Quality of perception that Gestalt Psychology started in the following decades.

The focus of the Gestaltists' experiments was precisely to study why we experience phenomena as wholes even if they are made up of separate components. In Wolfgang Köhler's words: 'Instead of reacting to local stimuli by local and mutually independent events, the organism responds to the *patterns* of stimuli to which it is exposed; and…this answer is a unitary process, a functional whole, which gives, in experience, a sensory scene rather than a mosaic of local sensations' (Köhler 1970, p. 103). At the basis of any experience there is an organisation of the stimuli into Gestalts—forms, configurations, closed shapes—and this native and autonomous organisational process operates according to the better configuration possible, that is, the most stable and complete. This is the general 'Law of Prägnanz'—'the tendency towards simple Gestalten' (Köhler 2013, p. 54)—which could be called 'Law of Good Configuration' and 'according to which every Gestalt becomes as "good" as possible' (Wulf 2013, p. 148)—with 'good' meaning as stable, complete, balanced as possible. Famously, Gestaltists said that 'the whole is different from the sum of its parts,'[12] and a musical example is, once again, brought into explain the concept:

> When the tones *c* and *g* are sounded together they produce a quality which in music is called the Fifth. That quality is neither in the *c* nor the *g*, nor does it depend on those particular notes. Any two tones with the ratio 2/3 will be recognised immediately as a Fifth no matter in what region of the scale they may be played. Fifthness is a Gestalt which is different from either or any of its parts, and no amount of knowledge about the parts in isolation would give the remotest hint as to what Fifthness is like. (Pratt 1969, p. 10)

Famous Gestalt experiments dealt with the spontaneous sorting of percepts into regular groups; the automatic completion of incomplete shapes or the perception of complete shapes where there actually are only edges and empty space; the figure/background separation whereas the brightest elements tend to be perceived as foregrounded; the stabilisation of ambiguous figures (like Rubin's vase) into only one at a time of the two possible configurations.[13]

Whilst Gestalt Psychology laid important foundations for the psychology of perception, showing the mechanisms of how we experience the world as we do, it has long been criticised for the unconvincing explanations given to the otherwise correctly observed phenomena. Gestaltists posited 'Psychophysical Isomorphism' as the basis of mental activity, a correspondence between the configurations of the external objects as we perceive them and the configurations of the energy field in the brain structures responsible for the perception of those objects: 'our experiences and the processes which underlie these experiences have the same structure. Thus we assume that when the visual field exhibits a thing as a detached entity, the corresponding process in the brain is relatively segregated from surrounding processes' (Köhler 1970, p. 344). The brain is hard-wired so as to perceive the world in a certain fashion—for example, similar and proximate objects tend to be grouped. Perception is the result of certain Gestalt qualities in the external world—the figure has lines that converge in acute angles—that trigger a 'dynamic self-distribution' of energy in the brain that, once it has reached an equilibrium in its distribution, produces in our mind a corresponding experience—in our example, that of 'edginess.' If the figure has other Gestalt qualities—say, curved lines—the energy fields in the brain take a different distribution and produce a corresponding different experience—of 'roundness.' In Köhler's words: 'A stationary visual field corresponds to a balanced distribution of underlying processes. When conditions change, resulting developments will always be in the direction of balance' (Köhler 1970, pp. 130–133). Indeed, Isomorphism can be used to explain those ambiguous stimuli known as multi-stable figures, such as the 'Rabbit/Duck' where we can see only one of the two configurations at a time, or the 'Necker Cube,' whose lower-left face can alternatively be seen as placed in the background or in the foreground, and the perception of the cube keeps undulating between these two configurations. The fact that it is impossible to perceive both configurations at the same time can be explained on the grounds of the one-to-one isomorphic rapport existing between the stimulus and the energy field in the brain. These multi-stable figures transmit *ambiguous* stimuli that allow for two possible configurations, but the brain energy fields cannot be conformed to both configurations at the same time: thus, the energy configuration keeps oscillating between the one and the other, causing perception to be equally oscillating, multi-stable. Gestalt Psychology soon expanded its interest and applied the theory of Psychophysical Isomorphism and Dynamic Self-Distribution to psychological areas of inquiry other than perception, including recalling, learning, thinking, and behaviour:

> Behaviour in the most *practical* sense of the world tends to be seen as organized in forms which copy the organization of corresponding inner developments....If my attention is attracted by a strange object such as a snake, this direction of my self goes with a feeling of tension. Naturally, a person who happens to be present will see my face and eyes directed toward the place of the object; but in the tension of my face he will also have a visual picture of my inner tension; and this tension will be referred to the same place....People in a state of pathological depression tend to assume drooping carriage, similar to the posture of a normal person in a period of extreme fatigue or sorrow. (Köhler 1970, pp. 232–234)

The fact that Gestaltists themselves had an interest in music—Köhler in particular[14]—made Gestalt Psychology a particularly interesting tool for music theorists, before Cognitive Psychology took over. Susanne K. Langer had already leaned on Gestalt theory in her definition of music as a 'unconsummated symbol' (Langer 1948, p. 195) capable of reproducing the 'morphology of feelings' (Langer 1948, p. 193). She explained that 'a composer not only indicates, but *articulates* subtle complexes of feeling that language cannot even name, let alone set forth; he knows the forms of emotion and can handle them, "compose" them' (Langer 1948, p. 180)—'morphology' and 'forms of emotion' betray the concept of 'Gestalt' behind them. Meyer further developed the application of Gestalt Psychology to music by basing his expectation theory on Gestalt laws of stableness and completion (Meyer 1956, pp. 83–127). But there was a tradition of Gestalt Psychology in Film Studies too. Rudolf Arnheim was the most notable exponent,[15] but influences can be detected in the theoretical work of Sergei Eisenstein and Béla Balázs too.[16]

Making the two realms converge, in film-music and audio-visual studies, Gestalt has recently been revived by K.J. Donnelly to discuss the phenomenon of audiovisual synchronisation: 'The grasping of situations as a whole is one of the most profound insights of Gestalt psychology.... Human hardware is determinedly pattern-seeking, looking for—and inevitably finding—some sort of sense, be it narrative, representational, relational, or whatever. A Gestalt-inspired approach might find something more or at least make us more aware of the process.' (Donnelly 2014, pp. 22–24). I am deeply indebted to Donnelly,[17] particularly as to his preference for Gestalt's holistic approach to the film experience over the more 'atomistic approach of cognitive psychology-inspired analysis' (Donnelly 2014, p. 23). Donnelly argues:

> Stimulus recognition takes place *before* cognition. Unconscious affect always creates emotion, whereas conscious cognition does not necessarily do so….Cognitive Psychology's notion of perception is that there is a small amount of stimulus and the 'work' all takes place as a cognitive process in the brain. This so-called mental model affirms that stimulus requires the considerable brain input of 'enriching' through hypothesis-testing.… Cognitive psychology has tended to deemphasize the process of perception, often merely declaring it an instrumental part of the more general cognitive process. Inspired by Gestalt psychology, in this book, I try to place more emphasis on perception. This reinstates a physical aspect to the process denied by cognitive psychology-inspired approaches. It also makes for a more solid demarcation between lower order and higher order brain processes, between those of basic understanding and a more culturally acquired sense of registering relationships between things and ensuing implications.…Although I am more than happy to accept the insights provided by cognitive psychology…there are distinct aspects of the aesthetic process (for film especially) that are poorly accounted for by such an approach. (Donnelly 2014, pp. 18–19)

Gestalt Psychology provides a fitting overarching framework to connect Meyer's theory and Neoformalism. Meyer's theory, as we have seen, is itself based on Gestalt Psychology, but the natural need for form and completion on which Neoformalism is based—'Artworks arouse and gratify our human craving for form.…The mind is never at rest. It is constantly seeking order and significance.…Artworks rely on this dynamic, unifying quality of the human mind' (Bordwell and Thompson 2010, p. 56)—also reminds of the Gestalt premises. Moreover, the original Russian Formalism was influenced by Gestalt concepts.[18] Bordwell mentions the 'canonical story format' as the basis of story comprehension: 'Nearly all story-comprehension researchers agree that the most common template structure can be articulated as a "canonical" story format, something like this: introduction of setting and characters—explanation of a state of affairs—complicating action—ensuing events—outcome—ending' (Bordwell 1985, p. 35). This transcultural 'canonical story format' does not sound too dissimilar from a type of narrative 'Gestalt.'

As a matter of fact, Neoformalism adopts Constructivism and Cognitivism, not Gestalt, which Bordwell passingly mentions only as a comparative background for Constructivism: 'For the Gestaltist, perception is the imposition of a mental order upon the world, but these *Gestalten* operate in a static, absolute manner. For constructivist theory, perception is a temporal process of building the percept in a probabilistic fashion' (Bordwell 1985, p. 101). While Cognitivism sees perception more as a matter of elaboration of data and information—it is modelled around the functioning of computers and Information Technology—Gestalt Psychology sees perception more as a matter of energy distribution that produces isomorphic percepts. As Donnelly pointed out, Cognitivism implies a major reliance on higher-order cognitive processing, while Gestalt presupposes a wider presence of lower-order autonomous activities. Besides our parochial usage for film analysis, part of the scientific community has also long defended Gestalt Psychology, and some concepts developed by the Gestaltists (in particular about the psychology of perception) have been integrated into the Cognitive framework—for example, object grouping or insight (Braisby and Gellatly 2012, p. 306). Some also claim that Cognitivism is the continuation of Gestalt, not a different thing altogether.[19] The transcultural presence of some perceptual categories that everyone is natively able to recognise—like the basic emotions: anger, fear, sadness, disgust, happiness (Braisby and Gellatly 2012, p. 513)—suggests that there might indeed be some Gestalt qualities at the basis of perception. And the recent discovery of mirror neurons (Rizzolatti and Craighero 2004)—neurons in the brain that fire in the same way both when we do an action and when we observe the same action performed by others, an automatic mechanism of imitation that have been explained as the basis for empathy and learning—has been linked to the Psychophysical Isomorphism postulated by Gestalt (Eagle and Wakefield 2007). Gestalt and Cognitivism can be seen not as competitive theories but as complementary ones; the latter is somewhat the continuation of the former through more validating empirical evidence and neuroscientific experiments.[20] Cognitivism is extremely handy at providing descriptions and explanations for single research questions and backs them with empirical evidence but somewhat lacks a unified theoretical position other than 'the mind works like a computer.' On the other hand, Gestalt can provide an overarching theory for the film-viewing experience: human beings are naturally inclined to search for stable and complete configurations (gestalts)—with the 'Law of Prägnanz' regulating such stabilisation and completion activities—and the Gestalts of the external objects trigger internal Gestalts in our mind (through 'Isomorphism'). So, if we wish to give an account of how the formal system of a film works, probably the holistic view of Gestalt is more apt for this global task. If in some instances we wish or need to go deeper and study a single phenomenon, then Cognitivism can be of better help—for example, the 'invisibility' of editing matches ('edit blindness', Smith and Henderson 2008)—can be explained with the blindness occurring during our saccadic eye movements (Shimamura et al. 2014).[21]

In support of the adoption of Gestalt, there is also the fact that the concept of 'Isomorphism' and the search for Gestalt quality are, I argue, a good solution to talk about music in films from a non-separatist perspective interested in music as a part of the audiovisual whole. We can think of Isomorphism as a correspondence between Gestalt qualities from one field of experience to another: 'Brightness and darkness, for instance, are attributes of both the auditory and visual experience. Again, if an object which we touch appears cool, its coolness somehow resembles visual brightness; comfortable warmth is dark in comparison' (Köhler 1970, p. 223). This correspondence is illustrated by Köhler's 'maluma/takete' experiment (Köhler 1970, pp. 224–225). Transculturally, when presented with these two non-words and two drawings (one with curvaceous features and the other with sharp edges and angles) and asked to associate one non-word to one drawing, people invariably associate 'maluma' with the soft-feature drawings and 'takete' with the edgy-feature one. This indicates that there is some Gestalt quality—softness in one case and sharpness in the other—that is present both in the visual and in the auditory phenomenon. 'Maluma' is isomorphic with the curvaceous figure, and 'takete' with the edgy one. Köhler further elaborates on this:

> Something arouses a 'bitter' feeling in us. Again, one talks about being in a 'soft' mood. 'Sweet' love seems to occur in all countries, also 'bright' joy and 'dark' grief. In wrath there is something which many call 'hot.'… Certain experiences of the inner and perceptual worlds resemble each others.…Quite generally, both emotional and intellectual processes have characteristics which we also know from music, i.e. from auditory experience.

Crescendo and *diminuendo*, *accelerando* and *ritardando* are obvious examples. But these terms are applicable not only to auditory facts but also to visually perceived developments. Hence, when such dynamic traits occur in the inner life of a person, they can be most adequately represented in his behavior as heard and seen by others....When somebody is reminded of an injustice which he has suffered, he will, while his indignation grows, probably walk with increased speed. Thus, the greater tempo and intensity of his emotional thinking are nicely rendered in the *accelerando* and *crescendo* of his movements as seen by others. (Köhler 1970, pp. 225–231)

Bringing in music, once again, the passage suggests that there is not only isomorphism between mental states and experience/behaviour but also between art expressions. Donnelly mentions that: 'in "The Gestalt Theory of Expression" (1949), [Arnheim] theorized that expressive aspects of art objects have a form of "structural kinship" with corresponding mental states' (Donnelly 2014, pp. 19–20). This implies that, if an artistic expression is isomorphic with an emotional experience, then the artistic expression must also be isomorphic with the mental process that produces that emotional experience. If negative events cause my mental processes to configure around certain energy distributions that make me experience sadness, then a piece of music that proficiently replicates the Gestalt qualities of sadness is able to make my mental process configure along the same patterns and hence make me experience sadness. Moreover, Donnelly adds that 'similar structures in different media are related in a way not dissimilar to the relation between an artistic stimulus and the configuration of the brain activity it causes' (Donnelly 2014, p. 98). The fact that different media are capable of configuring the same Gestalt—or possess the same Gestalt qualities—is of great importance to the study of how music combines with visuals. Another musical example from the Gestalt psychologist (and musicologist) Carroll C. Pratt illuminates the point:

> An auditory rhythm is auditory, and that's that; but the same rhythm —a Gestalt—may also be visual or tactual, and the graceful lilt, let us say of a waltz rhythm...will be present in all three modalities. Gestalten...reveal innumerable iconic relations and resemblances across modalities. Therein lies the great power of art, for the moods and feelings of mankind are capable of iconic *presentation* in visual and auditory patterns—a mode obviously far more direct and effective than symbolic *representation*. (Pratt 1969, pp. 25–26)

If there is a Gestalt quality ('fast') that causes the brain to configure its energy field in such a way that an isomorphic Gestalt is experienced ('Fastness') and if said Gestalt quality is present in different presentations ('fast music' and 'fast running character'), then these two presentations are isomorphic, and if combined, they are able to make us experience the 'fastness' Gestalt even more firmly than in their separate manifestations.

To analyse music in films from a non-musicological viewpoint, we should search for and concentrate on the Gestalt qualities of the music, which can be roughly identified with what Meyer calls 'secondary parameters.' While the 'primary parameters' of music (chordal progressions, syntactic relations between tones, etc.) are the structural parameters responsible for the formal construction of the piece and those typically focussed on in the musicological analyses, the 'secondary parameters' are the affective and expressive parameters.[22] The secondary parameters are such 'exterior' characteristics of the music as dynamics (is music's volume loud or soft?), tempo and agogics (is music fast or slow? Is it accelerating or decelerating?), register (is music in a high or in a low pitch?), timbre (is the music played by instruments or combination of instruments with a bright or dark colour?), rhythmic character (are the rhythmic patterns simple and regular or complex and irregular?), consonance/dissonance (very roughly: Is the music texture more or less agreeable to the ear or does it sound grating?), and melodic character and identification (Can a melody or melodic idea be first spotted and then recognised when it reappears in fragments or in its integrity throughout the film? Can we attribute a character to said melody—sad, happy, menacing?). Even if musicological skills are not indispensable here, *some* musical competence is to be 'competent listeners.' One is expected to be able to tell a flute from an oboe when one hears it, or to notice an *accelerando* or *decelerando*, and should possess enough ear training to discern the profile of a melody and recognise it when it is presented again, or to distinguish between dissonance and consonance.

Take, as an example, the major/minor mode difference. To be able to distinguish, while listening, if a piece is, on the whole, in major or in minor mode—the two scales of diatonic music—is a fundamental competence for film/music analysis, one that does not require the study of music treatises but certainly requires some ear training. Indeed, the traditional affective bipolarity associated with major and minor mode makes the capacity to distinguish one from the other quite necessary. Very basically, major mode is associated with happiness, minor mode with sadness, and evidence shows that this is perceived trans-culturally, that is, it does not depend on convention and culturally stratified associations but on the psychoacoustic qualities of the two scales.[23] The transposition of a theme from major to minor mode or vice versa has long been used for emotional effects in dramatic music. A famous example from the ballet repertoire is in Tchaikovsky's *Swan Lake* (1877). The main theme is presented in the 'Scene,' in a sorrowful minor mode tinged with nostalgia, and later in the piece a passionate modulating bridge seems to be struggling to bring the minor mode to the major mode, but the piece collapses back again to a resigned minor mode. In the final apotheosis when the evil spell that had transformed Odette into a swan is eventually broken, the theme is presented in major mode as Odette and Siegfried ascend to heaven, finally and forever united in their love: Good has triumphed over Evil. The major/mode transposition is similarly used in film music. In *Gone with the Wind* (1939, dir. Fleming), 'Tara's Theme' is presented in major mode in the opening title and then associated with the O'Hara plantation and Scarlet's home, Tara. Later in the film, when Scarlet returns home after her stint in Atlanta during the Civil War, we see the dilapidated Tara estate and hear a minor-mode rendition of the 'Tara's Theme,' effectively communicating that Scarlet's happy and affluent home (major mode) does not exist anymore, replaced by desolation, loss, and poverty (minor mode). In *Suspicion* (1941, dir. Hitchcock), Johann Strauss II's waltz 'Wiener Blut' (1873) in its original major mode is associated with Lina's happiness with her new husband Johnnie; but when she begins to suspect he might be plotting to kill her for the life-insurance money, the waltz switches to the minor mode—most notably, in the creepy version accompanying the famous scene of Johnnie bringing her a glass of milk, possibly poisoned. In *The Adventures of Tintin* (2011, dir. Spielberg), Captain Haddock is associated with a minor-mode faltering leitmotiv, which consolidates the unreliable nature of the forgetful and alcoholic mariner. In the finale, when Haddock acts heroically and restores his dignity, his leitmotiv modulates to major mode, expressing the radical positive change that the character has undergone. To have a further confirmation of how powerful this major/minor transposition can be, listen to how the originally minor-mode Darth Vader's theme (a menacing and merciless march) when transposed in major mode sounds like a cheerful and feel-good graduation tune.[24] The major and minor mode are precisely examples of the Gestalt qualities of music. A mode is a relational structure—one mode played in one key is recognisable as the same mode when played in a distant key—and they produce a predictable emotional response: dysphoric-ish the minor mode, euphoric-ish the major mode (Köhler 1969, pp. 53–54). By focussing on the secondary parameters of music and on the degrees of isomorphism between music and the other cinematic devices, film scholars and film critics can fruitfully address the roles and functions of music in films without the need for musicological investigations.

ANALYSING THE FILMIC SYSTEM: MACRO AND MICRO CONFIGURATIONS

When we blend Neoformalism with Gestalt, to give an account of the reciprocal interplay of the devices within the filmic system we can say that the configurations of the single devices (micro configurations) combine into the whole audiovisual configuration of the scene/sequence (macro configuration). Given that 'the whole is different from the sum of its parts,' the combination of these micro configurations is not merely additional but it is a product, it generates a surplus (of meaning, emotion, perception) that is not given by a single element, but it is the multiplied result of their combination. My theorisation here echoes Eisenstein's discussion of the productive capacities of montage, similarly based on elements of the Gestalt Psychology:

> The juxtaposition of two separate shots by splicing them together resembles not so much a simple sum of one shot plus another shot as it does a *creation*. It resembles a creation—rather than a sum of its parts—from the circumstance that in every such juxtaposition *the result is qualitatively distinguishable from each component element viewed separately*....The woman, to return to our first example, is a representation, the mourning robe she is wearing is a representation—that is, both are *objectively representable*. But "*a widow*," arising from a juxtaposition of the two representations, is objectively unrepresentable—a new idea, a new conception, a new image.[25] (Eisenstein 1957, pp. 7–8)

I prefer to think of the interaction of music with the other devices in these terms rather than as a music being a 'modifier' of the other devices, as suggested by Noël Carroll, who compares the function of music to that of adverbs (Carroll 1996). Carroll's view, as already pointed out by Robynn Stilwell (Stilwell 2007, p. 185), implies an imbalanced view in which the key semantic/affective element is already in the visuals and music only modifies it, as the key semantic element is in the verb and adverbs only modify it. The idea of two or more micro configurations producing a macro configuration that is more than its parts does not imply a dominance of one device upon the other and favours a non-separatist conception.

The holism of the Gestalt-based approach is not incompatible with analysis, that is, the breaking down of the whole into separate elements. Analysis is at the basis of any scientific enquiry, Gestalt simply takes the whole as a starting point to study the parts (Köhler 1970, p. 168). In everyday perception Gestalts are noticed beforehand and only later, and making a conscious effort of analysis, the determinants of those Gestalts are isolated: a face is immediately experienced as sad (Gestalt) before I analyse that such sadness is communicated by the particular frown of the eyebrows, the depressed vacuousness of the eyes, the droopy mouth corners, and so forth. Similarly, analysis can be said to be an act of backtracking to the factors that determined the product. It is like a reverse-engineering move, isolating, within the macro configuration of the film's system, the micro configurations of the single devices and then studying how they interact, combine, isomorphically fuse, and 'multiply' each other to create the stabilised and unified product of the macro configuration that we perceive.[26]

In noir films—think of *The Killers* (1946, dir. Siodmak) and its Miklós Rózsa score—the chiaroscuro low-key patterns, the dark shadows and the harshly contrasting beam of light of the cinematography are coupled with music in a low register and dark timbre, with occasional and dramatic outbursts of dissonant high-register brass chords, creating an analogous musical chiaroscuro. In action scenes, the break-neck pace of the editing is typically paired with a similarly frantically fast music, in an agogical/rhythmical isomorphism. Think of *Citizen Kane* (1941, dir. Welles): in the opening sequence, the dark and lugubrious images of the abandoned Xanadu mansion are coupled with music in an extremely low-register, in an almost lifeless slow tempo, played by dark-timbre instruments such as the bass clarinet and the contra-bassoons. Music helps convey the sense of death and ruin in the sequence. On the other hand, think of the sequence in *Hook* (1991, dir. Spielberg) in which Peter Banning retrieves his 'happy thought' and thus is able to fly again and reverse to his previous Peter Pan status. As soon as the happy thought is secured, music builds up, creating a *crescendo* in volume and orchestral texture, with flutes and piccolo bubbling in the higher register to express the excitement that is hardly containable and about to explode; then, when an exhilarated Peter takes off to fly over Neverland, the jubilant music explodes *fortissimo* with the full orchestra, exactly as Peter pops out like a missile into the sky, making the moment irresistibly joyous and liberating; then music continues to support Peter's flight with an airy melody of the high-register violins, punctuated by fast flights and runs of high-register woodwinds and celebratory fanfares of the trumpets in their brighter register—music is as bright as the sunny sky, as excited as Peter, as soaring as the flight it accompanies, as fizzy as the wind whirls up there. In all these examples, there is a correspondence, an isomorphism, between the configuration of the music and some configuration of the visual aspect or of the emotional tone of the narrative.

Music can replicate some visual and rhythmic configurations (as is the case with the dark light/dark timbre and fast editing/fast music coupling), but music can also replicate gestural and emotional configurations (as in the *Hook* example). Meyer's explanation is the following:

> Most of the connotations which music arouses are based upon similarities which exist between our experience of the materials of music and their organization, on the one hand, and our experience of the non-musical world of concepts, images, objects, qualities, and states of mind, on the other....Both music and life are experienced as dynamic processes of growth and decay, activity and rest, tension and release. These processes are differentiated, not only by the course and shape of the motion involved in them, but also by the quality of the motion. For instance, a motion may be fast or slow, calm or violent, continuous or sporadic, precisely articulated or vague in outline....If connotations are to be aroused at all, there will be a tendency to associate the musical motion in question with a referential concept or image that is felt to exhibit a similar quality of motion.... Mood association by similarity depends upon a likeness between the individual's experience of moods and his experience of music. Emotional behaviour is a kind of composite gesture, a motion whose peculiar qualities are largely defined in terms of energy, direction, tension, continuity, and so forth. Since music also involves motions differentiated by the same qualities, 'musical mood gestures' may be similar to behavioral mood gestures. (Meyer 1956, pp. 260–268)

Meyer calls this 'metaphoric mimicry': music mimics the Gestalt qualities of extramusical phenomena—emotional, visual, rhythmic, gestural, behavioural, and so forth. This mimicry is possible precisely because of the presence of Gestalt qualities that music shares with extramusical phenomena and experiences. In the following Meyer's passage there are clear echoes of Kohler's aforementioned discussion of cross-domain isomorphism, in this case applied to music:

> The pervasiveness of the correlation between music and other modes of sense experience is evident in the way we describe sounds: pitches are high or low; melodic lines rise or fall, or are sinuous or jagged; rhythms are emphatic or weak, smooth or jerky; timbres (tone *colors*) are brilliant or somber, piercing or dull; volumes are large or small, chords rough or smooth, and textures thick or thin; and, more generally, musical patterns are characterized as regular or irregular, exciting or calm, light or heavy, happy or sad. These attributes of sound are also the attributes of objects, actions, and affections outside the realm of music....Observe that in order to be re-presented in sound, visual phenomena...must be understood as having a characteristic motion or position. Such interpretation is possible because we know from experience how things move: save for special cases (airplanes and so on), large objects move slowly and their position tend to be low—close to the ground; small things generally move more rapidly, often seemingly irregularly, and their position is often high....Ordinary experience couples large size with heavy weight, and heavy weight with slow motion and low position. Similarly, the acoustics of sounding bodies links large size with low pitch, slow sound activation, large volume, and dark tone color. With the introduction of attributes such as color, sound, shape (round, sharp), and the like, we begin to border on the realm of cultural metaphor—a realm in which the constraints of the physical and biological worlds become the basis for valuation: *up* (high pitch) is connected with what is 'good' (light, life, heaven, birds, sun, and warmth); *down* (low pitch) is connected with what is 'bad' (Hades, death, cold, giants). (Meyer 1996, pp. 128–129)

Imagine a close-up of a character having just lost a dear friend: we recognise her/his face as sad because some physiognomic traits, the Gestaltic qualities of 'sadness,' produce a certain configuration that we experience as an expression of sadness. (Mind that the actress/actor interpreting the part might not be sad at all but has the skills to exteriorly replicate the Gestalt that we recognise as 'sadness.') The same happens with a piece of music: 'Music is sad…not in a literal sense, nor because the composer was sad when he or she wrote it, nor even because it makes us sad, but because it "presents the outward features of sadness"' (Stephen Davies in Cook 1998, p. 89). If that close-up is coupled with music that possesses 'the outward features of sadness' (Gestalt qualities that are experienced as sad, for a mix of native responses and cultural conventions), then the two micro-configurations of 'sadness'—physiognomic and musical—fuse to produce a macro-configuration of 'sadness' that is more powerful than the two taken singularly.

I have dealt here more extensively with the so-called 'parallel/synchronous' audiovisual relationship, one in which music 'communicates' the same thing as the visual (Cook's 'conformance'), because these instances—the majority of interactions between music and film—are generally neglected within the predominant communications model. What happens with the cases when music 'comments,' to continue with the familiar jargon of the communications model? When it comes to abstract concepts, detailed extra-musical phenomena, or fine-grain feelings that do not fall within the general basic emotions—for example, compassion—music is inadequate to express them: 'Their representation results not from the natural commonality of human experience, but from more or less arbitrary denotations contrived by the composer, usually in connection with a text' (Meyer 1996, pp. 128–129). To use Langer's term, music is a symbol but an 'unconsummated' one—that is, one that is not as referentially precise as the verbal or visual symbols. To be 'consummated,' music has to be associated with some other extra-musical phenomenon—the association being the 'more or less arbitrary denotations contrived by the composer' that Meyer mentions as regards programme music. Or, reworking Gorbman's concept, the 'ancrage' is not only music that anchors some ambiguous meaning in the visuals but also, vice versa, any other extra-musical elements that anchors the vague meaning of the music (Gorbman 1987, p. 32).

> Music presents a generic event, a 'connotative complex,' which then becomes particularized in the experience of the individual listener. Music does not, for example, present the concept or image of death itself. Rather, it connotes that rich realm of experience in which death and darkness, night and cold, winter and sleep and silence are all combined and consolidated into a single connotative complex. (Meyer 1956, p. 265)

A generically sentimental music can become the expression of compassion if coupled with the images of someone succouring another human being. As in Eisenstein's montage the conjunction of two visual segments is not an addition but a multiplication, similarly the coupling of micro-configurations that are not exactly isomorphic ('complementation', in Cook's proposal) produces a macro-configuration that is more than the sum of its parts, and music cooperates in the expression of ideas and abstract concepts—'compassion,' in our case.

What if music has a configuration that has nothing to share with that of the visual, what if there is no isomorphism at all, like in the radical cases of the so-called audiovisual counterpoint, or Cook's 'contest'? For example, we can have a funeral scene scored with a lively and carefree merengue. In such cases, we are faced with an interpretive problem that requires an act of 'productive thinking' on our part. We have to find a solution: What has a merry merengue to do with a sombre funeral? A problem is like an incomplete or unstable configuration, and the Gestalt theory of problem-solving posits that a solution is found when the configuration of the problematic situation is made stable. And this is done by examining the *relations* between the elements of the problem at hand:

> We have to recognize that probably all problems with which we may be confronted, and also the solutions of such problems, are matters of relations. So long as problems *are* problems, the materials in question exhibit *some* relation; but these special relations are such that a difficulty arises. However, we may now discover other relations in the material which make the difficulty disappear. In some instances, we are at first unable to see any relations in the material which are relevant to our task. When this happens, we have to inspect the given situation until, eventually, it does exhibit relations from which a solution can be derived. Consequently, not only does our understanding of the problem depend upon our awareness of certain relations; we can also not solve the problem without discovering certain new relations. For the most part, such relations are not...simple and directly accessible....Often they are of a far more abstract or conceptual kind; and, almost always, we have to deal not with one relation but, rather, with whole sets of them, and thus with relations among relations. (Köhler 1969, pp. 143–144)

The difference with Cognitivism is that Gestalt addresses problem-solving not so much as a cognitive effort of hypothesis-testing but more as a perceptive effort of relation-seeking; we have to 'observe' the problem from different angles until we find the right one from which the required relation is individuated that can illuminate a solution. Indeed, Gestalt theorised the 'Aha! phenomenon,' that is, an instance in which the solution to a problem does not arise from hypothesis-testing, inferences, reasoning, data processing, but suddenly presents itself to the mind.[27] This resolutive awareness of the problem's solution is more properly called 'insight,' which is achieved by restructuring the parts of the problematic situation in question: 'We suddenly become aware of new relations, but these new relations appear only after we have mentally changed, amplified, or restructured the given material' (Köhler 1969, p. 153). I argue that the interpretation activity of the general film-viewing is more a matter of insight than reasoning, or at least as much a matter of insight as of reasoning. The professional film analyst may intensively ponder on a particular interpretive conundrum or perform some sophisticate exegesis to write a research paper or scholarly criticism; the regular viewer has generally a problem-solving attitude that has more resemblance with the less conscious insight and re-configuration of relations, than with the more conscious cognitive effort of interpretation. If the latter were the case, while stuck and concentrated on pondering on a previous unsolved interpretive problem, the viewer would miss the subsequent developments in the film.

It may be useful, as a comparison, to resort to Nicholas Cook's previously mentioned spectrum of media relationships to sum up the different degrees of isomorphism that we can find between music and the other cinematic devices—an operation reminiscent of Cook's 'similarity/difference test'—and to show the different angle I use, in particular as regards interpretation of 'audiovisual counterpoint.' There can be a relationship of 'conformance' (if the configuration of the music and that of the other device[s] match), of 'complementation' (if the configuration of the music is not perfectly matching, and it is that discrepancy that provides the elements to stabilise the macro configuration), or of 'contest' (the micro configurations are in utter contradiction). Imagine these three cases. A romantic dialogue scored with sentimental violin music creates a macro configuration (romantic scene) obtained from two micro configurations (sentimental words and attitudes of the actors in the dialogue and sentimental music) in 'conformance,' in perfect isomorphism—the 'sentimental' Gestalt quality is present in both. The same romantic dialogue coupled with a sentimental music that becomes hesitant on the sentimental lines of one of the two lovers produces a different macro configuration (a romantic scene in which only one of the two is actually romantically involved) through two micro configurations (romantic dialogue with only partially 'romantic' music) that are 'complementary,' only partially isomorphic: the effect is a macro-configuration (romance with some hesitation) that is created by the combination of the Gestalt qualities of the micro-configurations. Finally, we can have the romantic dialogue scored with an absolutely incongruous dissonant and eerie music, one type of music one would expect in a horror film. The two micro-configurations (sentimental dialogue, threatening music), taken singularly and compared, are not isomorphic. Unlike Cook, this latter case of 'contest' is not seen here as a 'struggle' between elements but as a case in which the stabilisation of the macro-configuration is less immediate and automatic than in the previous cases. The resulting formal effect is one of incongruity and tension (romantic scene with incongruous eerie music)—which would have been of consistency and relaxation, in the case of two perfectly isomorphic micro-configurations. The incongruity of the two micro-configurations that we register has precisely the function of making such incongruity noticeable, creating a problem and alerting us that an act of interpretation (problem-solving) is required. A relation between the problematic elements is to be found. When it is found, the two micro-configurations reconfigure reciprocally and reach the isomorphism from which the macro configuration finally emerges (potentially dangerous romance). In the 'problematic' romantic scene, imagine that the visual and performative aspects of the scene are decidedly and markedly maudlin—with almost nauseating pastel tones in the scenery, high-key lighting and 'romanticising' soft-focus photography, actors over-tenderly whispering mawkish lines of dialogue. In this case, the relation between music and the other devices might be one of irony, even satire; the eerie music is related not to the romantic situation depicted here but to the general idea that, although idyllic they might appear, sentimental relationships are doomed to perish, they can look like a delightful bliss at first but in the long run they may even turn into nightmares, and so forth. In this case, the macro-configuration results to be a satire of romance, in which music eventually proves to be perfectly isomorphic with the subtended idea—mocking the blissful joys of love. Although seemingly in 'contest' and 'asynchronous' if compared as separate elements, music and visuals are actually working towards a common goal, the macro-configuration, which is achieved by combining two contradictory but *cooperating* elements. When we eventually interpret the contradiction—when we have an insight into the relation between the micro-configurations—the contradiction itself is removed. The elements in 'contest' are eventually revealed to be in 'conformance' with what narration planned to express.

Suppose a different outcome. Imagine that the romantic scene has no apparent trace of sarcastic overtones about the love relationships—no pastel tones, no caricaturally over-sentimental gestures—just the oddly contrasting music. Imagine that at a certain point the face of the male character changes position and thus falls under a chiaroscuro lighting pattern, with a side of his face now hidden in the shadow. Here, another device, besides music, is in contradiction with the romantic situation. And the two might be in relation, given the conventionally 'evil' Gestalt quality that such chiaroscuro pattern evokes. In this case, the eerie music may be a hint of something terrible that is about to happen, a hint that is reinforced by the strange light-pattern. Perhaps, through music, the narration is anticipating what is about to be revealed, maybe one of the lovers in the romantic scene is in fact a killer ready to strike the unaware partner. In this case, the impossibility of finding an answer to the contradiction between the two micro-configurations leaves the macro-configuration open and creates curiosity,[28] an alerted state that prompts us to search for elements in the following scenes that can retrospectively explain the previous anomaly and thus stabilise the macro-configuration. If, two scenes later, the lover indeed stabs her/his partner to death, the relation of the eerie music with the romantic scene is made clear, our curiosity is satisfied, and the macro-configuration of that scene comes to a stabilisation (the scene was a foreshadowing of the future outcome).

Having in mind this Gestalt-based theorisation of macro-configurations fusing into a macro-configuration and the previously presented Neoformalist approach, in the next chapter I formulate what the functions and motivations are that music can have in films.

Notes

1. An early and shorter starting point for this chapter was Audissino (2017). On other occasions I have been warned about using Leonard B. Meyer because it is 'old.' But if old theories have not been refuted but merely updated, as is the case with Meyer, and if the scope of one's study is not to advance one discipline but to borrow theoretical tools from an outside discipline that fit her/his research, I do not see why one shouldn't use them. Also, theories as old as or older than Meyer's, and more dubiously valid if not entirely refuted, are still around, like the 'Persistence of Vision' that is sometimes still used in the psychoanalytic circles to explain the basic mechanics of film viewing: see Anderson and Anderson (1993).
2. For an introduction on the psychology of music, see Gjerdingen (2002).
3. For simplicity's sake, I use 'emotional' and 'emotive' herewith to broadly refer to the psychological sphere of emotions, but most theorists

distinguish between emotions proper, moods, feelings, and affects. See Plantinga (2011).
 4. On the difference between 'designative' and 'embodied' meaning, see Meyer (1956, p. 35).
 5. On tropes in film music, see Scheurer (2008).
 6. The influence of Meyer's work is acknowledged in Bordwell (1985, pp. 284, 351, n. 54).
 7. Meyer (1967, p. 212, n. 61) acknowledges the similarity of his positions to those of Sontag (1966).
 8. Gestalt Psychology equally battled the atomistic premises of Introspectionism—objective experience of reality is belittled or denied altogether in favour of a subjective experience—and of Behaviourism—not access, and hence no scientific study, is possible of the internal mental processes (the so-called 'black box'): the only scientifically observable thing are external behaviours in form of reflex actions, which are modifiable through 'conditioning.' Gestalt psychologists aimed at giving an account of the whole experience—'the full-blown forms…of behaviour and consciousness' (Köhler 1969, p. 9)—and finding a connection between the external world of stimuli (the focus of Behaviourism) and the internal world of mental activity (the focus of Introspectionism). For a Gestalt-based criticism of Behaviourism and Introspectionism, see Köhler (1970, pp. 3–33, 67–99). A more essential comparison is in Parkin (2000, pp. 1–7). The classical text of reference for Gestalt Psychology is Koffka (1935). Yet, I find Köhler (1970) and Köhler (1969) more accessible for a first recognition in these territories. Other introductory texts are Katz (1950) and Ellis (2013).
 9. Ehrenfels's concept of Gestalt Quality is explained in Rollinger and Ierna (2016).
10. See Köhler (1970, p. 177). Also: 'The segregation of specific entities [gestalten] in sensory fields appears as only one, though surely a highly important, instance among the various issues which constitute the subject matter of Gestalt Psychology. In fact, the concept of "Gestalt" may be applied far beyond the limits of sensory experience. According to the most general functional definition of the term, the processes of learning, of recall, of striving, of emotional attitude, of thinking, acting and so forth, may have to be included. This makes it still clearer that "Gestalt" in the meaning of shape is no longer the center of the Gestalt Psychologist's attention' (Köhler 1970, pp. 178–179).
11. To make a more concrete example, when we see a chair we first see it as a whole, the 'chair' Gestalt, we do not see four legs plus a seat plus a backrest. And we recognise the 'chairness' regardless of what shape or materials a chair is made of. Either steel and leather or wood and straw,

the Gestalt transcends the elements and materials because the relation between the elements—the Gestalt quality of 'chairness'—remains the same: a sufficient number of legs that sustain a horizontally oriented seat connected to a vertically oriented backrest (if no backrest were in place, we would probably identify it as a stool, not a chair).
12. 'It has been said: The whole is more than the sum of its parts. It is more correct to say that the whole is something else than the sum of its parts, because summing is a meaningless procedure, whereas the whole-part relationship is meaningful' Koffka (1935, p. 176).
13. See Wertheimer (2013) and Kanizsa (1979).
14. See Köhler (1970, pp. 238–255).
15. See Arnheim (1957) and Higgins (2011).
16. See Eisenstein (1957) and Bauer (2016).
17. My consultations but also informal chats with K. J. Donnelly were seminal in steering my path from Cognitivism—which I originally aimed to adopt for my neoformalist method for film/music analysis—to Gestalt.
18. See Erlich (1980, p. 277).
19. For example, Rock and Palmer (1990), Sharps and Wertheimer (2000), Wagemans et al. (2012a) and Wagemans et al. (2012b).
20. See, for example, Kanizsa and Legrenzi (1978). Köhler himself admitted that Isomorphism was only a hypothesis (Köhler 1969, p. 66) and that the validity of the theory could not be checked because the brain functions could not be studied at that time (Köhler 1970, p. 271).
21. For comparison's sake, I stated that Cognitivism is more atomistic and concerned with higher-level processes than Gestalt, but within the Cognitivist field there are more holistic proposals—in the case of film music, Cohen (2000) and her following elaborations—and also studies that address lower-level perceptual operations—Zohar Eitan's work, for example, as in Eitan and Rothschild (2011).
22. On primary and secondary parameters, see (Meyer 1996, pp. 209, 322).
23. See Jourdain (1997), p. 313; Tan et al. (2013), pp. 93–95, 149, 270.
24. The composer Ian Gordon reworked the piece into 'Vader's Redemption': https://soundcloud.com/laztozia/vaders-redemption-the-imperial-march-in-a-major-key, and https://iangordon.bandcamp.com/album/theme-tweak-volume-one. Accessed 29 October 2016.
25. For a discussion of the Gestalt-inspired constructivist and formalist positions of Eisenstein and Arnheim, see Elsaesser and Hagener (2009, pp. 23–28).
26. The micro/macro-configuration approach that I am explaining has similarities with Jeff Smith's 'polarisation' and 'affective congruence': 'The first of these refers to an interaction in which the specific affective character of the music moves the content of the picture toward the emotional pole communicated by the music. The second interaction…refers to

a type of cross-modal confirmation in which the spectator matches the score's affective components to the emotional shading of narrative.... More than the sum of its parts, affective congruence produces a degree of emotional engagement that is stronger than either that produces by the music or visual track alone' (Smith 1999, 148). The difference is that Smith is concerned here with the emotional contribution of film music, while I aim at applying the micro/macro-configuration approach to all the potential agencies of film music. Also, despite the Gestalt-reminiscent wording, Smith develops his approach within a Cognitivist framework.

27. See Braisby and Gellatly (2012, p. 306). The Aha phenomenon is 'a sudden ability to see the solution to a problem without any intervening steps' (Parkin 2000, pp. 279–280).
28. On curiosity as the result of some past event left unspecified, see Bordwell (1985, p. 37).

References

Anderson, Joseph, and Barbara Anderson. 1993. The Myth of Persistence of Vision Revisited. *Journal of Film and Video* 45 (1): 3–12.
Arnheim, Rudolf. 1957. *Film as Art*. Berkeley, CA: University of California Press.
Audissino, Emilio. 2017. A Gestalt Approach to the Analysis of Music in Films. *Musicology Research* 2 (Spring): 69–88.
Bauer, Matthias. 2016. Béla Balázs: A Gestalt Theory of Film. *Historical Journal of Film, Radio and Television* 36 (2): 133–155.
Bordwell, David. 1985. *Narration in the Fiction Film*. Madison, WI: University of Wisconsin Press.
Bordwell, David. 2008. *Poetics of Cinema*. New York and London: Routledge.
Bordwell, David, and Kristin Thompson. 2010. *Film Art: An Introduction*, 9th ed. New York: McGraw and Hill.
Braisby, Nick, and Angus Gellatly. 2012. *Cognitive Psychology*, 2nd ed. Oxford: Oxford University Press.
Carroll, Noël. 1996. Notes on Movie Music. In *Theorizing the Moving Image*, 139–145. Cambridge: Cambridge University Press.
Cohen, Annabel J. 2000. Film Music. Perspectives from Cognitive Psychology. In *Music and Cinema*, ed. James Buhler, Caryl Flinn, and David Neumeyer, 360–377. Hanover, NH: Wesleyan University Press.
Cook, Nicholas. 1998. *Analysing Musical Multimedia*. Oxford: Clarendon Press.
Donnelly, K.J. 2014. *Occult Aesthetics: Synchronization in Sound Film*. Oxford and New York: Oxford University Press.
Eagle, Morris N., and Jerome C. Wakefield. 2007. Gestalt Psychology and the Mirror Neuron Discovery. *Gestalt Theory* 29 (1): 59–64.

Eisenstein, Sergei. 1957 [1942]. *The Film Sense*, trans. and ed. Jay Leda. New York: Meridian Books.

Eitan, Zohar, and Inbar Rothschild. 2011. How Music Touches: Musical Parameters and Listeners Audio-Tactile Metaphorical Mappings. *Psychology of Music* 39 (4): 449–467.

Ellis, Willis D. (ed.). 2013 [1938]. *A Source Book of Gestalt Psychology*. Abingdon and New York: Routledge.

Elsaesser, Thomas, and Malte Hagener. 2009. *Film Theory: An Introduction Through the Senses*. New York: Routledge.

Erlich, Victor. 1980. *Russian Formalism: History—Doctrine*, 4th ed. The Hague, Paris and New York: Mouton.

Gjerdingen, Robert. 2002. The Psychology of Music. In *The Cambridge History of Western Music Theory*, ed. Thomas Christensen, 956–981. Cambridge: Cambridge University Press.

Gorbman, Claudia. 1987. *Unheard Melodies: Narrative Film Music*. London and Bloomington: BFI/Indiana University Press.

Higgins, Scott (ed.). 2011. *Arnheim for Film and Media Studies*. Abingdon and New York: Routledge.

Huron, David. 2006. *Sweet Anticipation: Music and the Psychology of Expectation*. Cambridge, MA: MIT Press.

Jourdain, Robert. 1997. *Music and the Brain: How Music Captures Our Imagination*. New York: Harper Collins.

Kanizsa, Gaetano. 1979. *Organization in Vision*. New York: Praeger.

Kanizsa, Gaetano, and Paolo Legrenzi (eds.). 1978. *Psicologia della gestalt e psicologia cognitivista*. Bologna: Il Mulino.

Katz, David. 1950 [1948]. *Gestalt Psychology: Its Nature and Significance*. trans. Robert Tyson. New York: The Ronald Press Company.

Kivy, Peter. 1981. *The Corded Shell: Reflections on Musical Expression*. Princeton, NJ: Princeton University Press.

Koffka, Kurt. 1935. *Principles of Gestalt Psychology*. Brace: Harcourt.

Köhler, Wolfgang. 1969. *The Task of Gestalt Psychology*. Princeton, NJ: Princeton University Press.

Köhler, Wolfgang. 1970 [1947]. *Gestalt Psychology. An Introduction to New Concepts in Modern Psychology*. New York: Liveright.

Köhler, Wolfgang. 2013 [1920, 1938]. Physical Gestalten. In *A Source Book of Gestalt Psychology*, ed. Willis D. Ellis, 17–54. Abingdon and New York: Routledge.

Langer, Susanne K. 1948 [1941]. *Philosophy in a New Key: A Study in the Symbolism of Reason, Rite, and Art*. New York: The New American Library.

Meyer, Leonard B. 1956. *Emotion and Meaning in Music*. Chicago and London: University of Chicago Press.

Meyer, Leonard B. 1967. *Music, the Arts, and Idea: Patterns and Predictions in Twentieth-Century Culture*. Chicago and London: University of Chicago Press.
Meyer, Leonard B. 1973. *Explaining Music: Essays and Explorations*. Chicago: The University of Chicago Press.
Meyer, Leonard B. 1996 [1989]. *Style and Music: Theory, History, and Ideology*. Chicago and London: University of Chicago Press.
Narmour, Eugene. 1990. *The Analysis and Cognition of Basic Melodic Structures: The Implication-Realization Model*. Chicago, IL: University of Chicago Press.
Parkin, Alan J. 2000. *Essential Cognitive Psychology*. Hove and New York: Psychology Press.
Plantinga, Carl. 2011. Emotion and Affect. In *The Routledge Companion to Philosophy and Film*, ed. Paisley Livingston and Carl Plantinga, 86–96. Abingdon and New York: Routledge.
Pratt, Carroll C. 1969. Wolfgang Köhler—1887–1967. In *The Task of Gestalt Psychology*, ed. Wolfgang Köhler, 3–29. Princeton, NJ: Princeton University Press.
Rizzolatti, Giacomo, and Laila Craighero. 2004. The Mirror-Neuron System. *Annual Review of Neuroscience* 27: 169–192.
Rock, Irvin, and Stephen Palmer. 1990. The Legacy of Gestalt Psychology. *Scientific American* 263 (6): 84–90.
Rollinger, Robin, and Carlo Ierna. 2016. Christian von Ehrenfels. In *The Stanford Encyclopedia of Philosophy*, ed. Edward N. Zalta, Winter Ed. Accessed 4 Nov 2016. http://plato.stanford.edu/archives/win2016/entries/ehrenfels/.
Scheurer, Timothy E. 2008. *Music and Mythmaking in Film: Genre and the Role of the Composer*. Jefferson, NC: McFarland.
Seashore, Carl E. 1967 [1938]. *Psychology of Music*. New York: Dover.
Sharps, Matthew J, and Michael Wertheimer. 2000. Gestalt Perspectives on Cognitive Science and on Experimental Psychology. *Review of General Psychology* 4 (4): 315–336.
Shimamura, Arthur P., Brendan I. Cohn-Sheehy, and Thomas A. Shimamura. 2014. Perceiving Movement Across Film Edits: A Psychocinematic Analysis. *Psychology of Aesthetics, Creativity, and the Arts* 8 (1): 77–80.
Sloboda, John. 1999. *The Musical Mind: The Cognitive Psychology of Music*, new ed. Oxford and New York: Oxford University Press.
Smith, Jeff. 1999. Movie Music as Moving Music: Emotion, Cognition, and the Film Score. In *Passionate Views. Film, Cognition, and Emotion*, ed. Carl Plantinga and Greg M. Smith, 146–167. Baltimore, MD: Johns Hopkins University Press.
Smith, Tim J., and John M. Henderson. 2008. Edit Blindness: The Relationship Between Attention and Global Change Blindness in Dynamic Scenes. *Journal of Eye Movement Research* 2(2) 6: 1–17.

Sontag, Susan. 1966. *Against Interpretation*. New York: Farrar, Straus and Giroux.

Stilwell, Robynn J. 2007. The Fantastical Gap Between Diegetic and Nondiegetic. In *Beyond the Soundtrack: Representing Music in Cinema*, ed. Daniel Goldmark, Lawrence Kramer, and Richard Leppert, 184–203. Berkeley, Los Angeles and London: University of California Press.

Tan, Siu-Lan, Annabel J. Cohen, Scott D. Lipscomb, and Roger A. Kendall (eds.). 2013. *The Psychology of Music in Multimedia*. Oxford: Oxford University Press.

von Ehrenfels, Christian. 1988 [1890]. On Gestalt Qualities. In *Foundations of Gestalt Theory*, trans. and ed. Barry Smith, 82–117. Munich and Vienna: Philosophia Verlag.

Wagemans, Johan, Jacob Feldman, Sergei Gepshtein, Ruth Kimchi, James R. Pomerantz, Peter A. van der Helm, and Cees van Leeuwen. 2012a. A Century of Gestalt Psychology in Visual Perception: II. *Conceptual and Theoretical Foundations. Psychological Bulletin* 138 (6): 1218–1252.

Wagemans, Johan, James H. Elder, Michael Kubovy, Stephen E. Palmer, Mary A. Peterson, Manish Singh, and Rüdiger von der Heydt. 2012b. A Century of Gestalt Psychology in Visual Perception: I. Perceptual Grouping and Figure–Ground Organization. *Psychological Bulletin* 138 (6): 1172–1217.

Wertheimer, Max. 2013 [1923]. Laws of Organization in Perceptual Forms. In *A Source Book of Gestalt Psychology* [1938], ed. Willis D. Ellis, 71–88. Abingdon and New York: Routledge.

Wulf, Friedrich. 2013 [1922, 1938]. Tendencies in Figural Variation. In *A Source Book of Gestalt Psychology*, ed. Willis D. Ellis, 136–148. Abingdon and New York: Routledge.

CHAPTER 6

Film/Music Analysis II: Functions and Motivations of Music

Film/music analysis is about tracing the correspondence (or lack of correspondence, or the degree of correspondence) between the perceived micro-configuration of the music device and the micro-configuration of the other devices in the scene/sequence at hand. Gestalt provides us with a theoretical model to account for the mental activities of the viewer, and in particular—combined with Meyer's theories—offers us an explanation of how music can fuse with the other extra-musical devices in the film. Under this overarching theoretical framework, Neoformalism supplies us with the tools to analyse how the single devices work within the film's system and how they interact with the other to construe said formal system. If music is treated as a cinematic device, the key to the Neoformalist film/music analysis is to focus on what the *motivations* and *functions* are of a particular piece of music in a particular moment of the film, and how these functions and motivations influence one or more of the three levels—stylistic, narrative, thematic—within the overall formal system.

Music and Motivations

While the function of a device is what it does in the film (how a device achieves some effect), its motivation is the justification for its presence (why a device is there). We have previously seen that there are four motivations: realistic, compositional, transtextual, and artistic. A piece of music is *realistically motivated* when its presence is expected according to our knowledge of the real world; we expect 'Muzak' in the background of a sequence set in a supermarket and it would be strange, perhaps unsettling, to have such a scene without any music, because it would sound unrealistic compared to our knowledge of the 'supermarket prototype.' Music is *compositionally motivated* whenever its presence is needed to help us reconstruct the fabula: music makes the narrative progress, clarifies narrative information, helps us engage with the characters, reveals possible interpretations, and so on. A typical compositionally motivated instance is the leitmotiv in classical Hollywood cinema: by associating a musical motif with each character and narrative situation and repeating it in dramatically appropriate variations throughout the film, music makes the narrative passages and links stronger and clearer, and the overall narrative composition more cohesive. Music is motivated *transtextually* when a type of music or a type of action from music's part is prescribed by the conventions of, or to make a reference to, a given film genre, or for parodic purposes. In a Hammer or Hammer-styled horror we anticipate thunderous and sinister music with shocking blasts by the brass section. The shark motif from *Jaws* 1975, dir. Spielberg) in the false-excrement-in-the-swimming-pool scene in *Caddyshack* (1980, dir. Ramis) is transtextually motivated, being a humorous reference to a similar, though much more fatal, aquatic threat.

Music is motivated *artistically* when there's no apparent reason for it to be there other than authorial idiosyncrasy or aesthetic effects. A recent case was in *The Artist* (2011, dir. Hazanavicius), the French homage to silent Hollywood cinema. The film features an originally composed score by Ludovic Bource, in the style of silent-film accompaniment, until something happens in the finale, coinciding with the climactic moment of the protagonist attempting suicide. After a silent pause dramatically emphasising the seemingly fatal gunshot, the music resumes *pianissimo* and, to our surprise, it is not Bource's music but 'Scene d'Amour' from Bernard Herrmann's score for *Vertigo* (1958, dir. Hitchcock). Why use *Vertigo* here? The film is a patent tribute to classical Hollywood cinema and the references and quotes abound—the character of George Valentin, the silent-cinema star played by Jean Dujardin, is a reference to Rudolph Valentino as to the name, Douglas Fairbanks as to the on-screen persona, John Gilbert as to the tragically declining career. But *Vertigo* is quite out of place; it has nothing to do with silent cinema nor is it a reference to some narrative similarities between *The Artist* and the Hitchcock film. The choice stirred much controversy for its incongruity and anachronism, also being called a 'shameless theft' (Haggstrom 2012, online), and even escalating to the accusation of 'rape' made by Kim Novak herself (Kilday 2012, Online). Its use, most people said, was gratuitous, *unmotivated*. The director Hazanavicius stated in his defence that: '*The Artist* was made as a love letter to cinema, and grew out of my (and all of my cast and crew's) admiration and respect for movies throughout history. It was inspired by the work of Hitchcock, Lang, Ford, Lubitsch, Murnau and Wilder. I love Bernard Herrmann and his music has been used in many different films and I'm very pleased to have it in mine' (Anon 2012, Online). The unmotivated choice of *Vertigo* is ultimately motivated *artistically*, by a personal decision by the director that does not involve any other realistic, compositional, or transtextual motivation. A piece of music can also have more than one motivation at the same time; an instance of all the four motivations being simultaneously present is the opening title scene of *The Abominable Dr. Phibes* (1971, dir. Fuest), which I have analysed elsewhere (Audissino 2014, p. xx).

If we wished to expand the analysis from the artwork's formal system to the marketing dynamics and economical context in which the film circulates, we could add a fifth motivation—the *economical motivation*. The four we have reviewed so far can be called *endogenous* motivations, as the reason for the music being in the film originates from needs that are internal to the film's formal system—connecting two narrative elements, enhancing the realism, making a quotation, and so forth. Economical motivation is *exogenous* as the presence of music is, in this case, dictated by reasons others than formal, reasons that are external to the film's system and aesthetic design: economically motivated devices are dictated by the market. Songs are frequently added also, if not principally, with an economical motivation, their function being to promote the sale of tie-in albums and thus increment the box-office revenues with those of the record market. The film in this case is also a sort of advertisement for the song, and in turn the radio passages of the song advertise the film associated with that song—think of *Titanic* (1997, dir. Cameron) and its James Horner/Will Jennings song 'My Heart Will Go On.'[1] The song, in the more marked cases of economically motivated music, is so incongruously inserted in the film that no other compositional, realistic, or transtextual motivations can be found for its presence, and the impression is that the narrative has stopped to show us a sort of MTV moment—an often cited example is 'Raindrops Keep Fallin' on My Head' in *Butch Cassidy* (1969, dir. Hill).[2] If no other motivation is detectable, economical motivation can be confused with artistic motivation. The difference, I would say, is that a piece of music inserted with an artistic motivation is not expected to generate extra revenues, while one with an economical motivation is. The anachronistic use of the spiritual 'Sometimes I Feel like a Motherless Child' in *The Gospel according to St. Matthew* (1964, dir. Pasolini) is not likely to promoted the sale of tie-in albums; 'Raindrops Keep Fallin' on My Head' certainly is. For those interested in expanding the analysis of a film to its market strategies, the concept of economical motivation can be a useful one in trying to find the economical rationale behind the use of a given cinematic device.[3] And this is not limited to music; even the use of Marilyn Monroe in a film instead of a lesser known or lesser sexualised actress can be seen as economically motivated.[4] In this study, I will limit my focus on the 'endogenous' motivations, but a mention, even a passing one, of this exogenous economical motivation seemed dutiful.

We can test the set of motivations on an imaginary scene. Consider a scene where a waltz is introduced as a narrative device because the screenplay requires the two characters, who so far barely know each other, to make deeper acquaintance, and a good way seems to have them make acquaintance while casually engaging in a dance together during some sort of public gathering. The essential function of the waltz here is to make the characters stay closely together so that they can connect. Imagine such a scene in a realistic film. If the waltz suddenly started playing out of nowhere and the characters started dancing to it, the musical device would appear to be implausible, ill-integrated within the scene, maybe even risible: Why a waltz, suddenly?! The feeling would be that of a *deus-ex-machina* solution, that is, a theatrical and artificial trick to quickly solve a narrative problem. While in a musical film the sudden appearance of music would be not only accepted but expected, in a realistic film this would appear wrong. (Unless this anti-realistic violation is a device intended to break the conventions of realism, but in this case the narration has to make its anti-conformist intention clearly detectable, for example, framed within an 'art film' form featuring other stylistic violations—as in Godard's cinema—or within the terrain of parody and spoof, as in Mel Brooks's comedies. (I distinguish here the 'realistic film', the one in which the realistic motivation is preponderant, from the 'art film', the one in which the artistic motivation is stronger.)[5] If, on the contrary, the narration had first showed a small ensemble tuning their instruments, at the start of the waltz the musical device would have appeared well-integrated and credible. It is a matter of motivation.

(A narratologist would probably say that it is a matter of indeterminacy of the narrative level on which the source of the music is. In the first scenario the music sounds implausible because we do not clearly understand who the narrator is that emits it; the music is in the 'fantastical gap' as we are not sure whether it comes from a narrator outside of the narrative worlds (non-diegetic music), some unseen ensemble within the narrative world (diegetic), or perhaps even from the dancers' mind (meta-diegetic or internal diegetic music). Keeping the focus on the internal dynamics of the filmic system and dispensing with the need to postulate narrators, I prefer to say that the music sounds implausible because its presence is not properly motivated.) In our example, the 'unprepared' waltz can be seen to have a crude *compositional motivation*. We need the two characters to make acquaintances first, if we want them to start dating in the next scenes, and the waltz is inserted with the motivation of making the narrative composition progress to that dating point. Yet, as I have previously mentioned, compositional motivation is better integrated when 'fleshed-out' by some other motivation that hides the 'compositional skeleton' of the narrative. In our example, the waltz appears to be odd in the realistic scenario not only because there is no other motivation than the compositional but also because a device was chosen, the waltz, that in that realistic context draws too much attention to itself as artificially inserted. To sound right in that context, the musical device has to have a *realistic motivation* too, by showing that music comes from a source within the narrative world. In the case of the musical film, the waltz coming from nowhere would have been accepted because it would have had a *transtextual motivation*, that is, the motivation comes from the conventions of the musical genre, in which characters 'naturally' start singing or dancing to music that is not necessarily diegetic. On the other hand, if the coming-from-nowhere waltz were inserted to purposely subvert the realistic expectations that a realistic film generates, that would be an *artistic motivation*, that is, a deliberate foregrounding of some otherwise unmotivated device for aesthetic or authorial idiosyncratic reasons. For example, the sound jolts and sharp cuts to the musical flow and the 'wrong' sound levels that can be heard at the beginning of *A Woman Is a Woman* (1961, dir. Godard) at first sound like the result of 'faulty' post-production operations. But having noticed other stylistic subversions—like the 'Lights! Camera! Action!' backstage sounds that open the film, and later Anna Karina winking at the camera—in a film that clearly presents itself as an *auteur* revisitation of the Hollywood musical, we understand that the jolts and cuts are artistically motivated disruptions of the smoothness and seamlessness of the conventional norms of soundtrack construction, an artistic baring of the technical operations behind film-making.

Functions

Keeping with the division between more automated, lower-level mental processes and higher-level mental processes, I propose to name the three functions that music can perform in films after the three areas of activity of film-viewing: perception, emotion, and cognition. Perception and emotion are taken as lower-level mental processes, taking place more non-consciously and autonomously—a bright figure jumps to the foreground without any conscious mental effort from my part, a sad piece of music strikes me as such and I cannot do anything about it. Perception and emotion have to do, in my view, with the type of engagement with the film's narrative that does not require conscious elaboration, like basic story understanding: narrative patterns we instantly recognise either for innate dispositions (such as the 'Canonical Story Format' previously mentioned, which responds to our need for order and closure) or for repeated cultural exposure. If I see someone approaching a bank and wearing a stocking over her/his face before entering with a pistol in hand, I do not have to ponder about that—the 'Bank Robbery Gestalt' (or 'Prototype' in cognitivist terms: Kellogg 2012, p. 186) immediately materialises. If character A is the victim of some wrongdoing by character B in one scene and later in the film character A sets character B's car on fire, I do not have to consciously ponder about the cause/effect link between the two events; the two are almost automatically experienced as linked under the 'Revenge Gestalt.'

Music has an *emotive function* when its agency is mainly directed at configuring the 'emotion system' of the film. The term in quotation marks is taken from Greg M. Smith's theory of cinematic emotion (Smith 2003). The 'emotion system' of the film is seen as aimed at keeping a certain sustained mood throughout the scene/sequence/film by reinforcing said mood with moments of emotions of the same quality. Explains Smith:

> I argue that the primary emotive effect of film is to create mood.…Generating brief, intense emotions often requires an orienting state that asks us to interpret our surroundings in an emotional fashion. If we are in such an emotional

orienting state, we are much more likely to experience such emotion....Film structures seek to increase the film's chances of evoking emotion by first creating a predisposition toward experiencing emotion: a mood....To sustain a mood, we must experience occasional moments of emotion....Therefore, mood and emotion sustain each other. Mood encourages us to experience emotion, and experiencing emotions encourages us to continue in the present mood.' (Smith 2003, p. 42)

Unlike other theories of emotion—such as M. Smith (1995), Grodal (1997), or E. Tan (1996), which link the emotional engagement mostly to the characters—Smith's has the advantage of linking the emotion system to the formal system, i.e. any device can be responsible for sustaining the mood and creating emotion moments. And since film music is a film device, this makes Smith's theorisation very appropriate to explain how music takes part in the construction of the emotion system.[6] He provides a demonstration in his analysis of how music contributes to build the sad mood of the birthday party in *Stella Dallas* (1937, dir. Vidor) (Smith 2003, pp. 101–107). To illustrate Smith's theory, think of *Psycho*. The bulk of Bernard Herrmann's score is divided between a group of tension-building pieces—long sustained notes by the low strings creating unresolved dissonances that are experienced as anxiety-inducing music—and a group of musical shockers. The most notable of these is the infamous piercingly shrieking *Rhee! Rhee! Rhee!* introduced during the shower murder and replicating the violent and painful gestures of the stabbing: music is played ferociously with stab-like bowing of the violins, and the piercing dissonances are 'painful' to the ear. The ominous tension-building music is already presented before the shower murder— when Norman lewdly spies on Marion—creating a disturbing impression of the Bates Motel, as if something wrong had happened/were about to happen. The micro-configuration of the music (sustained and unresolved dissonance, low 'shady' tones but also unnaturally cold high-register violins), coupled with the shabbiness of the motel premises and Norman's odd behaviour, creates in the viewer anxiety and anticipation of something not good. Indeed, moments later we witness the shocking murder of Marion, the supposed protagonist who is surprisingly dispatched in the first third of the film. The tension-building music had already created a mood of anxiety before the shower scene; during the sudden murder— the emotion moment—it is music that makes it even more shocking. The burst of violence thus reinforces the general mood, confirming that indeed the Bates Motel is a dangerous place where sick things happen. The mood is further sustained in the following scenes, where the mysterious maternal presence and the house where she is secluded are scored with more tension-building music. In this mood, when the detective Arbogast, later in the film, enters the house to look for traces of the disappeared Marion, we cannot but expect for the worse. Tension-building music can be heard when he approaches the house, with a distinct three-note dark motif played by the low-register celli and basses that recurs in the film and, retrospectively, can be identified with madness. When Arbogast enters the hall we hear *tremolo* strings, a classical technique used—since Claudio Monteverdi—to express tension and suspense in music. When Arbogast starts walking up the staircase, the high-register violins freeze in a sustained tone of anticipation—of nothing good. Indeed, the door of Ms. Bates's bedroom slowly opens. The mood is at its highest point of tension. Them, we hear the *Rhee! Rhee! Rhee!* murder motif start instants before we see Ms. Bates storming out of her bedroom to stab the intruder to death. The emotion moment of Arbogast's gruesome death is prepared by the outburst of the murder music, which we know means 'murder' because we have previously heard it during Marion's death.

Similarly but not identically to these two actions in the emotion system (mood and emotion moments), the *emotive function* can be divided into two distinct sub-functions: *macro-emotive function* and *micro-emotive function*. The micro-emotive function is at work locally in one scene or sequence. In this case, the micro-configuration of the music meets the micro-configurations of the other devices, which by combination produces the emotive macro-configuration of the scene (this can be the 'mood' or an 'emotion moment,' depending on whether it is prolonged or instantaneous). Sentimental music with a sentimental dialogue creates a strong sentimental macro-configuration (in this case, a 'mood') that can be further boosted if, when the two lovers kiss, music soars to passionate heights, creating a stronger 'emotion moment' during the kiss. Or the mood can be subverted, if a slap in the face scored with a dissonant stinger is in place of the kiss. But the emotive micro-configuration of the music can be non-isomorphical with the other devices, as we have seen, and in that case the resulting macro-configuration can be a more complex mood—the romance with hesitation that I have mentioned in my previous example. In any case, I call micro-emotive function the case in which the action of music coincides with a distinct moment (slap in the face with dissonant stinger) or is circumscribed to a limited portion of the film, like a scene or a sequence (sentimental music that helps create the sentimental mood of a romantic scene). In the case of *Psycho*, the harsh grating *Rhee! Rhee! Rhee!* murder motif has the micro-emotive function of making us feel the violence and the pain of the stabbings in an almost tactile way in that moment of the film.

When the emotive agency of the music has a wider extension, I call that *macro-emotive function*, for example, when music acts as an emotive bonding frame for the film. This is not simply a matter of creating a prolonged and consistent mood (in Smith's usage of the word) throughout the film that takes part in the creation of the emotion system. Music fulfils a function that is emotive but above all architectural (macro as opposed to micro). A theme is presented at the beginning of the film and then reiterated consistently across it:

> A sound or a complex of sounds functions as a center not because of learned syntactic convention, but because of the innate cognitive proclivity that Gestalt psychologists have called 'the principle of return.' That is, the psychic satisfaction of returns enables the set of sounds to function as a center—a point of stability and relative closure. [T]o function as a center, the set of sounds not only must be distinctive in some way, but must be emphasized through repetition. (Meyer 1996, p. 343)

Music creates a sort of set of rhymes that stretches along all the film. The return of patterns in a score creates a psychological effect of closure (Meyer 1996, p. 329), and the consistency and closure of the configuration of the score makes the macro-configuration of the whole film's formal system felt as equally consistent and closed—even if this might not be the case.[7] Think of the use of Max Steiner's 'Tara's Theme' in *Gone with the Wind* (1939, dir. Fleming), which is presented during the opening titles in its original major-mode version, consistently reprised so as to consolidate it in the viewer's memory, presented in minor-mode during the downfalls, eventually reinstated to its major-mode version to celebrate hope for the future when Scarlet promises she 'will never be hungry again,' and finally closes the film majestically—with an added vocalising chorus. The constant and consistent reprises of Tara's Theme contribute to the macro-configuration of the whole film a sense of formal consistency and closure. Similarly, *Psycho* ends with a close-up of Norman Bates coupled with the 'madness motif' that we had already heard during the film—for example when Arbogast is about to enter the house. Contrary to the micro-emotive, the recurrences and wider extension of the macro-emotive function also engage our memory:

> Film music has a forward and backward priming effect....The implications...are manifold: [this] not only extends our understanding of musical effects in cinematic narration and characterization, but also suggests that these effects, starting as early as the title sequence, may aggregate over the course of a film and thus shape our memory of the entire film, especially when composers choose to endow the score with a coherent character. (Hoeckner and Nusbaum 2013, p. 256)

The recurrence of a theme—besides creating a coherent mood for the characters and settings—helps our comprehension of the story and helps us follow its development by creating emotive rhymes through music that make us recall previous events, and the emotion associated with those events.[8] An illuminating instance is in *The Night Walker* (1964, dir. Castle): Irene, a widow of a pathologically jealous husband, has a series of unsettling dreams involving a handsome man visiting her during the night. In the longest of these, he takes her to his apartment and then to a sinister chapel where he marries her before a congregation of mannequins. When Irene and her mysterious dream lover arrive at his house, we see the archway of the elegant facade and hear a conspicuous musical statement from the brass. Given the vivid nature of the dream, when Irene wakes up, she is convinced that it was not a dream, and asks her lawyer to accompany her around the city to identify the places of her supposed dream. At a certain point of the car tour, the narration shows us the facade with the archway and we are presented with the same brass music we heard in the dream sequence. As soon as we see the facade and hear the music that was previously associated with it, we instantly realise, with Irene, that the locale of her dream is a real place. The brass statement helps us recall the building by having consolidated a stronger memory trace of the dream man's house; it is a stronger memory trace because it is a richer one, made of both visual and aural elements.

Besides helping structural consolidation and recollection of events, the macro-emotive function builds and prolongs a certain mood (in Smith's usage) throughout the film's emotion system. For example, the use of jazz music in *The Man with the Golden Arm* (1955, dir. Preminger), instead of the still-dominant symphonic orchestral idiom, gives the film a certain grittiness and contemporary realism that a symphonic score would have failed to do. Less obviously, the macro-emotive function can also be responsible for a gradual build-up of the mood that leads to a particularly important emotion moment in the film. This has not only to do with the mood-orienting agency formulated by Smith; music creates a certain mood that makes us particularly ready to respond to the forthcoming emotion moment. It is the result of a combination of architectural score design, our recollection of the past musical presentation, and the delayed fulfilment of our expectations: 'The recurrence itself...creates closure and a feeling of completeness' (Meyer 1956, p. 152). This calculated repetition of the theme(s) makes it familiar to the viewers, who thus learn to recognize it and, as a consequence, experience a positive feeling each time the familiar theme appears again. Leonard B. Meyer calls this the 'Pleasure of recognition' (Meyer 1996, p. 210), an effect of the 'Principle of Return':

> [It] depends for its operation upon 'recurrence'....Recurrence is repetition which takes place after there has been a departure from whatever has been established as given in the particular piece....Because there is departure and return, recurrence always involves a delay of expectation and subsequent fulfilment....The recurrence itself represents, not tension, but the relaxation phase of the tonal motion. It creates closure and a feeling of completeness. (Meyer 1956, pp. 151–152)

Following a procedure of thematic development inherited by nineteenth-century music, some film composers present the main theme in the opening credits and only later in the film present it again—like Steiner in *Gone with the Wind*. Some even present only parts of the main theme at first, maybe only the first few notes, and then incrementally longer expositions later in the film. Meyer explains that 'motivic constancy is used because it allows for the perception of larger processes, and because the use of *part* of a previously established whole (a motive taken from a theme) is implicative of the return of the total pattern' (Meyer 1973, p. 54). The whole theme—the 'total pattern'—is presented only in a moment in the film in which a particularly strong emotional response is required. The long-awaited presentation of the 'total pattern' creates an emotional response of gratification both because of the 'Pleasure of Recognition' (I recognise the theme and welcome the comforting feeling of returning in familiar territories) and because I am finally given the chance to hear a closure in the micro-configuration of the musical piece. When this gratification given by the return and closure of a familiar theme coincides with a moment of the film in which an action finds a similarly satisfying completion and success, the overall macro-configuration produces a very strong emotional moment. John Williams is particularly noted for adopting this technique, which I have called 'gradual disclosure of the main theme' (Audissino 2014, p. 126). For example, in *Raiders of the Lost Ark* (1981, dir. Spielberg), the entire 'Indiana Jones Theme' is not presented at the beginning of the film, and only its first half is used in the first half of the film; the whole theme is finally disclosed in the triumphal moment in which Indiana manages to board the Nazi submarine to rescue Marion (Audissino 2014, pp. 177–178).

Music has a *perceptive function* when helps the viewer configure the spatio-temporal perception of the scene/sequence. The *perceptive function* operates when the particular micro-configuration of the music is isomorphic to the micro-configuration of some other element in the film, either within the time dimension or the space dimension. The *spatial perceptive function* is at work in those cases in which music can point the viewer's attention to some important visual detail or action by highlighting his presence or trajectory. Music mimics some extra-musical gesture; an obvious example is a character falling down a flight of stairs accompanied by a fast downward scale of the violins. The micro-configuration of the visual action (falling down) is matched with an isomorphic configuration of the music (falling down), which produces a macro-configuration (falling down) that acquires a stronger salience in the formal system of that scene and thus attracts our attention. Suppose you have a very crowded long-shot scene, with different layers and centres of action, and it is important that the viewer notices one character falling down in the lower left corner of the shot. Without music, the fall might pass unnoticed, our attention distracted by other actions. If some isomorphic musical gesture is exactly synchronised with the character falling, we will perceive aurally that there is some 'falling' going on, and our attention will be automatically engaged in the search of the visual action within the frame that is congruent (isomorphic) with that falling.

This type of spatial perceptive function is nowadays almost exclusively performed by sound effects rather than music—imagine that, instead of someone falling, the narration wants our attention to be directed to a door opening in the lower left corner—the sound of a squeaking hinge would do the trick. Yet, in the classical Hollywood cinema of the 1930s and 1940s, music covered many of such tasks, being characterised by following the visual action very adherently (Kalinak 1992, pp. 83–86). The so-called Mickey-Mousing (a technique in which musical gestures closely replicated visual gestures so as to emphasize the importance of such visual actions) is a primary trait of that Golden Age style (Audissino 2014, pp. 40–41). The term originates from the pantomime-like gestures of cartoon music—Jerry Mouse walks on tip-toes to go past the sleeping Tom Cat, and his tiny steps are precisely punctuated by *pizzicato* strings—but it was widely employed in live-action films as well: think of the swashbucklers and Errol Flynn swinging from vine to vine accompanied by swirls and flights of the strings and woodwinds in perfect synchronisation. But we have examples of this high level of 'metaphoric mimicry' and almost onomatopoeic music also outside of the classical Hollywood cinema. For example, in *Kind Hearts and Coronets* (1949, dir. Hamer) when the balloon that carries Lady Agatha D'Ascoyne is shot down and plummets, we hear a descending harp *glissando*. Even if today we don't have this kind of accentuated spatial-perceptive function anymore—with the exception of some old-fashioned adventure scores like Williams's—music is nevertheless an important device to point our attention to the detail in the narrative space that narration wants us to notice. In the ghost story *Crimson Peak* (2015, dir. Del Toro), the mother's phantom appears now and then to the young protagonist. The main apparition, as usual, is preceded by very quick manifestations, mainly in the background. In one shot, the ghost rapidly shows behind the protagonist, in the distance. If it weren't for the sudden chord that punctuates its appearance, we might fail to notice that something happened in the background. In this case, we have a static shot with static, ominous music; when something suddenly, quickly, and briefly happens in the music, we automatically scan the shot for the isomorphic element within, and thus we notice the sudden, quick, and brief appearance of the ghost. This 'Look There!' function of the music is quite common and very useful in making sure we catch the narrative elements we need to understand and follow the developments. For example, in the episode 'Child's Play' of the TV series *Castle* (2009–2016, prod. Marlowe),[9] Castle and Beckett are searching a bedroom, on the trail of a dangerous Russian hit-man. While they are there, a low-angle shot shows us the Russian fiend hiding under the bed—unbeknownst to our heroes, who are in a potentially deadly danger. The scene is set at night and the hidden killer is in the shadow. To create the suspense—we know that the killer is there, Castle and Beckett do not, and this creates anxiety in us about the outcome of this dangerous situation—it is essential that the viewer notices the killer under the bed. The average TV viewer, distracted by a number of things happening around her/his household, might miss the visual element—he might be sending a text right at that moment, or scolding the dog off the sofa. But the moment the narration shows us the hiding killer, we hear a dark and threatening chord. The music has suddenly changed and our attention is thus revived and we look for the cause of the sudden change; we pay attention and notice the killer. Again, in terms of configurations, the sudden and noticeable change in configuration of the music lets us know that there must be a similarly important change in the configuration of the narrative.

Besides focussing the attention on some elements of the narrative space, the spatial perceptive function can also be operative as a spatial binder in complex multi-setting sequences. In this cases, diegetic music aides in creating a more solid perception of the narrative space of the sequence, allowing us to experience it as a unified whole and/or helping us orientate within it. A typical case is when pieces of diegetic music identify different sections of a locale and the volume and reverberation[10] of one piece of music vis-à-vis the others clarify the position of the characters and their movements from one place to the others, as can be seen in the Cairo sequence of *Raiders of the Lost Ark*:

> Jones and Marion are taking a stroll in the streets of Cairo—instrumental Arabic-sounding diegetic music can be heard. Besides setting the 'local color,' the diegetic music serves here to define the position of the characters in space. The point of highest volume is the square, but the same music can be heard also from the room in which the villains are preparing to attack: thus the music locates the room in the environs of the square. A different vocal diegetic music is present in the scene under the arcade between the thug with the monkey and the Nazis, separating the indoor arcade space from the outdoor square space. (Audissino 2014, p. 168)

Music can operate on the other dimension of the film narrative as well, time, and have a *temporal-perceptive function*. Time configurations in the visuals may correspond to the rhythm and pace of editing or to the rhythm and pace of the movements and gestures of the actors, or to those of camerawork. For example, we can have a very regular and relaxed series of shot of the same long duration (five-second shot + five second-shot + five-second shot, etc.); a very regular but hectic series of the same short duration (one-second shot + one second-shot + one-second shot…); an irregular series of different-duration shots (one-second shot + three-second shot + half-second shot + two second-shot, etc.). If each cut in editing corresponds to a pulse, in the first instance, the rhythmic pattern is regular (the cut always falls after the same period of time) and the tempo is slow (five seconds pass between each cut); in the second instance, the rhythmic pattern is still regular but the tempo is fast (one second passes between each cut); in the third instance, we have an irregular rhythmic pattern (the period of time between cuts is variable) and an undefined tempo (there is not a fixed temporal duration between cuts). Similarly, an actor can talk and gesticulate in a slow pace and with regular rhythmic patterns, or have a frantic and irregular delivery. Music has its own rhythmic patterns and tempi and, coupled with the temporal/rhythmic configuration of the other devices, can produce a temporal macro-configuration that is perceived as different from the configurations of the separated elements. For example, if an actress/actor is shown marching in a 1–2; 1–2; 1–2 pace, her/his gait will appear more resolute and perhaps even faster if coupled with a music that doubles the pulse, matching the 1–2; 1–2; 1–2 with (1–2)–(3–4); (1–2)–(3–4); (1–2)–(3–4).

An action scene can be perceived as more fast-paced because of the music's tempo and rhythm. For example, think of the final chase on the Mount Rushmore in *North by Northwest* (1959, dir. Hitchcock). Once the protagonists and the villains reach the presidential monuments, there is not much fast-paced action in the visuals but mostly people stalling on some ledge trying to figure out what direction to take without risking falling down, or people slowly crawling along from one ridge to the other. It is Herrmann's fiery main theme, with its relentless and urging fandango rhythm, that makes the macro-configuration of the sequence more hectic than the micro-configuration of the visuals alone. Or music can be the binding element that harmonises the pace and rhythm of editing and actors' performance into a well-synchronised whole. This case of temporal-perceptive function of music is particularly noticeable in musical films, in which the coordination of the tempi and rhythmic patterns of the music with those of the gestures, dance movements, camerawork, and editing are a central part of the choreographic form of the dance numbers of this genre. An example from a non-musical film is in *Pauline et Paulette* (2001, dir. Debrauwer), a story of two sisters who try not to be assigned the custody of their mentally impaired sister Pauline. Pauline has a special love for flowers: she has a scrap book that she covers in flower drawings, flower clippings from newspapers, and flower-ornate wrap paper. She also relishes in taking care of Paulette's luxuriant garden. In one scene we are given access to Pauline's inner world in a particularly salient way: she waters the flowers with joyous and ample gestures of her arm, the watering-can swinging semi-circularly, in synch to the beat of the first three full-orchestra measures (1–2–3; 1–2–3; 1–2–3) of the main theme from Tchaikovsky's 'Waltz of the Flowers' from *The Nutcracker* (1892). On the fourth measure of the theme (by the woodwinds), narration cuts to and pauses for one second on close details of flowers (1–2–3), and then cuts back to Pauline's choreographic gardening as the main theme reprises from measure one (1–2–3; 1–2–3; 1–2–3)—Fig. 6.1 replicates this tight and almost choreographic coupling of music and visuals, as if Paulette and all the garden were dancing to Tchaikovsky's music.

As the spatial perceptive function can also have a unifying role, so can the temporal-perceptive function. A typical example is the montage sequence, that is, those summarising sequences typical of the Classical Hollywood cinema that compress a number of events in a short presentation. For example, in *Dishonored* (1931, dir. Von Sternberg) the interest is for the spy played by Marlene Dietrich and the seductive manoeuvres she employs to fulfil her duties. World War I itself is of little interest but nevertheless provides the context for the narrative; the solution was to compress some war events in a quick montage. Tellingly enough, in an epoch like the early sound cinema

Fig. 6.1 Pauline waters the flowers, *Pauline et Paulette*

in which non-diegetic film music was seldom present in films, this is the only part of *Dishonored* with non-diegetic music. Montages are very fragmentary editing sequences in which the causal links and timeline can be unclear or confusing; with music they may acquire not only a stronger cohesion but a clearer chronological orientation too, because of the music's uninterrupted and logical temporal flow—what Chion calls 'vectorisation' (Chion 1994, p. 14).[11] An example of a temporal perceptive function that both unifies and orients is from *Sorry, Wrong Number* (1948, dir. Litvak). The main character, Leona, is at home, bedridden and alone, and happens to find out, from a phone interference, that a hired killer will visit her that night at 11:15. In the film's finale, the arrival of the murderer at Leona's house, his slow approach to her bedroom, and her increasingly desperate helplessness, are scored by Franz Waxman with a passacaglia, a musical form from the Baroque era in which an ostinato bass line keeps playing throughout the piece. The use of a passacaglia (a formally cohesive and developing piece, instead of some general 'suspense' music) not only imposes a stronger temporal unit to this final sequence of the film; it also casts on the sequence a sense of inevitability (given by the unstoppable ostinato) and of climatic progression of the drama (given by the gradual and teleological development of the piece).

In the set of functions introduced so far, music helps the viewer connect emotionally and perceptually with the film. When music helps the viewer comprehend more complex narrative relations or even interpret implicit or symptomatic meanings, I call it music with a *cognitive function*, because higher-level mental processes are involved, including productive thinking, in the case of interpretation. Music has a *denotative cognitive function* (denotation is a direct relation between a sign and its meaning) when it highlights relations amongst elements in the narrative and thematic levels that help us comprehend the narrative in a better and less equivocal way. The combination of the micro-configurations of the devices in the film segment at hand might not produce a macro-configuration that is stable enough to be unequivocally comprehensible.[12] As in the case of the multistable figures where we can stabilise our perception on one of the two if we focus on a selected element of the image—for example, in the Old Lady/Young Lady image, if we focus on the necklace interpreting it as a mouth we see the Old Lady—similarly here the music is used by narration to stabilise the desired macro-configuration.

Music can anticipate a narrative turning point. In the Italian comedy *Letto a tre piazze* (1960, dir. Steno) a couple is celebrating the tenth anniversary of their wedding. The wife is a widow, her first husband declared dead during the Russian campaign of World War II. Early on the anniversary day, we see the second husband—a jealous Mediterranean type—ask the housemaid to get rid of the first husband's portrait, which the wife had so far kept on the wall. He comments about the long-delayed removal of the portrait: 'I've finally got rid of this jinx.' We cut to the party, that same night, with a detail of the tenth-anniversary cake. On that, we hear an ominous version of Wagner's 'Wedding March' from *Lohengrin* (1850), played in minor mode and by ghostly ethereal celeste and glockenspiel: some 'jinx' seems to be about to strike the celebrating couple. The party goes on and one of the guests comments: 'Looking at this most happy wedding, I am astonished and I ask myself if anything in the world does exist that can possibly spoil it!' Right after that, the narration cuts to the condominium's staircases, where we see a detail of some man's feet, wrapped in coarse boots made of cardboard and rags, wearingly walking up the stairs. On that, we hear an exhausted instrumental rendition—with a plodding heavy bass line—of the quintessentially Russian 'Song of the Volga Boatmen,' which continues to accompany the new character as he walks all the way up to the couple's apartment, to finally ring the doorbell. As music clearly anticipated, we soon find out that the unexpected guest is the supposedly dead husband, eventually come back from Russia.

Music can clarify our understanding of a character's motive for a certain action. In *The Treasure of the Sierra Madre* (1948, dir. Huston) three gold-diggers have formed a society and are working in a mine. There is an accident and the ceiling of the gallery collapses on one of them, Dobbs, burying him. Curtin, one of his partners, rushes to the mine to rescue him but, suddenly, he stops and lingers at the entrance. We hear a slightly sinister musical motif, previously associated with gold. Music is helping us understand Curtin's ruminations: if Dobbs dies, the remaining two partners will receive bigger shares. But eventually the music moves from the 'gold motif' to the jaunty one previously associated with the friendship between the partners, and indeed Curtin stops pondering, rejects the greedy temptation and rescues Dobbs.

Music can also bring in a decisive contribution to the comprehension of the narrative. In the comedy/drama *Macaroni* (1985, dir. Scola), the narrative closure is totally left to the agency of music and sound. At the end of the film, Antonio is beaten to death by some mobsters after rescuing his son from dangerous liaisons with the local organised crime. Previously in the film, Antonio had told his American friend Robert that he had been dead twice but both times had resurrected at 1:00 p.m., right on time for lunch, signalling his awakening by ringing a bell that was left there for him. The final scene of the film shows us Antonio's corpse on his dead-bed, a string tied to his hand and connected to a bell. In the adjacent dining-room all the family and Robert are seated at the lunch table, in a mournful but slightly hopeful mood. In trepidation, Robert keeps watching the wall clock, a few minutes to 1:00 p.m. The narration suddenly leaves the dining-room, pans away from the house to stop on the outdoor view seen from the balcony. For a moment we are led to think that we are left with an open ending, not knowing whether Antonio will wake up for his third time. But on the view of the rooftops, we hear a bell excitedly ringing, and music soars cheerfully: the third miracle has happened. It is not presented visually but announced with music and sound.[13]

In other cases—in particular with the classical Hollywood cinema's commitment to absolute narrative clarity at the cost of being an 'excessively obvious system' (Bordwell et al. 1985, p. 3)—music plays a lesser role: not really providing the missing clues as in the previous examples but introducing a micro-configuration that redundantly over-stabilises the macro-configuration. In *The Rat Race* (1960, dir. Mulligan), an out-of-towner moves to New York to start a career as a jazz saxophonist. He ends up sharing an apartment with a tough-skinned girl who has been living in the city for years, modelling and dancing. The romantic and trusting one in the couple is Pete, while Peggy is cynical and distrustful. It is obvious from the beginning that Pete is sentimentally involved with Peggy, but she is resisting him behind a coriaceous no-nonsense pose. In one scene, Peggy is reading at the presence of her bartender friend a letter that Pete sent her—he is away for a musical gig on a cruise ship. During the letter reading, we hear sentimental violin music, and Peggy seems to miss Pete. When the bartender notices that and remarks: 'You're stuck on the guy!' she defiantly quips, resuming her tough-girl attitude: 'Oh, don't be corny! I don't care if he's living or not!' and as soon as she says that, street-wise jazz music replaces the violins. But as the bartender elaborates on his argument, the gradual return of the sentimental violin music confirms that Peggy is indeed missing Pete and she is romantically involved as well, and she is starting to accept that. In *It Started in Naples* (1960, dir. Shavelson), Michael (Clark Gable), a divorced mature man about to re-marry, travels to the Italian city to settle an inheritance. A clash of cultures ensues, with his American customs and way of life contrasting with the Neapolitan more relaxed ones. Accordingly, local Italianate music for mandolin is contrasted with American music—including quotations of 'Yankee Doodle.' During his sojourn, Michael has a legal dispute with Lucia (Sophia Loren) over the custody of his late brother's son—the mother, Lucia's sister, having died in the same accident as Michael's brother. Despite the litigation, the two start falling in love. At the end, Lucia wins custody and Michael prepares to go back to America to marry his fiancée, reluctantly at this point. At the train station, Michael, already on board, eventually decides to stay in Naples and surrender to his love for Lucia. As he gets off the train and heads back to the city centre, we hear 'Yankee Doodle' played by mandolins, an eloquent musical equivalent of America-meets-Italy and of the Michael/Lucia couple.

Music has a *connotative cognitive function* in those instances in which its function and motivation are less immediately graspable than in the denotative cases. Music seems oddly coupled with the other devices, incongruous, counter-intuitive—as the eerie music in the romance scene we have previously discussed. In this case it is not a matter of 'comprehension' but one of 'interpretation.' To reprise Köhler's words: 'we have to deal not with one relation but, rather, with whole sets of them, and thus with relations among relations' (Köhler 1969, p. 144). We notice that the music is apparently inconsistent with the visuals, and this inconsistency seems to point to something else. Music suggests some connotation, that is, an indirect meaning.

Consider the case of the joyful march played against the images of defeat in *Deserter* (1933, dir. Pudovkin). The micro-configuration of the images we are seeing—Defeat—is coupled with a non-isomorphic micro-configuration of the music—Triumph. We are thus faced with an interpretive problem, an unstable or incomplete macro-configuration, and we have to search for the set of relations that can make us see the solution to the problem. In this case, given the propaganda nature of the film, the reasons behind this choice become clear: any defeat or the Revolution is only temporary and victory can eventually be achieved everywhere. We have finally reached an isomorphism between the micro-configuration of the music—Triumph—and the micro-configuration of the visuals—Defeat—under the macro-configuration of 'Temporary Defeat eventually followed by Triumph.' In this view, music is not at all 'asynchronous' but perfectly 'synchronous' with narration's intent, communicating that one defeat will not prevent victory eventually.

A similar 'commentary' role about the depicted events is in *Taxi Driver* (1976, dir. Scorsese). Anyone familiar with Herrmann's music or having a good recollection of *Psycho* will notice that this film is closed with the quotation of the 'madness motif' from that Hitchcock film. In *Taxi Driver* the 'madness motif' can be seen as a self-quotation of one of Herrmann's most famous scores but, less superficially, also as a commentary about the Travis Bickle character that is celebrated as an accidental hero at the end of the film. Actually, the music tells us, Travis is a psychopath—not too different from *Psycho*'s Norman Bates— but he happened to kill the 'right' people and thus he passes for a hero.

This last case of connotative cognitive function might not be graspable by anyone—if you don't know Herrmann and have never seen *Psycho*, you cannot pick the reference. Indeed music can also have a connotative cognitive function that we do not notice, a covert one that does not activate an interpretive effort. Music here is meant to point to some symptomatic meaning or some reference external to the film's system that, even if not noticed by everyone, does not impede the comprehension of the film. But to those who notice, the reference opens new perspectives on the film. *The Adventures of Robin Hood* (1938, dir. Curtiz-Keighley) boasts a score by Erich Wolfgang Korngold, a former child-prodigy and highly respected opera composer who, as a Jew, had to flee from Vienna and take shelter in Hollywood because of the Nazi annexation of Austria— the *Anschluss*. The film was being shot at the time of this event, and the story of the fight for freedom of Robin and his men against the tyrannical Prince John instantly acquired political connotations because of the parallels with what was happening in Europe. Even more so because the film opens with a herald who reports bad news from Vienna—in the film, the legitimate King of England, Richard Lionheart, being kept a captive; in fact, Austria being kept a captive by Hitler. It is probably to strengthen this parallel with the current events—to sustain this symptomatic meaning of the Hollywood version of this old medieval tale—that Korngold took a waltz called 'Miss Austria' that he had written in 1929 and transformed it into Robin's theme, a rousing march.[14] If we do not know this, the film and its score can be appreciated anyway as an enjoyable Technicolor adventure. If we know the story behind the musical choices, the film reveals a deeper layer and the political connotations—hinted at in that 'News has come from Vienna' announcement that opens the film and in the re-use of 'Miss Austria'—become even more evident.

Consider a more articulated case of cognitive function. In *The Seven Year Itch* (1955, dir. Wilder), the over-imaginative and temporarily single husband Richard—his wife and kid are out of town on summer vacation—daydreams of having an affair with the gorgeous new girl living upstairs—played by Marilyn Monroe. Since he owns an air-conditioning system, he invites her to spend an evening at his apartment downstairs, to enjoy some refreshing solace from the heat waves. Eagerly awaiting the arrival of the object of his desire, Richard mentally rehearses the scene, putting on a record to help his imagination: 'The good old Rachmaninov. The second piano concerto. Never misses,' he says. His fantasy materialises and we, with him, see the girl appear, with a haughty poise, wrapped in a stunning evening gown with a tiger-stripe pattern, cigarette in hand. The camera pans and we now see Richard in a crimson satin dinner jacket, salt-and-pepper hair, sitting at the piano and playing the Rach 2 flawlessly, to the spell of which the girl desperately tries to resist. 'This is unfair!' she nobly protests as soon as she recognises the piece. 'Why?' asks him detachedly (with theatrical British accent). Replies the girl, 'Every time I hear it, I go to pieces.' In Richard's fantasy the girl soon surrenders and falls into his arms in a passionate kiss brought about and then accompanied by Rachmaninov's impetuous orchestral *tutti*. When the girl actually arrives at the apartment, things go quite differently. She is quite far from being the haughty goddess of Richard's fantasy; she couldn't be more indifferent to the Rach 2; Richard, when asked to play the piano, cannot but produce a basic rendition of 'Chopsticks,' a piece which reveals to be surprisingly endearing to the girl, who enthusiastically joins Richard at the piano for a four-hand (or better, four-finger) version; when Richard tries to kiss her on the piano bench as he did in his fantasy, the girl falls off the bench and lands on her derrière. The sequence is built as a satirical comparison between idealisation/fantasy and reality, and the Rach 2 is the musical symbol of the idealised romance to which the prosaic 'Chopsticks'—the musical symbol of down-to-earth extramarital affair—stands in contrast. So, the function of the music can be seen as a denotative cognitive one: music is a major comparison term to appreciate the difference between the two situations. It can also be seen as having a micro-emotive function; music infuses a sense of mastery, control and high proficiency in the first situation, and one of awkwardness, inadequacy, and amateurism in the second—the discrepancy in the musical performance easily alludes to the discrepancy between Richard's ideal and his actual sexual prowess.

But why choose that particular piece? The choice of the Rach 2 is a quotation of another famous—and romantically ill-fated—story of extramarital affair: *Brief Encounter* (1945, dir. Lean). In that film, the Rach 2 is the main musical presence—both diegetically and non-diegetically.[15] Thus, the use of this particular concerto is a way to make a parody of the love-story genre, on which Richard's fantasies has evidently been feeding. The satirical comparison between the two situations—ideal and real—is not only a comparison between what Richard would like to be and what he really is but also a comparison between romance as seen in the movies and romance as it is in real life.

As is clear from the previous instance, two or more functions can be performed by a piece of music at the same time. Consider the so-called stingers' in horror films (sudden dissonant chords that punctuate some shocking revelation or appearance). A stinger can be said to fulfil a spatial-perceptive function in that it replicates musically some visual action—the sudden appearance of the monster. But it also fulfils a micro-emotive function; not only the grating dissonance makes us experience the macro-configuration as unpleasant, disturbing or unsettling, but the very nature of the stinger—a loud and sudden sound—exploits the 'Startle Effect,' a physiological response that is inescapable. When we hear a loud and sudden sound we tend to recoil and enter into a defensive and alerted mode—'fight or flight'—because we register said sudden and violent noise as a potential danger. The emotional effect of this physiological startle is one of scare, agitation, and anxiety.[16] Another example of more than one function at work can be spotted in *Citizen Kane* (1941, dir. Welles). During the famous 'breakfast montage' the gradual deterioration of Kane's marriage is shown as a compressed series of breakfast moments in which, from the tenderly affectionate first one, we gradually see the spouses becoming more and more sour and eventually glacially indifferent to each other. The montage is scored with a waltz that not only provides temporal cohesion for the fragmentary nature of the montage but is also coordinated with the couple's descending slope: Herrmann's waltz deteriorates itself as the relationship deteriorates, ending up as an almost formless and static music in which the original pulse of the waltz is hardly noticeable. The music can be said to have a micro-emotive function appropriate to the mood of each segment of the montage—for example, romantic waltz when the couple is still in their honeymoon mood. It can also be said to fulfil a macro-emotive function over the whole montage; the comparison of the final deconstructed variation with the original waltz theme casts a sad light on the final phase of the couple's marriage—love and happy days are irremediably lost. Or music can also be said to have a denotative cognitive function, as a deterioration of the music so parallel to the deterioration of the couple is a way to make the macro-configuration 'Marriage Deterioration' stronger and more evident. The previous *Taxi Driver* example, for those who do not notice the quotation, will not be seen as an instance of connotative cognitive function but as one of micro-emotive function—those three dark notes makes the strange 'happy ending' more disturbing. And the previously mentioned example from *Macaroni* can be seen both as a denotative cognitive function (completing the narrative) but also as a micro-emotive function within the scene (the mourning is turned into joy) or even as a macro-emotive function within the film (the reprise of the main theme in the finale gives emotional closure to the narrative: 'all's well that ends well').

It is up to the analyst to investigate as deeply as possible what function/functions music is performing, and part of the analysis is also to study how music can function on multiple levels—for example, both emotionally and cognitively. In *The Legend of Lylah Clare* (1968, dir. Aldrich) the budding actress Elsa is approached to impersonate in a biopic a deceased movie star, Lylah Clare, whom she has an uncanny resemblance with. In her hotel room Elsa is uneasy, trying to make up her mind whether to accept the contract or not. She takes a walk outside, on Hollywood's 'Walk of Fame' and all the way to Grauman's Chinese Theater. Early in the morning, Elsa walks in the dawn lights, a potential hint that a new star is about to be born. A no-lyrics version of Frank DeVol's pop song 'Lylah' accompanies her stroll. Elsa seems fascinated by the vestiges of Hollywood's past, she admires herself CCTV-ed in the set of screens displayed in a window of a television store, and also makes playful grimaces. Maybe a splendid new career in Hollywood is indeed about to grace her? But in front of the Chinese Theater she stops before a memorial billboard of Lylah. The theme song is now replaced by more tense music with dissonances, and sentimental high-register violins are disturbed by dark ominous bass notes. There is a tormented quality in the music. When Elsa puts her foot in Lylah's footprint on the pavement, it is a perfect match. But this *Cinderella*-like test is punctuated by an alarmed *gruppetto* of the muted trumpets, quasi a warning signal, and Elsa steps back, as frightened. If we focus on the emotive function, this configuration of the music, coupled with Novak's acting, can be seen as a confirmation that Elsa is very nervous about and uncertain whether to take this big step and sign, excited and scared at the same time. But consider the glaring references to *Vertigo*, first of all the presence of Novak, who played in the Hitchcock film the similar role of a woman paid to impersonate a deceased woman. In the hotel scene before the morning stroll we saw the blinking light of the exterior neon sign filtering through the window, decidedly reminiscent of the hotel scene in *Vertigo* when Judy completes her transformation into Madeleine. These references are motivated transtextually—a New Hollywood film's homage to a past masterpiece—but are also compositionally motivated; they anticipate the ending by pointing out that this story is similar to that story, with the same tragic finale. Considering the bigger picture, the music here is not merely expressing what Elsa feels but is also foreshadowing the ending, thus orienting our comprehension of the narrative towards that direction—building a mood. Elsa is indeed about to go from Cinderella to Hollywood Princess, but her destiny will not be a happy one. As in *Vertigo*, there are deadly consequences for impersonating a deceased woman for an obsessed man.

Richer conclusions can be attained if the analysis of the functions is paired with the analysis of the motivations. In *The Seven Year Itch* example, if we examine the music as motivated compositionally, our analysis will focus on the denotative cognitive function; it is there to help us appreciate the ironic comparison between the two situations (Richard's fantasies and reality). If we also examine the music as motivated transtextually—the Rach 2 as a reference to *Brief Encounter*—then we find out that it also has a connotative cognitive function: to make fun of film-genre conventions. Consider another example. Within the conventions and aims of the 'Historical Materialistic Narration' of which *Deserter* is a specimen, there is the centrality of sending a strong and clear political message, an explicit meaning, through storytelling: '[Historical Materialistic Narration] has a strong rhetorical cast. It uses narrational principles and devices…for purposes that are frankly didactic and persuasive….There is a tendency to treat the syuzhet as both a narrative and an argument' (Bordwell 1985, p. 235). In this case, the connotative cognitive function of the victory march in *The Deserter* can be said to be motivated compositionally: propaganda is a central feature of the film's system—the dominant—and every device has to cooperate to the clear composition of the political meaning. On the other hand, the reference to the Austrian *Anschluss* in *The Adventures of Robin Hood* is not so much motivated compositionally; it is irrelevant for our understanding of the narrative that we notice the reference. The primary scope of the 'Classical Narration' is not that of sending overt political messages. The reference to the *Anschluss* is not an explicit meaning of the narrative but rather a symptomatic meaning, which means that it is not paramount that everyone in the audience grasps it, and the reference is not a central device for the narrative construction. More than motivated compositionally, the musical reference has a connotative cognitive function that is motivated artistically, a comment that Korngold made about the hard times his homeland was suffering. And further cases of distinction are the abrupt soundtrack jolts in Godard's *A Woman is a Woman*. We said that they are artistically motivated, but what function do they fulfil? One can argue that they have a connotative cognitive function—they help us interpret the film as homage to Hollywood musicals that at the same time rejects its technical conventions, such as continuity editing, because they represent ideological conventions. Another one can argue that they have a denotative cognitive function; they help us *comprehend* the film first, before interpretation. The musical jolts are congruent with the jump cuts, the violations of the don't-look-at-the-camera rule, and the narrative non-sequiturs. The shared and systematic infringement of the classical norms and conventions by such a large number of devices makes us comprehend that we are not facing some 'technical mistakes' or 'sloppy film-making' but deliberate choices. We understand that this is a different style and form altogether, 'Art-Cinema Narration,' with conventions and norms that are different from those of the Classical Narration.[17]

It may be useful, at the end of the chapter, to summarise the functions that we have discussed so far (Fig. 6.2):

The set of functions is limited to a number that can be easily managed mnemonically, and the names of the functions are derived from the types of activity the viewer is engaged with when s/he watches the film. The set of functions is not meant to theorise by distillation all the possible and nuanced interventions that music can have in films but serve to the analyst as a pointer of where to look, thus helping her/him focus her/his eyes on the broad domains of intervention. S/he can, then, further describe, theorise, explain, or interpret that specific film/music moment. In the next chapter I further demonstrate this set of functions in more extended pieces of film/music analysis.

Emotive Function	Micro-emotive (produces mood and emotion locally – in a shot, scene, sequence)
	Macro-emotive (builds mood, emotion and recollection throughout the film)
Perceptive Function	Spatial-perceptive (guides attention to actions and details within the shot)
	Temporal-perceptive (affects the perceived rhythm, pace, and temporal direction)
Cognitive Function	Denotative (helps comprehend narrative developments and relations)
	Connotative (prompts interpretation of ambiguous or hidden meanings)

Fig. 6.2 The set of functions

Notes

1. A study that investigates the economical synergy between cinema and the record industry is J. Smith (1998).
2. For example in Prendergast (1977, pp. 25–26).
3. Further on this in Audissino (2013).
4. This line of enquiry is somewhat in line with Douglas Gomery's 'Theory of technological change' (see Gomery 2005, p. xii), which explains technical and aesthetic changes in cinema on the basis of 'industrial organisation economics.' See also Gomery (1981).
5. On realism in films, see Thompson (1988, pp. 195–244); on art films, see Bordwell (1985, pp. 205–233).
6. This is also acknowledged in S. Tan et al. (2013, p. 120).
7. An experiment has demonstrate that a film narrative that is per se inconclusive is perceived as having closure if music with a strong closure is coupled with it. See Forde Thompson et al. (1994).

8. Music as a vehicle for recalling visual content is studied in Hoeckener and Nusbaum (2013). In *The Night Walker* example, music has a role in recollection by participating in the phenomenon of 'encoding specificity': 'remembering depends on activating precisely the same cues at retrieval that were originally encoded with the event in question' (Kellogg 2012, p. 146).
9. Season 7, Episode 4, aired on 20 October 2014.
10. The spatial location of diegetic sound is rendered through a balance of the ratio of direct to reflected sound (reverberation): the louder the direct component, the closer the sound source. See Altman (1992, pp. 20–23).
11. Similarly, what I have called 'spatial-perceptive function' can be seen as similar to what Chion calls 'punctuation' (Chion 1994, pp. 48–55).
12. This is similar to what Claudia Gorbman calls 'ancrage,' that is, music that 'anchors' some meaning that might be ambiguous as experienced in the visuals alone (Gorbman 1987, p. 32).
13. It is interesting to compare this resurrection scene in which only music and sound are used to stage it with other two in which music is used quite differently. In *E.T. The Extraterrestrial* (1982, dir. Spielberg), both the visuals and the music are coordinated to make E.T.'s resurrection as emotionally striking as possible. On the other hand, in *Ordet* (1955, dir. Dreyer) there is not music at all and the poignancy of the wife's resurrection is staged in a starkly realistic way.
14. A thorough analysis of the Korngold score is in Winters (2007).
15. For a description of the use of Rachmaninov's Piano Concerto no. 2 in Brief Encounter, see O'Connor (2013). The 'Rach 2' as used in the film is classified as 'musical camp' in Jarman-Ivens (2016, p. 195).
16. See Koch (1999). The implications for the film-viewer are discussed in Baird (2000).
17. On the conventions of Art-Cinema Narration, see Bordwell (1985, pp. 206–213).

References

Altman, Rick (ed.). 1992. *Sound Theory. Sound Practice*. London and New York: Routledge.
Anon. 2012. The Artist Director Responds to Kim Novak Slam Over Vertigo Music. *Hollywood Reporter*, 9 January, Online. http://www.hollywoodreporter.com/race/artist-kim-novak-michel-hazanavicius-279757. Accessed 12 Oct 2016.
Audissino, Emilio. 2013. The Aesthetic Cost of Marketing. The Economical Motivation of Pop Songs in Films. In *Pratiques et esthétiques. Le coût et la gratuité. Tome 3*, ed. Catherine Naugrette, 41–46. Paris, France: L'Harmattan.
Audissino, Emilio. 2014. *John Williams's Film Music: 'Jaws,' 'Star Wars,' 'Raiders of the Lost Ark,' and the Return of the Classical Hollywood Music Style*. Madison, WI: University of Wisconsin Press.

Baird, Robert. 2000. The Startle Effect: Implications for Spectator Cognition and Media Theory. *Film Quarterly* 53 (3): 12–24.
Bordwell, David. 1985. *Narration in the Fiction Film*. Madison, WI: University of Wisconsin Press.
Bordwell, David, Janet Staiger, and Kristin Thompson. 1985. *The Classical Hollywood Cinema: Film Style & Mode of Production to 1960*. New York: Columbia University Press.
Chion, Michel. 1994 [1990]. *Audio-Vision: Sound on Screen*, trans. Claudia Gorbmam. New York: Columbia University Press.
Forde Thompson, William, Frank A. Russo, and Don Sinclair. 1994. Effects of Underscoring on the Perception of Closure in Filmed Events. *Psychomusicology* 13 (Spring/Fall): 9–27.
Gomery, Douglas. 1981. The Economics of US Film Exhibition Policy and Practice. *Ciné-Tracts* 12 (Winter): 36–40.
Gomery, Douglas. 2005. *The Coming of Sound*. Abingdon and New York: Routledge.
Gorbman, Claudia. 1987. *Unheard Melodies. Narrative Film Music*. London and Bloomington: BFI/Indiana University Press.
Grodal, Torben. 1997. *Moving Pictures: A New Theory of Film Genre, Feelings, and Cognition*. Oxford: Clarendon Press.
Haggstrom, Jason. 2012. Homage or Theft? *The Artist*, and the Sound of *Vertigo*. *Reel 3*, 26 February, Online. http://reel3.com/homage-or-theft-the-artist-and-the-sound-of-vertigo. Accessed 12 Oct 2016.
Hoeckner, Berthold, and Howard C. Nusbaum. 2013. Music and Memory in Film and Other Media: The Casablanca Effect. In *The Psychology of Music in Multimedia*, ed. Siu-Lan Tan, Annabel J. Cohen, Scott D. Lipscomb, and Roger A. Kendall, 235–263. Oxford: Oxford University Press.
Jarman-Ivens, Freya. 2016. Notes on Musical Camp. In *The Ashgate Research Companion to Popular Musicology*, ed. Derek B. Scott, 189–203. New York and London: Routledge.
Kalinak, Kathryn. 1992. *Settling the Score: Music and the Classical Hollywood Film*. Madison, WI: University of Wisconsin Press.
Kellogg, Ronald T. 2012. *Fundamentals of Cognitive Psychology*, 2nd ed. Thousand Oaks, CA: Sage.
Kilday, Gregg. 2012. *Kim Novak Cries "Rape" Over The Artist's Use of Music From Vertigo*. *Hollywood Reporter*, 9 January, Online. http://www.hollywoodreporter.com/race/the-artist-kim-novak-rape-vertigo-279690. Accessed 12 Oct 2016.
Koch, Michael. 1999. The Neurobiology of Startle. *Progress in Neurobiology* 59 (2): 107–128.
Köhler, Wolfgang. 1969. *The Task of Gestalt Psychology*. Princeton, NJ: Princeton University Press.
Meyer, Leonard B. 1956. *Emotion and Meaning in Music*. Chicago and London: University of Chicago Press.

Meyer, Leonard B. 1973. *Explaining Music: Essays and Explorations*. Chicago and London: The University of Chicago Press.

Meyer, Leonard B. 1996 [1989]. *Style and Music: Theory, History, and Ideology*. Chicago and London: University of Chicago Press.

O'Connor, Sean. 2013. Soundtrack to a Love Story: The Use of Rachmaninov's Second Piano Concerto in the Film *Brief Encounter*. *Sean Michael Connor.com*, 22 April, Online. https://seanmichaeloconnordotcom.files.wordpress.com/2013/11/brief-encounter-soundtrack-to-a-love-story.pdf. Accessed 25 Nov 2016.

Prendergast, Roy M. 1977. *Film Music: A Neglected Art. A Critical Study of Music in Films*. New York: W. W. Norton.

Smith, Greg M. 2003. *Film Structure and the Emotion System*. Cambridge: Cambridge University Press.

Smith, Jeff. 1998. *The Sound of Commerce. Marketing Popular Film Music*. New York: Columbia University Press.

Smith, Murray. 1995. *Engaging Characters: Fiction, Emotion, and the Cinema*. Oxford: Clarendon Press.

Tan, Ed S. 1996. *Emotion and the Structure of Narrative Film: Film as an Emotion Machine*. Abingdon and New York: Routledge.

Tan, Siu-Lan, Annabel J. Cohen, Scott D. Lipscomb, and Roger A. Kendall (eds.). 2013. *The Psychology of Music in Multimedia*. Oxford: Oxford University Press.

Thompson, Kristin. 1988. *Breaking the Glass Armor: Neoformalist Film Analysis*. Princeton, NJ: Princeton University Press.

Winters, Ben. 2007. *Erich Wolfgang Korngold's The Adventures of Robin Hood: A Film Score Guide*. Lanham, MD: Scarecrow.

PART III

Pars Demonstrans

CHAPTER 7

Five Illustrations of Film/Music Analysis

Here I wish to offer some illustrations of how the method proposed so far can be applied. Single problems are addressed, film sequences are brought in to illuminate the method, and points that were previously mentioned are further developed and cast into a new light.

Are All Gaps 'Fantastical' and Meaningful?

We have already mentioned the 'Fantastical Gap' (Stilwell 2007) and the risk that, using this as an analytic tool, too much attention is pointed to where the music comes from rather than on what function the music is fulfilling—see Chaps. 2 and 3. The concept is a fascinating theoretical description of the presence of the music in one intermediate dimension between the diegetic and the non-diegetic, of its fluctuation between these two levels, and the adjective 'fantastical' is evocative enough of the powerful immateriality and transcendence of music that escapes precise locations and defies those boundaries that other elements of the film are subject to. I can think of two film examples in which music can be seen as literally acting in a fantastical gap between two worlds.

Laura (1944, dir. Preminger) is a noir film about a detective who grows an inescapable infatuation for the (presumably) murdered woman he is investigating. The film is built as a complex system of temporal layers and flashbacks, with the final act—where Laura suddenly reappears alive and oblivious of the investigation on her death—famously interpreted as the detective's dream (Thompson 1988, pp. 162–194). In terms of music, the peculiarity of *Laura* is David Raksin's monothematic score. 'Laura's Theme' is heard in the opening credits and then extensively presented and re-presented throughout the film, not only in its string-based 'Hollywood romance' incarnation but also in an out-worldly rendition with electronically manipulated piano.[1] 'Laura's Theme' appears not only non-diegetically but also diegetically, played by a small orchestra in a restaurant scene. The principal motivation may have been 'economical,'[2] that is, to advertise 'Laura's Theme' as much as possible in the film so as to sell the music as a tie-in commodity—which indeed happened, with the successful song version with lyrics by Johnny Mercer. Yet, the choice is perfectly motivated also compositionally, and indeed the music adds a fantastical element to the story. The main (and only) musical theme is clearly identified with the eponymous woman from the very beginning of the film. The opening titles introduce 'Laura's Theme' over the image of a painting of Laura, and then the film's title appears—LAURA—making it very clear who Laura is, what her semblance is, and even what her musical sound is. The ubiquitous presence of her music, then, is the aural manifestation of Laura herself, or better, of Lt. McPherson's romantic obsession; we cannot hear anything but Laura because he cannot think of anything but Laura. Besides the obvious micro-emotive function of making the romantic moments more 'romantic' and making Gene Tierney more glamourised, the music also has a connotative-cognitive function: it anticipates what is developing in McPherson's mind well before the apartment sequence in which he clearly romanticises about the deceased woman. McPherson is falling in love with a ghost. The 'fantastical' free movement of the music between the non-diegetic and the diegetic and its unstable positioning is the aural correlate of the ghost woman, capable of coming back from the beyond (non-diegetic) to inhabit the mundane (diegetic) and haunt McPherson and the other men who knew her (meta-diegetic). 'Laura's Theme,' like a ghost, can cross the walls of the narrative. As in *Jaws* (1975, dir. Spielberg) the music is a vicarious device for the unseen shark, so here the music is for the unseen Laura.

A less diffused case can be spotted in *The Witches of Eastwick* (1987, dir. Miller). In the final act, Daryl Van Horne (the Devil in human/Jack-Nicholsonian form) enters an ice cream shop and whistles John Williams's main theme ('The Devil's Dance').[3] That musical theme was never played within the narrative world of the film. How can a character know this music? He must have trespassed the diegetic borders to have access to the non-diegetic level where the music was played. In this case, the character in question is the Devil, whose supernatural powers can well enable him to cross any narrative or natural borders. There can also be a humorous touch here: the Devil knows really everything, even the non-diegetic main theme! And the musical joke acquires further satirical connotations if we consider what is about to happen at this very moment in the film: the three 'witches' are preparing their revenge plot against an oblivious Daryl. So the joke goes like this: the Devil may know everything, even the non-diegetic score, but women know better!

I have applied the 'fantastical gap' literally and provided interpretations of such 'fantastical' status of the music. In such cases as *Laura* and *The Witches of Eastwick*, it is a useful interpretive tool because the films possesses fantastical tones, *Laura* in particular.[4] What about those films that do not possess such overtones? Do we have to push 'fantastical readings' onto the film just because the music is doing some allegedly 'fantastical' action? Even a reception of the concept less literal than the one I have adopted—and intentionally exaggerated—still shows a problem. Stilwell wrote that 'the phrase "fantastical gap" seemed particularly apt for this liminal space because it captured both its magic and its danger' (Stilwell 2007, p. 186). Even taken poetically and not literally, the term 'fantastical' nevertheless colours this concept with magical and mysterious implications. Mystery and magic cannot be closely analysed but tentatively interpreted, or merely contemplated as inexplicable phenomena. Calling such fluctuations 'fantastical' gives them an excessive salience that often they do not have. This inflated salience favours interpretation over analysis. Indeed Stilwell herself peremptorily claims: 'When that boundary between diegetic and nondiegetic is traversed, it does always *mean*' (Stilwell 2007, p. 186). I beg to differ. As already pointed out by Jeff Smith, this generalisation renders the concept an 'all-too-blunt instrument for film music analysis' (Smith 2009, p. 2) because such moves across the gap should always be 'read' as something of great significance, which often they are not.

The famous anecdote comes to mind of Hitchcock not wanting any music for his *Life Boat* (1944)—which was set on a boat in the middle of the ocean—because he objected, 'Where is the music coming from?' and the composer, sternly replying, 'From the same place the camera comes from.'[5] This reminds us to keep in mind that music is simply one of the technical/artistic devices that are used to construct a film. In most occurrences of the diegetic/non-diegetic dialectics there is nothing 'fantastical' and extremely significant, but only instances of formal consolidation; the main musical theme is reiterated not only in the non-diegetic score but also thrown into the diegetic world, so as to fix it even further in the viewers' ears. Such a case is in *Bachelor in Paradise* (1961, dir. Arnold), in which the Henry Mancini main theme can be also heard diegetically as the tones of the doorbell. It can also be a matter of playing around, more or less ironic and metatextual, with the film's devices. Consider the *Witches of Eastwick* example, with one character that 'mysteriously' has access to the non-diegetic music. I can think of two other instances from Italian cinema in which characters whistle the main theme without being supernatural creatures or foreshadowing some meaningful fantastical thing happening. In *The Bigamist* (1956, dir. Emmer), Mario, the character played by Marcello Mastroianni, enters the scene whistling the very theme we have just heard in the non-diegetic opening titles; the same happens in *The Swindle* (1955, dir. Fellini), in which the very Rota-esque jaunty main theme is presented in the opening credit and then whistled by Picasso on his way to another mission with his con-artist pals. What is the 'meaning' of this musical trespassing? Mario does not repeat such 'fantastical' whistling anywhere else in the film, nor is the Rota theme a particular musical motto that the trio of swindlers whistle while on the job—the only occurrence in the film is in the first scene. This is a formal embellishment, a musical bridge between the opening credits and the first scene. The music trespassing upon the characters' world—or vice versa—sometimes can prompt interpretation (have a cognitive function) but *not* always; it can have an emotive/perceptive function, one of consolidation of the formal system, or even be a 'stylistic exercise' and have only an artistic motivation.

Consider *The Sea Hawk* (1940, dir. Curtiz), a classic swashbuckler featuring Errol Flynn as the privateerman Captain Thorpe, fighting the Spaniards for Queen Elizabeth of England. During the second act, he and his men are captured by the enemies and sentenced to be chained to the oars of a galley. In a night sequence Thorpe and his crew manage to set free and capture the ship. Erich W. Korngold's battle music can be heard obtrusively during the mutiny operations, with a high degree of temporal perceptive and, above all, spatial perceptive function that makes the music adherently synchronised with the visual action, in line with the scoring style of the classical Hollywood cinema—each thrust of sword, each jump from sail to sail has a corresponding musical action that mimics the configuration of the visual action. The non-diegetic score, at this point, is already so entangled with the diegetic action that, as suggested by Winters, music could be indeed said to be produced by the characters themselves. The walls of the narrative levels get thinner and at times immaterial, and the risk for the communications model-oriented analyst is that of getting lost in ruminations about whether the music is non-diegetic, intradiegetic, at times diegetic, what narrator is its sources, and so on. Things get even muddier, in a communications model, after the mutiny, when Thorpe and his crew prepare to sail back to England. After an excited *crescendo* and *accelerando*—in which we hear fragments of Capt. Thorpe's leitmotiv returning after a long silence corresponding with his captivity—music stops on a *tutti fortissimo* sharp chord. This is immediately followed by a sustained high strings tremolo that leaves aural room to this exchange of maritime commands:

- Thorpe: 'Aloft There! Clean your leech line!'
  (Followed by another *fortissimo* orchestral chord, one step higher.)
- First Officer (backed by tremolo strings): 'Clear away your mizzen vangs!'
  (Followed by another *fortissimo* orchestral chord, another step higher.)
- Second Officer (backed by tremolo strings): 'Heave taut your halyard!'
  (Followed by another *fortissimo* orchestral chord, another step higher.)
- Third Officer (backed by tremolo strings): 'Slack away your true lines!'

The music is so intertwined with the dialogue that this passage sounds like an operatic *recitativo*. The four commands/orchestral chords build a harmonic progression that creates an excited musical suspension in need of a resolution. And the musical resolution is achieved right after this exchange of commands, when we suddenly hear a men's chorus, accompanied by a full orchestra, singing at the top of their lungs 'Strike to the Shores of Dover', on the very notes of Thorpe's non-diegetic leitmotiv.[6] Is the chorus diegetic and the orchestra non-diegetic? Actually, we assume that the male crew is singing but there is no visible lip synch. Who is singing? Given the ambiguity, is the music in the fantastical gap? These questions here are quite inane. The point is Korngold fully unleashing his operatic background and pulling all the stops musically to enhance to his best this moment of excitement for the regained freedom and to give it the most appropriate and effective emotional punch. Not only did Korngold triumphantly bring back Thorpe's leitmotiv after the long silence of the humiliating imprisonment, but he also added an arresting chorus to make the music more striking and enthralling, and more connected to the freed men's joy, as they become themselves part of the celebratory music. It is not a matter of meaning here, it is a matter of style: the sequence is blatantly operatic, a stylistic 'excess'[7] that defies narrative and thematic purposes, which produces a moment of sheer spectacle, as in the numbers in musical films. The choral musical number here surprises us because it is not motivated transtextually—we expect such moments in musicals because of the genre's conventions, but we do not expect this in swashbucklers. The motivation for the spectacular jump from the non-diegetic to the diegetic is no other than an artistic one to create an excessive operatic moment.

It would be perhaps more productive to drop the equivocal term 'fantastical' and call such ambiguous locations and moves 'diegesis-level dialectics' or 'diegesis-level trespassing,' or even dispense with too rigid labels altogether. After all, if the communications model narrator/narrative dualism is dropped in favour of a perception-model unitary narration process that articulates the formal system, then every element is part of, and internal to, the process and the system, including both the so-called non-diegetic and diegetic music. For practical reasons, I retain the classical and well-established diegetic/non-diegetic distinction because I am not interested in replacing those familiar terms, given I am interested in analysis of what the music does rather than in theorising about where the music comes from/belongs to. The two terms can be kept as indicators of where narration places the source of the music. The term 'diegetic' indicates some music that narration ostensibly presents as having some source within the narrative world; non-diegetic refers to music that has not. And when the boundary between diegetic and non-diegetic is traversed, it does *not* always mean.

Anempathetic Effect, Proper

Like the 'Fantastical Gap,' Michel Chion's 'anempathetic effect' is another widely diffused theoretical concept (Chion 1994, pp. 8–9). And, likewise, it entails some risks. If applied mechanically and uncritically, it can be an analytical tool as 'blunt' as the 'Fantastical Gap.' In its original formulation, the 'anempathetic effect' happens in those instances in which some diegetic sound is playing before a dramatic event and continues playing after it, undisturbed as if nothing happened. A classic example is the shower murder in *Psycho*, in which the sound of the running water is dominating the scene before and after Marion's death. The course of that particular sound remains unaffected by what happened, and the resulting effect is one of indifference and lack of empathy with the tragic incident. This anempathetic effect produces in a scene an unsettling sense of futility and purposelessness: not only has a violent death just taken place, but this death is completely irrelevant to the economy of the Universe. Music can produce the anempathetic effect too. An instance is indicated by Claudia Gorbman: the scene from *Hangover Square* (1945, dir. Brahm) in which a diegetic street organ keeps playing outside during a murder that happens inside a nearby shop. Gorbman says that in that murder scene 'music doesn't care.' (Gorbman 1987, p. 159). Is it really so? Here we can see one risk inherent to this concept: the tendency to confuse the effect with the cause. Not only is the effect 'anempathetic'—we perceive that Universe does not care—but thus is also called the sound or music that produces the effect—music does not care. This overlapping is promoted by Chion himself, who talks of both 'anempathetic music' and 'anempathetic effect' (Chion 1994, p. 8). The confusion can be explained with the more or less conscious influence of a separatist and communications-based model; music and visuals are conceptualised as two separate codes of communication, and the narrator responsible for the musical enunciation can be either empathetic (confirm) or anempathetic (oppose) to what is happening in the visuals. But attributing the anempathetic intention to an entity or agent creates controversy. In the narrative world of *Hangover Square* the organ grinder is the diegetic source of the diegetic music, and therefore it would be more precise to say that it is him, not the music, who does not care and keeps playing notwithstanding. However, from the very scene it is evident that he is oblivious of the murder being committed while he is playing. So, he clearly keeps playing not because he doesn't care but because he doesn't know. Anempathy entails indifference from someone who is aware of a situation and simply does not care about it, and this is not the case with the organ grinder. One could object that, in terms of film-making, music is obviously not produced by the organ grinder but placed in the scene by the film-makers for dramatic effects. And from this viewpoint, one could contend that it is the music that does not care. But to say that the music is anempathetic implies either a personification of the music or the postulation of a source of enunciation external to the visual action. In either case, there is, again, a conceptual separation of the music from the film; something is happening in the visual but *the music is anempathetic*. A non-separatist approach based on the perception model would say that it is the narration that coordinates sound and visual devices so as to contrast a gruesome murder with a cheerful tune in order to *produce an anempathetic effect*, a disconcerting feeling of tragic loneliness and desperate helplessness before death.

This may sound as hair-splitting philosophising, but confusing the effect with the cause is something that can lead to another pitfall. It might lead to automatically think that every time some music sounds 'anempathetic' there is an anempathetic effect to be found—a top-down move that imposes a predetermined interpretive template on the film. Actually, there are instances of music that would be called 'anempathetic' but do not produce the 'anempathetic effect' proper. Such cases are those in which music is used not to convey a sense of 'cosmic indifference' but to express the insane anempathy of one character. An example is the first episodes of the omnibus *Tales that Witness Madness* (1973, dir. Francis). A child with constantly fighting parents has an imaginary friend, a tiger. Soon it turns out that the tiger may indeed be invisible but it is not imaginary at all. In the final scene, where the beast mangles the adults, the child is in the same room and carries on playing his toy piano, indifferent to what is happening. Here the music can indeed be called anempathetic because it expresses the anempathy of the one who produces it in the diegesis, perfectly conscious of the tragedy but untouched by it—unlike the organ grinder of the previous example. Another instance is *Twisted Nerve* (1968, dir. Boulting), in which the deranged juvenile killer whistles a cheerful tune each time he is about to take someone's life. In both these instances of literally anempathetic music there is no anempathetic effect; in both cases we are not anguished by the indifference of the Universe but horrified by the sociopathic behaviour of the characters. The anempathetic effect is not directly and automatically caused by the intrinsic anempathy of some music or sound. The 'anempathetic effect' is a macro-configuration resulting from two micro-configurations that are emotionally not isomorphic.

From Chion's account we can infer that the anempathetic effect is mostly carried out by diegetic sound. He provides examples of diegetic noises—like the *Psycho* shower murder—and, when referring to music, he mentions diegetic musical sources: 'player pianos, celestas, music boxes, and dance bands' (Chion 1994, p. 8). Gorbman's musical example is diegetic too. I gather that it is the diegetic presence of the sound in the same space and time in which the tragic event happens that produces the effect. It inhabits the same world as the one in which the incident happens; it was there when the event happened and yet it remains untouched. If the indifferent sound is part of the narrative world, then said sound and its lack of reaction can be assumed to be a symbolic representation of the indifference of the whole world itself. This would not be the case with non-diegetic music; it would seem a synonym for 'audiovisual counterpoint.' The triumphant march in the finale of *Deserter* (1933, dir. Pudovkin) is 'anempathetic' with the defeat of the protesters, but since the music is non-diegetic—and thus not part of the narrative world—we perceive it not as a symbol of cosmic indifference but as a political commentary. Seemingly, the difference between 'anempathetic effect' and 'audiovisual counterpoint' is that the former has to do with diegetic sound and the latter with non-diegetic. Yet, when Chion mentions music as a potential agent of the anempathetic effect, he contrasts such anempathetic music with 'empathetic' music that 'can directly express its participation in the feeling of the scene, by taking on the scene's rhythm, tone, and phrasing; obviously such music participates in cultural codes for things like sadness, happiness, and movement' (Chion 1994, p. 8). This sounds like a description of the typical *non-diegetic* musical accompaniment, music that is written 'sartorially' to fit the film, unlike the generally self-contained forms of the pieces that are used diegetically. Apparently, non-diegetic music too can produce the anempathetic effect. And because of such ambiguity in the Chion text, the term is indeed also used for non-diegetic music when it contrasts emotionally with the visuals.[8] The difference with 'audiovisual counterpoint' would be, I suppose, that in the former case music stresses the emotional effect of contrast, while in the latter the meaning-making effect of the contrast is stressed.

I would like to close this discussion with an example in which the conflation of non-diegetic anempathetic music with audiovisual counterpoint and the mechanical application of the concept lead to an analysis that misses a more productive angle on the film. David Sonnenschein thus explains and exemplifies Chion's concept: 'When music does not care what is happening [*sic*], irony can build a strong counterpoint for the spectator to seek more actively what is really happening. This involvement can be heightened when there is a great tragedy or catastrophe depicted, using the juxtaposition of happy music that simply challenges us to identify more closely with the victims, as in *A Clockwork Orange*' (Sonnenschein 2001, p. 156). In the first sentence, Chion's 'anempathetic effect' is equated with 'audiovisual counterpoint', and this audiovisual contrast is said to be prompting us to 'seek more actively what is really happening' (music has a connotative cognitive function, in my parlance). This seems to imply that music is used in a 'commentary' mode to prompt some interpretation. Yet, in the second sentence, the cause/effect automatism of anempathetic music silences the active meaning-seeking function of the audiovisual counterpoint and imposes a mechanical application of the equation 'if there is anempathetic music there must be an effect of cosmic indifference.' Thus, the happy music we hear in *A Clockwork Orange* (1971, dir. Kubrick) would make us feel how irrelevant the victims' sufferance is to the Universe, and thus we pity them—'identify more closely.' I think there is a more interesting way to tackle the use of music in the Kubrick film. Consider the scene in *A Clockwork Orange* in which the gracefully carefree 'Overture' from Rossini's comic opera *The Thieving Magpie* (1817) is used non-diegetically during the gang-bang rape scene in the abandoned theatre. Simply saying that music is anempathetic does not contribute much to explain what is happening here emotionally. Without music, the rape scene would have been experienced, by most people, as a dramatic moment of violence but, given it is framed from a distance in long-shot, it might have also been experienced with some emotional detachment—there is not a single close-up of the victim.[9] If appropriately 'empathetic' dramatic music had been used, we would probably have experienced this from a closer vantage point because the micro-configuration of the music would have been emotionally isomorphic with the situation as experienced by the girl—violence, terror, violation, captivity, and so forth—and thus the macro-configuration would have been consolidated around her as the subject at the centre of the experience. Instead, Kubrick's choice is to use music that is 'anempathetic' with the girl. But this does not necessarily and automatically means that the sought effect is the anempathetic effect. The micro-configuration of the music is isomorphic and empathetic with another viewpoint in the scene. Kubrick's choice, disturbingly enough, is to use music that has a micro-configuration that is isomorphic with Alex, his droogs, and the rival gang in action here. For all those violence-addicts, this is but a pleasant pastime. Indeed, the scene opens with Rossini's music, followed by Alex's casual voice-over recountal: 'They were getting ready to perform a little of the old in-out in-out on a weepy young devotchka they had there.' The merry music is isomorphic with Alex's feeling, and classical pieces—Beethoven's 'Ode to Joy' and the *joie de vivre* typical of Rossini's music—are consistently featured throughout the film during his 'ultraviolence' moments as a manifestation of the inner joy and the invigorating feel-alive sense that he experiences. The macro-configuration resulting from the long-shot-styled visuals (with no close-ups of the victim) and the merry music is one in which the subjects of the experience are the rapists, and the girl is just an objectified plaything they pass around—like a marijuana bong. Because of the micro-configuration of the music, we are provoked to empathetically align with the gang; we have access to their emotional world. This is why this musical choice makes the scene so effective and unsettling: we are forced to be part of the gang. And this is why applying Chion's concept mechanically can lead to questionable results; in *A Clockwork Orange* the music does not 'challenge us to identify more closely with the victims' but exactly the opposite. In this case, music that might superficially seem anempathetic is actually *empathetic*, but it is with the rapists, not with the victim.

TELL IT WITH A SONG: COGNITIVE FUNCTION OF THE LYRICS

Compared to instrumental music, songs have an extra element that can combine with the visual action: lyrics.[10] Songs can be used diegetically to provide a period mood to the scene—the 1960s in *American Graffiti* (1973, dir. Lucas), with their source identified in the many car radios. Or they can be used non-diegetically with a 'commentary' purpose, with configuration more or less congruent or contrasting with that of the visuals. In $9^{1/2}$ *Weeks* (1986, dir. Lyne), the Joe Cocker song 'You Can Leave Your Hat On' has lyrics that basically describes what is happening visually—Kim Basinger is stripping—and the music is appropriately sassy and enticing, with the sultry sound of the sax(sex)ophone, possessing a long-time association with sensuality and hot affairs.[11] In the *Breaking Bad* episode 'Ozymandias' (2008-2013, prod. Gilligan)[12] there is a scene in which Walter White—the school teacher turned into methamphetamine kingpin—is plodding on across the New Mexico desert, dragging along a heavy barrel of cash. He has just caused the death of his brother-in-law, has just been betrayed by his long-time associate, has lost all his wealth but the barrel, and, with his criminal activities now unmasked, he is the most-wanted public enemy and certainly about to lose his family too. He lost everything, he is alone, the only thing he has is the remaining barrel of cash. As we watch Walter toiling through the desert, we hear the Limeliters country ballad 'Take My True Love by the Hand' (1960, lyrics by Oscar Brand, Lee Hays Gene Raskin). Musically, the piece is rather serene, with just a bit of nostalgia, a pretty harsh contrast with what is happening. But parts of the lyrics actually are relatable to Walter's situation—they tell about times getting hard, scarcity of money, the loss of one's job and home, the need to leave the town. It is the refrain, though, that makes the scene sarcastic. While Walter is dragging his money, we hear: 'Take my true love by her hand/ Lead her through the town/Say goodbye to everyone.' What Walter has consistently stated as a justification of his heinous actions—'All I have done, I have done it for my family'—is debunked and ridiculed: his 'true love' is not his wife or kids, but money.

With songs, we have two micro-configurations to take into account: the musical qualities (minor mode = sad, major mode = happy, etc.) and the content of the lyrics. They are often isomorphic—happy music comes with happy lyrics—but nevertheless attention is to be paid to what the song is telling. Indeed, the nature of the music might distract from lyrics that have an opposite polarity, or controversial contents, particularly if they are not clearly discernible or are in a language we are not familiar with. Viewers not versed in Italian might find the song 'Faccetta Nera' (1935) musically pleasing and congruent if coupled with images of a merry parade. The realisation that its lyrics are profoundly racist and celebratory of the colonial exploits of the Fascist regime would change how the music is experienced. The merry micro-configuration of the music is reshaped by the racist micro-configuration of the lyrics, producing a macro-configuration of enthusiastic political extremism. Without lyrics, the music sounded retro and enjoyable; with the lyrics, the same music sounds disturbing. A case in which the qualities of the music can make us miss interesting connotations in foreign-language lyrics is the use of 'Die Wacht am Rhein' in *Casablanca* (1942, dir. Curtiz).

In *Casablanca* music reinforces the interventionist theme, in a period of time in which the USA had just entered WWII and Hollywood cinema was amongst the socio-cultural forces 'drafted' to explain the reasons of interventionism.[13] In particular, 'La Marseillaise', the French national anthem, is used as the central musical symbol of anti-fascism.[14] 'La Marseillaise' opens and closes the film, and recurs a number of times throughout it, the most prominent of which, as diegetic music, is in the famous musical battle.[15] The sequence takes place in 'Rick's American Café' in the Moroccan French protectorate, during WWII. The anti-fascist leader Victor Laszlo is in Rick's office, trying to convince the former activist now turned into a cynical businessman to hand him some smuggled letters of transit, and to join again the fight against fascism. Neither the praise of Rick's past deeds nor the offer of a conspicuous sum of money seems to be persuasive. Suddenly, a German chant starts in the main room. Rick and Laszlo get out of the office and find that Gestapo Major Strasser and a small group of Nazis have taken possession of the saloon and are defiantly singing. Rick watches at a distance, not approving but also not intervening to stop them. Outraged by the provocation, Laszlo instead heads towards the resident band and tells them to play 'La Marseillaise'. The musicians cast a questioning look at their boss. Rick, who has in the meantime joined Laszlo at the centre of the café, surprisingly gives a go-ahead nod. The band starts playing 'La Marseillaise' and, immediately, everyone in the café—regardless of their nationality—joins the chorus and sings poignantly, until they silence the Nazis. It is interesting to note that opposing 'La Marseillaise' in this singing battle we do not find the more famous 'Deutschlandlied' (the German national anthem) as one could expect—this is even more surprising because at the time it still opened with 'Deutschland über Alles' (Germany above all), quite fittingly. What we hear is 'Die Wacht am Rhein' (The Watch at the Rhine). The probable reason is that the 'Deutschlandlied' is already used non-diegetically, in an ominous minor-mode version, as Major Strasser's leitmotiv. Reportedly, the first choice as the German contender was the 'Horst Wesser Lied', the official hymn of the Nazi party, but it was copyrighted (Neumeyer 2015, p. 278, n. 8). Yet, 'Die Wacht am Rhein' is a very felicitous replacement. If one stops at the musical level, it is Teutonic and martial enough to sound like a Nazi song—even if it is not—and so it is a good fit in the scene. But if some research into the song's history is undertaken and, above all, if its lyrics are examined, one finds that this musical choice adds implications that the other options would not have supplied. First of all, 'Die Wacht am Rhein' was composed during the Franco-Prussian War of 1870 and has strong anti-France connotations, which neither the 'Deutschlandlied' nor the 'Horst Wesser Lied' possess. Such connotations make 'Die Wacht am Rhein' a better adversary of the French anthem. 'La Merseillaise' was composed during the Austro-Prussian invasion that led to the battle of Valmy in 1792—it was originally called 'Chant de guerre pour l'Armée du Rhin' (Battle Hymn of the Rhine Army)—and had similar anti-Prussian connotations. But it is the lyrics of 'Die Wacht am Rhein' that are particularly significant, because they create a contradiction with the martial configuration of the music and the Nazis' reputation. While 'La Marseillaise' tells about fighting for homeland and liberty against the attack of a ferocious invader, on the contrary 'Die Wacht am Rhein' is a defence song: the lyrics tell, worryingly, about guarding and defending the homeland's borders.

'La Marseillaise'

Allons enfants de la Patrie [Let's go, children of the Nation] /

Le jour de gloire est arrivé! [The day of glory has arrived!] /

Contre nous de la tyrannie, [Against us tyranny's] /

L'étendard sanglant est levé [Blood-drenched banner is raised,] /

Entendez-vous dans les campagnes [Can you hear, in the countryside,] /

Mugir ces féroces soldats? [The roar of those ferocious soldiers?] /

Ils viennent jusque dans nos bras [They're coming right into our arms] /

Égorger nos fils, nos compagnes! [To cut the throats of your sons, your women!] /

Aux armes, citoyens [To arms, citizens,] /

Formez vos bataillons, [Form your battalions,] /

Marchons, marchons! [Let's march, let's march!] /

Qu'un sang impur [Let an impure blood] /

Abreuve nos sillons! [Soak our fields!]

'Die Wacht am Rhein':

Es braust ein Ruf wie Donnerhall, [A call roars like thunderbolt,] /

wie Schwertgeklirr und Wogenprall: [like clashing swords and splashing waves:] /

Zum Rhein, zum Rhein, zum deutschen Rhein, [To the Rhine, the Rhine, to the German Rhine,] /

wer will des Stromes Hüter sein? [who will be guardian of the river?] /

Lieb Vaterland, magst ruhig sein, [Dear fatherland, do not fear,] /

Fest steht und treu die Wacht, die Wacht am Rhein! [Firm stands, and true, the Watch, the Watch at the Rhine!]

Moreover, 'Die Wacht Am Rhein' was associated with the Great War, a disastrous defeat that the Nazis would have hardly evoked.

Let's have a look at how these two songs interact with the other devices of the stylistic system. The narration shows us the small group of Nazis—accompanied by the piano, typically a solo instrument—isolated in a corner, crammed under an arch in front of a flat background and having a hard moment trying to keep their chant audible. It is also worth noticing the oppressive presence of a rotating ceiling fan, reminiscent of an aeroplane propeller and prefiguring the final airport sequence where Strasser will be defeated for good. In contrast, the international multitude sings powerfully—accompanied by the band, an ensemble of different kinds of instruments cooperating towards a common goal—and is showed in deep-focus and in an open and deep-spaced staging. The visual contrast between the isolation of the cornered group of Nazis and the deep-staged multitude of the international peoples can be appreciated in Fig. 7.1.

Fig. 7.1 Nazis singing 'Die Wacht am Rhein'/The peoples singing 'La Marseillaise', *Casablanca*

Moreover, the Nazis have no close-ups, which is the primary stylistic device to strengthen the empathy and the emotional engagement between a character and the viewer.[16] On the contrary, three extreme-close-ups—a shot size rarely brought in for classical cinema, and only to highlight to the maximum the emotive expression of a character—prompt us to connect with those who are singing the French anthem. The first one is for Yvonne, a French escort girl who we previously saw opportunistically familiarising with a Nazi officer. When Yvonne hears *her* national anthem, she breaks into tears and joins the chorus with passion and commitment. Her ECU is in soft-focus, with a back light delineating and detaching her face from the background, isolating it to make it more emblematic. And narration cuts to her exactly when she sings, in regretful tears, a stanza charged with significance, particularly resonating with her opportunistic 'betrayal': 'Do you hear, in the countryside, The roar of those ferocious soldiers? They're coming right into our arms.' Figure 7.2 provides an illustration of this highly emotional close up and its perfectly timely appearance on a particularly meaningful section of the song's lyrics—transcribed in the caption.

Fig. 7.2 'Those ferocious soldiers…are coming right into our arms…', *Casablanca*

And Yvonne is shown again, in ECU, at the end of the song, shouting 'Vive la France! Vive la liberté!' The other ECU is for Ilsa, Lazlo's wife, and it follows the CU of Laszlo singing: 'To arms, citizens /Form your battalions!' Stylistically similar to Yvonne's, it is also as emblematic: in Ilsa's wet eyes we can see not only the love for her husband but also her admiration. (By the way, this is one of the most rousing musical passages of the French anthem and the narration coordinates editing and music so that the first verse—'To arms, citizens!'—explodes exactly on Laszlo passionate CU, and then we cut to Ilsa's ECU exactly on the second verse—'Form your battalions!'—which reprises the same musical cell as the first one. Fulfilling a micro-emotive function, the music/image coordination adds poignancy and conviction to the two shots, and also connect Victor and Ilsa, whose shots share the very same musical cell.)

The shallow-staged and cornered small group of Nazis sings a defence song about the worry to guard the national borders and reassuring the 'Lieb Vaterland' to have no fear. This is contrasted with the deep-staged international multitude singing an attack song. The coupling of these micro-configurations—music and lyrics, camerawork, lighting, editing, acting, art direction, and so on—produces this macro-configuration: Nazis are a minority that can be defeated if the international majority coalesces to fight back. The connotative cognitive function of the music—and its lyrics in particular—has a central role in strengthening the interventionist meaning of the scene.

Opening Credits, Prefiguration, and Title Music

Like the Overture or the Prelude in an opera or ballet, title music often provides a foretaste of the tone and type of atmosphere we are about to experience. Opening title sequences are like the cover of a book from which the genre and main features of the text are already identifiable. While these have become rarer after the 1950s, brief but telling title sequences were common in classical films from Hollywood and other cinemas.[17] The font of the cast and crew credits, the background illustrations or images, the tone of the lighting and greyscale (or colours, for prestige films), and the music were all coordinated so as to provide immediate and informative indications: 'The classical aesthetic of "planting" and foreshadowing, of tagging traits and objects for future use' (Bordwell et al. 1985, p. 44). *Captain Blood* (1935, dir. Curtiz) announces its status as a pirate film by raising the curtain to

Korngold's heroic fanfares and sweeping strings, illustrations of galleons and swords engraved on treasure-map-like parchments, and wood-chiselled-like typeface for its credits. *Arsenic and Old Lace* (1944, dir. Capra) clarifies its nature of black-humoured comedy by flaunting Halloween-like spooky/comic imagery coupled by Max Steiner's music alternating romance, parodical horror/drama gestures, and light-hearted dance moves. More refinedly, *Lady in the Lake* (1947, dir. Montgomery) plays with the viewer's expectation; based on a well-known Raymond Chandler novel, it does not open with imagery proper of the hard-boiled detective story but with Christmas-themed title cards coupled with a carolling chorus. It is only revealed at the very end of the opening credits that, below the last Christmas card, a gun is hidden—thus confirming the film's genre but also informing us that the violence, cynicism, and loneliness typical of noir films will take place at Christmastime and thus be magnified by contrast. *The Women* (1939, dir. Cukor) not only presents the (all-women) cast member in vignettes, showing us the actress's name, her face, and her character in the film, but also humorously compares each of them to an animal, anticipating what attitude and inclinations are to be expected from them in the tale—Norma Shearer is a deer, accompanied by sentimental high-register violins; Joan Crawford is a leopard, accompanied by flirtatious jazz trumpets; Rosalind Russell is a hissing black cat, accompanied by a petulant comic *staccato*, and so on. Deservedly famous are the title sequences designed by Saul Bass in the 1950s and 1960s, particularly memorable in Hitchcock's film when they fuse with Herrmann's music. They both anticipate the dizzying vortex of love and death in *Vertigo* (1959, dir. Hitchcock)—the spiral is visible in the graphics and audible in the music—or the shattered-mind homicidal fury in *Psycho* (1960, dir. Hitchcock)—broken lines are visible in the graphics and audible in the music. An old-fashioned and subtly foretelling title sequence from more recent cinema is in *The Hateful Eight* (2015, dir. Tarantino).

Announced as the new Quentin Tarantino 'western' (Chitwood 2015, Online), or as his 'first true spaghetti western' (Niola 2016, Online), the film is actually quite distant from the typical imagery and action one would expect from that genre. The first reviewers called it 'more Agatha Christie than Sergio Leone' (Duralde 2015, Online), 'stubbornly theatrical' (Vishnevetsky 2015, Online), a 'Jacobean western' (Bradshaw 2016, Online), also noting its parallels with Tarantino's 1992 film *Reservoir Dogs* (Alter 2015, Online). Indeed, mystery elements of the

And-Then-There-Were-None whodunit, moments of kammerspiel-like minimalism and psychological dialogue, the annihilating chain of bloodshedding *vendetta* of Elizabethan/Jacobean theatre, and Tarantino's own circular narration form all coalesce into a hybrid that shows only some superficial elements of the western genre—the period, the costumes, certain types like bounty killers and bank robbers, the civil war theme. The opening title sequence is very clear in dispelling the western-genre expectations. A major contributor is Ennio Morricone's music, through its apt use of timbres and stylistic traits.

The film opens with a black screen and a low dark note of the basses. As we fade into a snowy mountain landscape, high-pitched layers of strings slowly pile up and *piano* brass chords are added, gradually expanding the musical texture into a slightly dissonant static mass. We see a flock of birds suddenly leave a meadow—as if they sensed some danger—and we hear an interrogative four-note motif by the flutes that introduces some suspense in the musical stasis. The motif is reprised and expanded, and a pan shows us the first sign of human presence in the otherwise untamed natural surroundings: the remains of a corral—a western icon—empty and lifeless. The middle-range musical texture is feeble: on one extreme we have a low-pitched pedal point (a long sustained note) by the basses, on the other a high-pitched pedal point by the violins. The two pedal points, in their stasis, build up the suspense and create expectation for something to happen (the prolonged musical immobility creates psychological tension because we cannot see any pattern in such motionless musical figures, and yet we expect music to move on sooner or later). The high-pitched violins are also isomorphic with the visuals: music is static, frozen as is the landscape we see. The sound of these violins in their extreme high range is poor in harmonics, a 'cold' sound—as opposed to, say, the 'warm' sound of a cello in its middle range. The high-pitch tones and the bright white of the snow share a common high-frequency quality—a bright light is the effect of high frequencies in the visual dominion and a high-pitched sound is the effect of high frequencies in the auditory one.[18] We see the snow, but through metaphorical mimicry (the reproduction in music of characteristics of non-musical entities) music makes us also *feel* the bitter cold of those snow-clad mountains.

The icy music continues, combined with the gloomy sound of gusting wind. As the first title appears—'The Weinstein Company presents'—a stalking low drum pulse is introduced, which breaks the stasis and puts the music (finally) in motion. The previous part was an introduction: the opening credits really start now, as does the second musical section. The screen goes to black, a new title appears—'The 8th Film of Quentin Tarantino'—and more musical ingredients are introduced: a driving rhythmic pattern of the high-hat combines with the drum pulse and sets the music in steadier motion, and a very-low-pitched note of the contrabassoon (the instrument with the darkest timbre) casts ominous and obscure nuances. Next, the film's title appears, in a typeface reminiscent of the 1960s and 1970s westerns. The main musical motif is now presented, a conspiratory and elusive phrase played by the dark timbre of the bassoons. We fade in again from the black, revealing the face of a crucified Christ roughly carved in wood. The main motif is repeated, with an added line of the flutes recalling the interrogative 'danger' motif presented in the introduction, while the camera slowly cranes up and moves away from the Christ to show the larger desert of snow behind and around it. Galloping timpani beats announce the third musical section, as we see something approaching from the distance: a stagecoach—a black spot of civilisation in the snowy whiteness of Nature, and another icon of the western genre. The musical excitation grows, with isolated stabs and harsh swirls of the violins leading to a full-orchestra burst of raging violence, followed by the *tutti* reprise of the main motif, now having lost its stealthy nature and having turned into a theatrically irate statement. When the stagecoach finally reaches the camera and runs past it, the opening-credit sequence ends with a brusque cut on black and a *staccato* chord of the violins.

What idea of the film is this opening sequence passing? The panoramic and larger 70 mm format and the yellow typeface and grouping of the credits are visual reminiscences of the western genre—for example, the opening credits of *The Shootist* (1976, dir. Siegel). We also have spotted a couple of elements, the stagecoach and the corral, that are iconic of the genre. Even if the snowy mountains are not the commonest setting, this is certainly not something unprecedented—for example, in the Italian spaghetti western *The Great Silence* (1968, dir. Corbucci) or in *McCabe & Mrs Miller* (1971, Altman). The name of Morricone itself, appearing onscreen, is famously associated with the spaghetti western. Figure 7.3 gives a clear idea of the key visual elements of the sequence: a deserted and inhospitable snowy landscape; a solitary and neglected crucifix; an

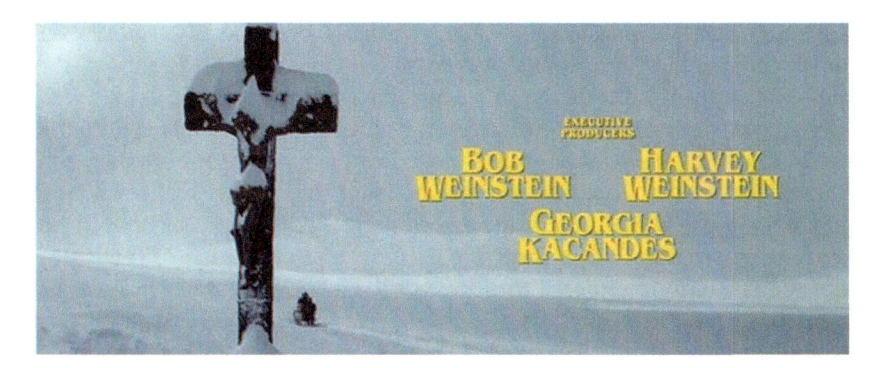

Fig. 7.3 Opening credits, *The Hateful Eight*

approaching stagecoach; 2.75:1 aspect ratio with retro graphics, both pointing back to the 1960s/1970s late westerns.

Visually, we have a western-film configuration. But Morricone's music here is far from his western models: no harmonica, no ocarina, no guitar, no Mariachi trumpet. The suspenseful pedal points and the high-hat driving rhythm make it sound like music for a thriller or crime film, and the prominent use of the bassoon for the conspiratory main motif is reminiscent of Morricone's grotesque and similarly conspiratory main theme for the political thriller *Investigation of a Citizen above Suspicion* (1970, dir. Petri). The audiovisual combination produces a macro-configuration that prompts us not to expect a traditional western, or even not to expect a western at all.

Let's now try some hermeneutic scrutiny of this sequence—a 'reading', some would say—to demonstrate that formalistic analysis does not preclude interpretation. Why is the Christ ostensibly put at the centre of the opening sequence? The film is not only set in wintertime; it is set in Christmastime. The Christ can be an anticipation of the Christmas theme, which is a key background for the central dialogue scene between the Unionist black Major and the Confederate racist General. Is the Cross there to introduce a religious theme? The Cross is an obvious Christian sign that may refer to this Christian solemnity, but, if so, Christ's birthday is interestingly paired with Christ's death—the Cross is more typically associated with Easter. And what we see is not simply a Cross—the generic Christian symbol—but a Cross with the crucified Christ, a *Christus Patiens*, one of two typical modes in the iconography of the crucifix (Derbes 1998, p. 5). While the

Christus Triumphans accentuates Christ's resurrection and His victory over death and sin, the *Christus Patiens* focusses on Christ's death because of the sins of humankind. So the meaning of the Christ is enigmatic: Is the dead Christ a further reminder of death in the already gloomy landscape? Is it a rough piece of art, representing a vestige of humanity in the surrounding wilderness? Or is it a comforting religious sign that suggests that Salvation and hope are possible even in those seemingly God-forgotten lands? If—in an experiment like Philip Tagg's 'commutation' (Tagg 1999, Online)—the snowy landscape, the Christ, the slow crane-up, and the arrival of the stagecoach had been paired with Bach's 'Christmas Oratorio', the produced macro-configuration could have prompted some religious interpretation. But setting aside the Tarantino connoisseurs that would immediately discard this interpretation as highly improbable, the musical configuration contributes to a macro-configuration that smothers the religious interpretation and leads also the casual and uninformed viewers to expect nothing good—the image of the dead Christ is paired with dark and violent music. And, after all, the eight in the title are 'hateful' not 'merciful.' I think that the enigmatic presence of the religious symbol is there to anticipate the 'Christmas deceit' that Tarantino plays on the viewers later in the film.

In the cabin in which all the strangers happen to get trapped in the snowstorm, a tense climate of reciprocal suspect is soon established. In addition to this, bitter resentment grows between people who fought in the opposing factions of the Civil War, the Unionists (who wanted to abolish slavery), and the Confederates (who wanted to preserve slavery). In particular, Major Warren is a black Unionist famous for having dispatched a number of confederates and Southern anti-abolitionists, and General Smithers is a now-old Confederate known for his radical racism and for summarily executing black Unionist soldiers—the General is there now on the trail of his son, disappeared and probably deceased on those mountains. The two arch-enemies find themselves in the same room, and immediately voice their contempt for each other. In a quiet moment halfway through the film, the Major stands up and brings a bowl of hot soup to the old General. 'You leave that old man alone!' promptly warns another former Confederate, ready to defend his General from further verbal attacks. Major Warren reassures him: 'I shared a battlefield with this man!' and gracefully asks for permission to join the General and sit in the armchair in front of him. 'Yes, you may,' replies the old confederate. The two enemies sit before each other; silence is only broken by the snowstorm gusting outside. One of the guests removes his gloves and sits at the piano. On the out-of-tune instrument, he starts playing a tentative rendition of the Christmas song 'Silent Night.' 'So, how's life since the war?', asks the Major. 'I've both my legs. I have my arms. I can't complain,' replies the General. A polite conversation has started, and it evolves to touch more intimate and affective confidences; the General talks about his beloved wife, who recently died, and nostalgically reminisces of the pre-war times. The scene is configuring like an attempt at reconciliation, made possible by the magic of Christmas: a warming fireplace, hot soup, cosy armchairs, peaceful conversation, and Christmas music. Every element seems to be pointing to one macro-configuration: Forgiveness. This is reminiscent of the 'Silent Night' scene in *Joyeux Noël* (2005, dir. Carion), which narrated the true story of a spontaneous truce between the Franco-English and German trench soldiers during the Christmas night of 1914—the enemies sing 'Silent Night' together, putting aside their rivalry and making room for the Christmas spirit.

But the music is regularly punctuated by wrong notes—and the cursing of the struggling pianist—a musical configuration that gradually unsettles the Christmas magic macro-configuration. Something is not quite right. Indeed, at one point the Major, with a provocative gleam in his eyes, mentions that he met the General's son. The General's face is now worried when he asks: 'You knew my boy?' And when he apprehensively asks again: 'Did you know my son?' the diegetic piano music is abruptly stopped with a dissonant cluster. The Major replies: 'I know the day he died. Do you?' With a confused look, the General says no. 'You wanna know what day that was?', asks the Major. And the General implores, 'Yes.' 'The day he met me', defiantly articulates the Major. The Christmas tune resumes here, and it is played a second time, but it is now clear that we are not heading towards a reconciliation. Another film is evoked here, but the Christmas situation is rather different: *McCabe & Mrs Miller*, in which a man is killed during a fist fight on Christmas night, while 'Silent Night' is played in the near saloon. As the Major slowly makes it clear that he is the one who killed the General's son, music continues, but now with freer and even insolent variations, and stops with theatrical major-mode chords as the Major prepares to detail how he not only killed the General's son but also tortured him. 'Silent Night' has now been revealed as a deceitful curtain opener for the main attraction of this scene, which is not the misleading Christmas reconciliation but a tale of sadistic retaliation. Narration—with the seminal cooperation of music—has tricked us into believing, for a brief moment, that some forgiveness might have been possible. And when it is eventually disclosed that the exact opposite is happening—the scene will end with the Major killing the General—'Silent Night' is played a second time, almost tauntingly, to remark how absurd it was for the viewers to even imagine that such a thing could happen. Nothing can stop the hateful and their thirst for revenge, not even Christmas. The meaning of the Christ in the opening sequence is now clearer: Christ is dead, there is no Salvation, Christmas is but an empty and exterior exercise, like the faltering rendition of 'Silent Night.'

Music as the Connective Tissue of Emotions: The Umbrellas of Cherbourg

As I have proposed, the 'macro-emotive function' is a type of action that music can perform on the emotive level of the viewer's activity. Contrary to the 'micro-emotive function,' the 'macro-emotive function' does not so much produce the emotive response because of its musical qualities and its presence in a punctual moment but articulates its effect and builds it up through meaningful recurrences across the film. It is not only a matter of creating a consistent mood throughout the film; besides the configuration of the music, the 'macro-emotive function' also exploits our memory (the ability to recognise a given theme each time it reappears) and the stratifications of meaning and associations that accumulate on the music during its many presentations. Because of the 'Pleasure of Recognition' and our craving for stable and closed configurations ('Law of Good Configuration' and 'Law of Return') each time a melody is restated and we recognise it, there is an emotive response of pleasure. In turn, such pleasure creates a stronger memory trace and makes it easier to recognise it in the subsequent presentations and to recall its previous appearances, thus creating a set of musical rhymes across the film. Often, the macro-emotive function works towards a pay-off moment in the film, in which the particular scene is thus charged with emotive qualities that are stronger than those achievable with the sole micro-emotive function (sad music in a sad scene). This is due to the emotive charge and significance that the music has accrued throughout the film and its power to evoke recollections of the previous film moments and to connect them. An outstanding instance can be found in Michel Legrand's score to *The Umbrellas of Cherbourg* (1964, dir. Demy).

This all-sung musical—a continuous musical flows in three acts, with set pieces and *recitativi*—tells the love story of two young people, Geneviève and Guy, abruptly separated when he is drafted during the Algerian War.[19] The two had planned to marry—despite her mother's disapproval—and were already fantasising about their children and their future together. The news is a shock to Geneviève, but she promises to wait for him. During their last night together she gets pregnant. The girl misses Guy very much, and the war prevents him from writing to her as often as desired. Moreover, the pregnancy is about to become visible—a potential stigma— and the girl and her widowed mother have serious financial issues with their umbrella store. Roland, a wealthy and handsome diamond dealer, offers his help. Sincerely in love with Geneviève, he asks her mother for her hand—the pregnancy does not show yet—telling them to take their time to think about it: they can give him an answer in three months, when he returns again to Cherbourg. The mother is clearly in favour of Roland over Guy—who is just a mechanic with few career prospects—and tactfully but relentlessly presses the daughter to seriously consider the proposal. Some mail correspondence between the two lovers continues—they agree on the name François, in case it is a boy—but the distance progressively takes its toll and Guy is now becoming only some words on too rare letters and a face on a photograph. After taking time to reflect on such a painful choice, Geneviève decides to marry Roland if he will embrace her pregnancy, which he does effortlessly, thus showing true love and commitment. Guy returns to Cherbourg after more than one year, and only then he finds out that Geneviève has married another man and left the town. Embittered, he is saved from a self-destructive slope by Madeleine, a girl who used to assist his aunt and who had always been in love with him. The two marry, have a boy, and Guy manages to buy a gas station. After six year, Geneviève stops at that gas station and meets Guy again, presumably for the last time.

The film opens with a high-angle view on the Cherbourg harbour and then tilts down and stops perpendicularly to a street nearby. It starts raining and the people walking by open their umbrellas. It is as if some superior entity—let's call it 'Fate'—were observing from a distance (and with a distance) the human events down there. Over this image, the main theme is introduced in an instrumental version—what later is revealed to be the 'Love 'Theme'. The music is in minor mode and played melancholically by the woodwinds and then reprised by violins backed by a dreamy arpeggio of the celeste. The 'Fate's view' configuration of the shot and the sad/melancholic configuration of the music fuse to foretell that this is the story of an ill-fated love: two people who think they are destined to be together but they actually are not. The 'Love Theme' reappears—and is now identifiable as a love theme—in the café scene after Guy breaks to Geneviève the news of his drafting. Here lyrics are associated to the bittersweet melody we heard in the opening titles. Devastated, she sings: 'I'll never be able to live without you....Don't go! I'll die!' Guy reassures her: 'My love! I have to go! I want you to know that I'll think only of you. And I know you will wait for me.' She sobs: 'Two years of our lives. I can't face it!' And he again: 'We'll be together again and we'll be stronger!' She worries: 'You'll meet other women. You'll forget me.' He promises: 'I will love you until the end of my life.' The sad and melancholic character of the music is confirmed and reinforced by the lyrics; Fate is tragically separating these two young lovers. Back home, Geneviève in tears reports the news to her mother, who consoles her and says: 'People only die of love in the movies....Time fixes a lot of things.' This piece of dialogue/singing highlights the dialectics between an idealistic view of life and love typical of the young ('I will die without you!') and a realistic one proper to the more experienced people—mother's answer. Geneviève and Guy meet once more at the train station, and she sings: 'My love, I will wait for you all my life.' When the train leaves, thus separating their lives, the 'Love Theme' is picked up by the orchestra in a dramatically rousing *tutti*. With this new rendition, the now-familiar melody has acquired more sorrowful overtones, which has turned the bittersweet melancholy into outright tragedy.

Time is passing, and fixing: mother seems to be right. We hear again an instrumental rendition of the 'Love Theme' when Geneviève replies to Roland, while she watches a black-and-white photograph of Guy, now becoming more and more a discoloured fading memory. Later, in a scene that contrasts the gaiety of the Carnival celebrations on the streets with Geneviève's inner anguish, her mother asks, 'Are you still waiting?' on which we hear a fragment of the 'Love Theme'; yes, she is, Guy is still in Geneviève's mind. The mother points out that marrying Roland is the sensible choice, 'He's rich, refined and enamoured of you. Guy's been your ideal but what future did he offer you?' The 'Love Theme' returns in a following dialogue, in which Geneviève sorrowfully asks her mother, 'Why is absence so heavy to bear? Why is Guy fading away from me? I would have died for him. Why aren't I dead?' The scene marks the moment in which the girl decides to accept Roland's proposal, and an instrumental version of the 'Love Theme' by the strings provides a sound bridge to 'April 1958,' Roland's return and the 'sensible' marriage. The musical theme is acquiring here a further trait: nostalgia. In this moment in which practical realism has overcome ideal love, the music summons to our mind the previous moment where Geneviève and Guy were together, and the pledge of their unending love that they expressed in lyrics. It is as if we could hear 'I will wait for you!' over the instrumental melody, but Geneviève could not wait for Guy because of the facts of life.

When Guy finally returns to Cherbourg and experiences himself the absence of Geneviève, we hear the 'Love Theme' in three moments: when he sees the umbrella store empty and closed, with a 'New Owner' sign, a relic of the past; when he stops in the same café where Geneviève had promised him she would be waiting for him; and when he later returns to the umbrella store to find it turned into a house-ware store, the old-fashioned umbrellas and colourful wallpaper replaced by washing machines and cold white walls. The music in these moments is nostalgic but also a bit hardened by resentment; it is played not by strings but by brass in a more jazzy style, telling of a more disenchanted and mature attitude that has taken the place of the youthful romanticism. In particular, the transformation of the umbrella store into the aseptically white store of practical pieces of domestic technology has a strongly nostalgic effect, it is the visualisation of a romantic past that has disappeared and become irretrievable. Guy himself eventually decides to put his past romantic fantasies aside and accept the practicalities of reality; he buys the gas station and marries Madeleine. He too plays along with what Fate prepared for him.

Is everyone content, if not happy, with their lives and marriages? The finale provides us with an answer, and it is the point in the film in which the music fully fulfils its macro-emotive function. It is December, it is snowing, it is Christmas time—what better (worse) time of the year for nostalgia of the past and of the loved ones who are no longer with us? Madeleine and her son, François, have just left the office at the gas station for some Christmas shopping, leaving Guy alone. From the window we see a car pull over at the gas pump. The 'Love Theme' starts, played demurely by the horns—the music already tells us who is in the car. Guy heads to the vehicle and, to the surprise of both, the two former lovers are face-to-face after six years. A little girl is in the car, their daughter. Geneviève says that it is cold outside and Guy invites her to the office while her car is serviced. The interaction is polite but cold, in particular Guy is avoiding eye contact and lights up a nerve-soothing cigarette. Geneviève is looking at him more insistently and tries to make a conversation, also stressing that she made an impromptu detour to Cherbourg on her way back to Paris and would have never expected to run into him: *excusatio non petita accusatio manifesta*, her offering an unsolicited justification for being there gives us a good reason to think that she deliberately sought Guy and wanted to see him. The 'Love Theme' plays on as the awkward dialogue continues. She mentions her daughter, and Guy asks: 'What did you name her?' 'Françoise,' she replies. Françoise and François: both have christened their offspring with other spouses with a name strongly associated with their past relationship and with their unrealised plans for a future together. 'She is a lot like you,' she points out. 'Do you want to see her?' she proposes. But Guy faintly head-shakes 'no' and adds, 'I think you're ready to leave.' The children's name are a clear tie with a past that has not been pacified or gotten over, a wound that is liable to re-open and it is better not to, despite the declaration of the contrary: 'Are you well?' she asks before leaving. 'I'm very well,' he replies. Neither of them is well, both have complied with what Fate has given them but have not managed to entirely accept it. As Geneviève drives away, the 'Love Theme' soars, with an added vocalising chorus. Madeleine and little François come back and Guy runs towards them merrily. The whole family enters the office as the camera lifts up to a 'Fate's view' shot similar to the opening one. As can be seen in Fig. 7.4,

Fig. 7.4 Gentle rain/Frigid snow, *The Umbrellas of Cherbourg*

in this 'Fate's view' shot coldness, snow and an almost monochromatic landscape have replaced the gentle rain and the colourful and romantic umbrellas that we had seen in the opening of the film.

The music gets more and more dramatic, and even desperate, speaking of a sentimental laceration that will probably never get mended, and tellingly the film closes on a minor chord, the exact contrary of a happy ending. The macro-configuration of deep sadness and poignancy that characterises this closing sequence is augmented not only by the micro-configuration of the music (minor mode and dramatic orchestral and choral writing) coupled with the micro-configuration of the visuals (sad and nostalgic glances, awkward detachment, Christmas time, coldness, and snow) but also by the fact that, at this moment in the film, the appearance of the 'Love Theme' is like a powerful and multi-layered recapitulation of the whole love story. Music recalls all the moments and existential developments that it has accompanied, and the idealistic lyrics that were associated with the melody materialises in our mind: 'We'll be together again'—No, they will not. 'I will love you until the end of my life'—Yes, they probably will, painfully so; 'You'll meet other women'—Yes, he did. 'You'll forget me'—No, he cannot. These past memories that have become associated with the music make the present situation of 'realistic compromise' even more painful and nostalgic: Geneviève and Guy will indeed love each other until the end of their lives, but Fate has separated them.

Notes

1. A discussion of the score is in Prendergast (1977, pp. 58–64).
2. See Chap. 6.
3. Reportedly, Nicholson's whistling was dubbed by John Williams himself. See Bond (2006).
4. On the 'fantastic' as a category between the 'strange' and the 'marvellous', see Todorov (1975).
5. The anecdote sometimes refers to David Raksin (at that time a staff musician in the Music Department at Twentieth Century Fox), sometimes to Hugo Friedhofer (composer of the film score) as the Hitchcock's respondent. See, respectively, Prendergast (1977, p. 211), and Sullivan (2006, p. 104).
6. Music by Erich W. Korngold, lyrics by Howard Koch and Jack Scholl. The full lyrics can be found here: http://lyricsplayground.com/alpha/songs/s/striketheshoresofdover.shtml. Accessed 24 March 2017.

7. '[Excess is] an inevitable gap in the motivation for the physical presence of a device.' Thompson (1988, p. 259).
8. My concern about the potential lack of clarity about this concept is shared by others: 'Chion's work presents a regrettably superficial discussion of how music specifically, as distinct from other sources of sound in film, may impact upon perception of filmic meaning, and how filmic context may impact upon perception and cognition of music' (Phillips 2013, Online).
9. The close-up is the key stylistic device to make viewers empathise with a character. See the Casablanca analysis later in this chapter.
10. A discussion of songs in media products is in Cook (1998, pp. 147–173). See also the more recent Dyer (2012).
11. This association in film can be traced as back as Max Steiner's score for *The Informer* (1935, dir. Ford), in which the prostitute Katie has a jazzy theme for saxophone, while the 'honest girl' Mary is scored with romantic strings. See Kalinak (1992, pp. 120–122).
12. Season 5, Episode 14, aired on 15 September 2013.
13. See Nachbar (2000) and Raskin (1990).
14. A famous discussion of the film is Eco (1985). Raskin (2002) is a journal issue entirely devoted to the film, as is Merlock (2000). Specifically on the music, see Marks (2000) and Scheurer (2004).
15. The musical duel is inspired by a similar scene in *La Grande Illusion* (Renoir 1937).
16. On the emotional power of close ups, see Plantinga (1999). The emotive design of the film is analysed in Eder (2008) and Gabbard and Gabbard (1990).
17. Opening title sequences in classical films are discussed in Bordwell et al. (1985, pp. 25–26).
18. High-pitched violins are also used to depict coldness in *Quintet* (1979, dir. Altman). Yet, it cannot be said that they automatically equal coldness. The experienced effect depends on the combination of the music's configuration with the ones of the other devices. High-pitched violins are also used to mimic the dazzling sunshine in scenes set in extremely hot locales, as happens in Maurice Jarre's score to *Lawrence of Arabia* (1962, dir. Lean). In such torrid desert scenes, high frequencies in the music are isomorphic with the high frequencies of the blinding sunshine.
19. The following is an analysis focussed on the music's macro-emotive function across the film. Those interested in broader accounts can find a political interpretation of the film in Virtue (2013); and a study of how the film fits into the French Nouvelle Vague in Hill (2008).

References

Alter, Ethan. 2015. Film Review: The Hateful Eight. *Film Journal International*, 18 December, Online. http://www.filmjournal.com/reviews/film-review-hateful-eight. Accessed 7 Feb 2017.

Bond, Jeff. 2006. Liner Notes. The Witches of Eastwick, CD. Collector's Choice Music, CCM-685-2.

Bordwell, David, Janet Staiger, and Kristin Thompson. 1985. *The Classical Hollywood Cinema: Film Style & Mode of Production to 1960*. New York: Columbia University Press.

Bradshaw, Peter. 2016. The Hateful Eight Review—Tarantino Triumphs with a Western of Wonder. *The Guardian*, 7 January, Online. https://www.theguardian.com/film/2016/jan/07/the-hateful-eight-review-tarantino-triumphs-with-a-western-of-wonder. Accessed 7 Feb 2017.

Chion, Michel. 1994 [1990]. *Audio-Vision: Sound on Screen*, trans. Claudia Gorbmam. New York: Columbia University Press.

Chitwood, Adam. 2015. The Hateful Eight Trailer Unleashes Quentin Tarantino's New Western. *Collider*, 12 August, Online. http://collider.com/hateful-eight-trailer-quentin-tarantino-new-western. Accessed 7 Feb 2017.

Cook, Nicholas. 1998. *Analysing Musical Multimedia*. Oxford: Clarendon Press.

Derbes, Anne. 1998. *Picturing the Passion in Late Medieval Italy: Narrative Painting, Franciscan Ideologies, and the Levant*. Cambridge: Cambridge University Press.

Duralde, Alonso. 2015. The Hateful Eight Review. *The Wrap*, 15 December, Online. http://www.thewrap.com/the-hateful-eight-review-quentin-tarantino-samuel-l-jackson-kurt-russell. Accessed 7 Feb 2017.

Dyer, Richard. 2012. *In the Space of a Song: The Uses of Song in Film*, rev. ed. Abingdon and New York: Routledge.

Eco, Umberto. 1985. Casablanca: Cult Movies and Intertextual Collage. *Substance* 47: 10–11.

Eder, Jens. 2008. Casablanca and the Richness of Emotion. *Journal of Literary Theory* 1 (2): 231–250.

Gabbard, Krin, and Glen O. Gabbard. 1990. Play It Again, Sigmund: Psychoanalysis and the Classical Hollywood Text. *Journal of Popular Film and Television* 18 (1): 6–17.

Gorbman, Claudia. 1987. *Unheard Melodies: Narrative Film Music*. London and Bloomington: BFI/Indiana University Press.

Hill, Rodney. 2008. Demy Monde: The New-Wave Films of Jacques Demy. *Quarterly Review of Film and Video* 25 (5): 382–394.

Kalinak, Kathryn. 1992. *Settling the Score: Music and the Classical Hollywood Film*. Madison, WI: University of Wisconsin Press.

Marks, Martin. 2000. Music, Drama, Warner Brothers: The Cases of Casablanca and The Maltese Falcon. In *Music and Cinema*, ed. James Buhler, Caryl Flinn, and David Neumeyer, 161–178. Hanover, NH: Wesleyan University Press.

Merlock, Ray (ed.). 2000. Introduction: Casablanca–Popular Film of the Century. *Journal of Popular Film and Television* 27 (4): 2–4.

Nachbar, Jack. 2000. Doing the Thinking for All of Us: *Casablanca* and the Home Front. *Journal of Popular Film and Television* 27 (4): 5–15.

Neumeyer, David. 2015. *Meaning and Interpretation of Music in Cinema*. Bloomington and Indianapolis: Indiana University Press.

Niola, Gabriele. 2016. The Hateful Eight, il primo vero spaghetti western di Tarantino. *Wired*, 28 January, Online. https://www.wired.it/play/cinema/2016/01/28/tarantino-spaghetti-western-hateful-eight. Accessed 7 Feb 2017.

Phillips, Nicola. 2013. Book Review: Michel Chion Audio-Vision—Sound on Screen. *FilmSound.org*, Online. http://filmsound.org/philips.htm. Accessed 25 Feb 2017.

Plantinga, Carl. 1999. The Scene of Empathy and the Human Face on Film. In *Passionate Views: Film, Cognition, and Emotion*, ed. Carl Plantinga and Greg M. Smith, 239–255. Baltimore, MD: Johns Hopkins University Press.

Prendergast, Roy M. 1977. *Film Music: A Neglected Art: A Critical Study of Music in Films*. New York: W. W. Norton.

Raskin, Richard. 1990. *Casablanca* and United States Foreign Policy. *Film History* 4 (2): 153–164.

Raskin, Richard (ed.). 2002. *P.o.v. A Danish Journal of Film Studies* 14.

Scheurer, Timothy E. 2004. You Know What I Want to Hear. The Music of Casablanca. *Journal of Popular Film and Television* 32 (2): 90–96.

Smith, Jeff. 2009. Bridging the Gap: Reconsidering the Border Between Diegetic and Nondiegetic Music. *Music and the Moving Image* 2 (1): 1–25.

Sonnenschein, David. 2001. *Sound Design: The Expressive Power of Music, Voice and Sound Effects in Cinema*. Studio City, CA: Michael Wiese Production.

Stilwell, Robynn J. 2007. The Fantastical Gap Between Diegetic and Nondiegetic. In *Beyond the Soundtrack: Representing Music in Cinema*, ed. Daniel Goldmark, Lawrence Kramer, and Richard Leppert, 184–203. Berkeley, Los Angeles and London: University of California Press.

Sullivan, Jack. 2006. *Hitchcock's Music*. New Haven and London: Yale University Press.

Tagg, Philip. 1999. Music, Moving Image, Semiotics and the Democratic Right to Know. *Tagg.org*, Online. http://tagg.org/articles/xpdfs/sth99art.pdf. Accessed 8 Feb 2017.

Thompson, Kristin. 1988. *Breaking the Glass Armor: Neoformalist Film Analysis*. Princeton, NJ: Princeton University Press.

Todorov, Tzvetan. 1975 [1970]. *The Fantastic*, trans. Richard Howard. Ithaca, NY: Cornell University Press.
Virtue, Nancy. 2013. Jacques Demy's Les Parapluies de Cherbourg: A National Allegory of the French-Algerian War. *Studies in French Cinema* 13 (2): 127–140.
Vishnevetsky, Ignatiy. 2015. Quentin Tarantino Gets Theatrical in the 70 mm Western The Hateful Eight. *AV Club*, 16 December, Online. http://www.avclub.com/review/quentin-tarantino-gets-theatrical-70mm-western-hat-229377. Accessed 7 Feb 2017.

CHAPTER 8

Close Encounters of the Third Kind and *E.T. The Extraterrestrial*: The Bonding Power of Music

Close Encounters of the Third Kind (1977) and *E.T. The Extraterrestrial* (1982) are very closely related films, for obvious reasons—both are directed by Steven Spielberg and scored by John Williams—but also because they similarly centre on extraterrestrial visitors coming to Earth and their encounter with earthlings. These films can be seen as two incarnations of the same concept: the visitors are benign and with good intentions. According to Andrew Gordon, they are part of Spielberg's 'suburban trilogy,' basically telling the same highly autobiographical tale from different perspectives (Gordon 2008, p. 55).[1] Both have already been the object of a number of studies, mostly *interpretations*. Is *Close Encounters* an ideologically fascist film? (Entman and Seymour 1978).[2] Is it superficially anti-authoritarian but in fact encouraging an extreme escapism in the form of psychic fantasies of regression? (Gordon 2008, pp. 70–73) Is it a metaphor of the cinematic apparatus—with the presence of the famed French director François Truffaut as the leader of the earthling community—and its inescapable powers of subject positioning? (Morris 2007, pp. 8–19). Is it 'a purified, Disneyised version of religion...an unchallenging faith for the simple-hearted and the simple-minded?' (Gordon 1980, p. 156). Is *E.T.* an ideologically deceiving product of the conservative Reaganian era? (Britton 2009). Is its appropriation of Christian iconography a manifestation of America's religious syncretism and 'vernacular religion' in the attempt of recovering from the 1970s paranoia and build a feel-good new decade? (Friedman 2006, pp. 39–46). Is it a critical statement about the superficial American lifestyle epitomised by the seemingly florid and smile-all-around suburban neighbourhoods? (Kendrick 2014, pp. 23–68).[3] Readers interested in answers to these and other questions—for example, whether the mother-ship is a maternal breast (Gordon 2008, pp. 65–66) or the E.T. character is a 'walking phallus' (Gordon 2008, p. 86)—will not find them in the following pages.

In the following pages I analyse these two films as to how music operates on the emotive, perceptive, and cognitive levels to help the formal system secure the viewers' comprehension of the explicit meaning (what the overt meaning is of the story being told) and the interpretation of the implicit meaning (what covert meanings are suggested by the film's form). In terms of comprehension, in *Close Encounters* music is fundamental in assisting the narration in its principal strategy across the film: keeping the viewers uncertain as to the intention and nature of the extraterrestrial visitors. What viewers—and certainly the first batch of them back in 1977—are primarily curious about is to comprehend whether the visitors from outer space are good or bad. In *E.T.*, music guides our comprehension of the gradual development of the friendship between Elliott and E.T. and makes their increasingly stronger bond vivid. In terms of interpretation, music is the key element in both films to gain access to the connotative level, which in *Close Encounters* is a celebration of the escapist power of fantasy, while in *E.T.* the healing and uniting power of love. Finally, by comparing my findings with those of a recent musicological analysis of these two films, this chapter also offers the opportunity to highlight how score-centric analyses that do not consider music in its interaction with the other cinematic devices often tend to miss important cues in the film's stylistic system that would further corroborate the analysis.

CLOSE ENCOUNTERS OF THE THIRD KIND (1977)

'The score for *Close Encounters* has the most pivotal musical role in any Spielberg film,' wrote Ian Freer (Freer 2001, p. 68). Indeed, music is a key part of the narrative world because it is the code and channel through which extraterrestrials and earthlings communicate. And universal communication is one of the film's central themes.[4] From the outset, the effectiveness of human verbal communication is somewhat derided. In the opening sequence, an old Mexican man—an eyewitness of a UFO manifestation—reports in Spanish to a police officer who repeats the report in English to an interpreter who finally translates it into French so that the ufologist Claude Lacombe can get the gist of what happened. The same awkward process occurs later in the Indian sequence—a Hindi-English-French translation chain. Lacombe himself is seen struggling with his non-fluent English throughout the film, and he even apologises for it during the conference scene—a further hint that the narration gives us of this communication-difficulty theme. Not only linguistic communication proves difficult; emotional, affective communication too shows its hurdles. The protagonist, Roy, is introduced in a family environment of boring routine and interpersonal detachment, where communication is sparse and the understanding of each other's desires and feelings is scarce, and this situation will further deteriorate as the narrative progresses.

If even creatures from the same planet can hardly understand each other, how could communication be possible between creatures from different planets? The film's answer will be: through music, a more immediate medium. This task is fulfilled by the famous diegetic five-note motif—also referred to as 'sky tones'—the creation of which was reportedly quite painstaking, thus attesting its importance in the film. Spielberg wanted a very incisive musical signal—'I just want a greeting' (Bouzereau 1998a)—insisting on having five notes instead of seven or eight. 'He said it shouldn't even be a melody. It should be more like if someone pushes a doorbell,' recalls Williams (Bouzereau 1998a). Throughout the film, the extraterrestrials transmit this mysterious acoustic sequence in every possible way—through radio waves, hijacked telephone lines, and even telepathically, reaching the old man in Mexico, little Barry in the States, and large crowds in India. Lacombe and his fellow scientists are puzzled by the meaning of this insistent musical messaging, until they realise that the tones are actually geographical coordinates, which point to the Devil's Mountain in Wyoming. The five tones are revealed to be like an invitation card sent to the earthlings.

The chosen combination—tone; one major second up; one major third down; one octave down; one perfect fifth up—has the peculiarity of ending with a perfect-fifth ascending leap to the dominant degree of the scale. It is worth pointing out that this ascending perfect-fifth leap that closes the motif is a prominent stylistic trait of Williams's that can be found in most of his uplifting themes depicting heroism and good nature—for example, in *Superman the Movie* (1978, dir. Donner), *Star Wars* (1977, dir. Lucas), *JFK* (1991, dir. Stone), *Harry Potter and the*

Sorcerer's Stone (2001, dir. Columbus), and prominently in *E.T. the Extraterrestrial*, as we shall see shortly.[5] The perfect-fifth interval is particularly consonant because it derives from the first and second overtones in the natural harmonic series, and is the pillar of tonal music. Some point out that it is a universal interval shared by most cultures (Sloboda 1999, p. 257). Moreover, the ascending perfect-fifth leap, say, from C to G, is an opening musical action, moving from the tonic (the starting point of the scale) to the dominant (the step of the scale that is harmonically closest to the tonic), a typical move to get a musical discourse started. This gives a feeling of openness, as to promote conversation and to invite people to join in. Williams explains: 'Ending on the fifth in music is, as you know, like ending a sentence with the word 'and'. It's unfinished: you can either repeat it ad infinitum or go on to something else' (in Elley 1978a, p. 23). The motif can indeed be 'repeated ad infinitum'—the insistent loop transmissions we keep hearing in the first part of the film—or 'go on to something else,' when the musical signal has finally fulfilled its primary function as an invitation card. At that point it evolves, from a one-way signal, into something more elaborate, a two-way exchange, a dialogue.

During the sequence at the Devil's Mountain, the mother-ship finally lands at the rendezvous point. After moments of awkward silence in which the multicolour-lighted spacecraft and the group of scientists study each other with trepidation and some anxiety, the interaction is timidly opened by a human keyboardist playing the five tones. After all, this is the only tested piece of communication that the humans and the extraterrestrials have managed to share, and both have successfully met by following the indications of the five tones. Then, why not continue the communication by building on what they have in common, though little it might be? The mother-ship responds with more tones and the musical conversation begins. That little and practical piece of aural information—a doorbell—is developed into a theme-and-variations musical piece synchronised with coloured lights—following a time-honed tradition of music/colour synaesthetic association that, most notably, Alexander Scriabin had tried to put into practice with his *clavier à lumières* for the tone poem *Prometeus* (1910).[6] This musical sequence is the gate-opener that leads the film to the denouement: the mother-ship unlocks its door after the musical conversation has successfully taken place. Communication—so hard to achieve linguistically between different cultures and also emotionally between members of the same family—is eventually achieved musically. That utilitarian five-tone code, simply communicating coordinates, has eventually evolved into a full-fledged musical discourse. Similarly, the UFOs' apparitions are not merely a casual manifestation of curiosity but will eventually develop in a seemingly long-term cultural exchange between the two civilisations; in the finale Roy departs with the aliens, in a sort of intergalactic 'Erasmus Programme.' The five-note motif is so effective and appropriate because the feeling of openness and the universality of its ascending perfect fifth come to aptly represent universal communication, the film's main theme.

Spielberg points our attention to a second role of the music in the film: 'Most of John's scores are characters in films....On *Jaws* there were three main characters and the shark, and John had the fifth role in that film. On *Close Encounters*, it was very important that John become a major character' (in Bouzereau 1998b). As the shark motif in *Jaws* (1975, dir. Spielberg) was the musical proxy for the mostly unseen creature—signalling its presence, position, and movements—similarly in *Close Encounters* the music is a substitute for the mostly undisclosed outer-space visitors.[7] While the five-note motif constitutes the *diegetic* voice of the aliens—they speak through music—in the *non-diegetic* score the presence of aliens is signalled by tone clusters (highly dissonant masses of contiguous tones that, put in rough words, sound halfway between music and noise). Tone clusters can be found, for example, in the modernistic music of Krzysztof Penderecki, like his *Threnody for the Victims of Hiroshima* (1960). The score itself begins with a tone cluster. The opening credits run on a black background; we hear a dissonant mass of tones (the tone cluster) emerging in *pianissimo* from the silence; the dissonant mass grows thicker in layers and louder in dynamics, till the *crescendo* brings the music to resolve to a *fortissimo* C-major blast, exactly synchronized with the white flash that closes the title sequence and leads into the narrative. This musical device of the *crescendo* tone cluster is employed throughout the film to accompany the apparitions of the various spaceships and extraterrestrial objects. The music replicates acoustically the visual movement of the alien aircraft: as little luminous points appear in the night skies out of the darkness and get increasingly bigger and brighter, so the tone cluster emerges from the silence and gets louder and shriller. Through 'metaphoric mimicry,' attributes of the visual objects (movement from far to close and from darkness to light) are translated into isomorphic musical attributes (crescendo from *ppp* to *f*, from low register to high register). As in *Jaws* the underwater movements of the shark are signalled by music, similarly this is an instance of spatial perceptual function: music highlights a presence or a visual movement within the film's space.

Clusters also have another function. Their harsh dissonance and lack of tonality have a micro-emotive function too; such music sounds unsettling and produces an effect of tension and anxiety in the audio-visual macro-configuration.[8] This choice has also a transtextual motivation: it is aligned historically and genre-wise with the standards of 'alien music.' In classical Hollywood scoring, the norm was tonal romantic music. Consequently, when dealing with abnormal subjects—aliens, monsters, mad-persons, and so on—composers would turn to dissonance or even atonality. For example, Miklós Rózsa composed the only twelve-tone piece of his entire musical career to depict the devil in *King of Kings* (1961, dir. Ray).[9] There is a long tradition of dissonant, non-tonal, even electronic music associated with extraterrestrial-themed films. Think of Louis and Babe Barron's 'outlandish' electronic score for *Forbidden Planet* (1956, dir. Wilcox) or the eerie sound of the Theremin (a 1928 electrophone) used in many 1950s films—to name one, *The Day the Earth Stood Still* (1951, dir. Wise)—or, more recently, the presence of György Ligeti's avant-garde concert pieces in *2001: A Space Odyssey* (1968, dir. Kubrick). Following the tradition, Williams's music depicts the extraterrestrials using tone clusters and atonal music to project a sense of unknown and sinister mystery on the space visitors. The sense of menace is also created through other musical devices than the clusters. During the sequence in which Roy is chasing a UFO with his car, we hear an interrogative and insistent chromatic motif, reprised later in the film and associated with the mystery behind the UFO apparitions and the search for answers. Besides the micro-emotive function of producing tension in the sequence through the use of chromaticism (although not atonal, chromaticism is not tonal either) and the anxiety-building repetition of same musical cell (working as an *ostinato*, another staple of thriller music),[10] the 'Mystery Motif' also performs a subtler connotative cognitive function. As pointed out by Neil Lerner, the motif is based, ominously enough, on the 'Dies Irae' sequence—used in the Latin Requiem Mass—and, for those educated enough to identify this musical reference, this connection further connotes the extraterrestrial as a potential grave danger (Lerner 2004, p. 104). Through the use of atonal idioms and chromatic *ostinati*—and the subtle reference to the ill-boding 'Dies Irae'—the score, locally, produces a sense of mystery and anxiety for a potentially impending danger. Employing Greg Smith's theory of the emotion system, we can say that this transtextually motivated non-tonal music seems to produce a mood that orients us to expect negative developments and danger, as in the thriller and horror films. Yet, this apparently negative mood is not clearly confirmed with negative emotion moments. The expected manifestations of danger are delayed. More than a mood of fearful tension and anxiety, it is a mood of frustratingly prolonged curiosity. Music adheres to the overarching strategy of the film's narration: keeping the viewers as uncertain as possible as to whether the extraterrestrials are dangerous or not.

To fully understand the point, we must reconstruct the original *background*: 'Every viewing occurs in a specific situation, and the spectator cannot engage with the film except by using viewing skills learned in encounters with other artworks and in everyday experience' (Thompson 1988, p. 21). Part of a critic's job, as previously mentioned, is to *defamiliarise* for the viewers' films that may now be watched against a background that has become different from the original. Currently, we all know that *Close Encounters* was to the extraterrestrials what *Soldier Blue* (1970, dir. Nelson) and other revisionist Westerns had been to Native Americans: it is considered the first film to show extraterrestrials as peaceful and gracious creatures (Taylor 1999, p. 127). The film and its 'pro-alien' theme is quite familiar to us, and has since become a rather common option in the sci-fi paradigm.[11] Back in 1977, however, the viewers had different experiences and expected other conventions: a sci-fi film about extraterrestrials coming to Earth meant cruel invaders wishing to destroy and subjugate. Even *The Day the Earth Stood Still*, which had human-like and unusually well-mannered visitors, nevertheless showed planet Earth 'blackmailed' with a mortal threat: if you earthlings do not stop engaging in warfare, we shall have to destroy you for the sake of universal peace. And *2001: A Space Odyssey*, despite not featuring alien monsters, had a killer computer who threatened humans. The filming of *Close Encounters* took place in strictly closed sets (Combs 2000, p. 30), and great care was taken in avoiding any leak to the press about the film's narrative: 'The entire project was shrouded in such secrecy prior to the film's release that the crew nicknamed it "No Encounters of the Publicity Kind"' (Taylor 1999, p. 91). Audiences at that time could not foresee that *Close Encounters* would be an exception, a 'pro-extraterrestrial' narrative, but expected the norm. Moreover, Spielberg's post-*Jaws* reputation as a thriller/horror director further validated those expectations—his credits also included the man-versus-mechanical-beast thriller *Duel* (1971) and the diabolical-possession TV movie *Something Evil* (1972). Banking upon these set of presumptions, at the time of its release, *Close Encounters* came with an ominous poster—a nocturnal landscape with a road leading nowhere to a mysterious bright light—and an ambiguous catchphrase, 'We are not alone.' How were those words to be interpreted? We are not alone…*unfortunately?* For about three quarters of the film's running time, the narration sustains this ambiguity. Accordingly, we see eyewitnesses with burnt faces and post-traumatic semi-insanity; ominous lights probing the night sky; sudden power black-outs affecting a gas station and a McDonald's restaurant—as if fuel and food supplies were at stake; a scaring kidnapping, with unseen extraterrestrials taking little Barry away from his desperate mother; and, last but not the least, atonal music traditionally signifying abnormal threatening situations. Moreover, authorities are also depicted as deceitful and untrustworthy, trying to deny and cover up the existence of extraterrestrials, thus also aligning the film with the post-Watergate conspiracy theory paranoia cinema of the 1970s—such as *The Conversation* (1974, dir. Coppola) and *The Parallax View* (1974, dir. Pakula). Yet, along with these menacing elements, we are also shown elements of the opposite sign. The main character Roy is enthusiastic about meeting the visitors and little Barry shows a confident and friendly attitude towards them. Narration is ambivalent and does not show a straightforward position on the events: this determines the aforementioned mood of uncertainty and curiosity, with too few and contradictory emotion moments that can stabilise the mood in either polarisation—negative/positive.

The most ambiguous sequence is Barry's kidnapping by the aliens. Stylistically, it foregrounds all the devices typical of the horror scenes: night setting; atonal shrill music and startle-reaction-inducing stinger chords; helpless victims (a woman and a child), whom we can emotionally align with, being isolated and unable to ask for help (the phone won't work); the house, everyone's private and intimate *sanctum sanctorum*, surrounded by invaders; supernatural lights and (maybe toxic) fumes entering from all the vents and openings; ominous sounds telling us that the invaders are working hard to break in; chiaro-scuro cinematography with violent slashes of lights; point-of-view shots of the invaders aimed at showing their movements while keeping their semblance mysteriously hidden; everyday objects and house appliances animated by inexplicable forces. There is even an instance of Chion's 'anempathetic effect' (see Chap. 7) when a turntable supernaturally switches on and diffuses the soothing Johnny Mathis romantic song 'Chances Are,' in palpable contrast with the havoc being wreaked on the house and with Jillian's desperate screams.[12] Yet, the most disturbing and puzzling thing is that, in this horrific sequence, while the mother is aghast, little Barry is oddly amused. He invites the invaders to come into play and when he sees the vacuum cleaner self-activate and run through the house, he cheerfully shouts, 'Clean everything up!' Does little Barry know better than his mum and hence there is really nothing to be afraid of? Or is little Barry possessed? After *Rosemary's Baby* (1968, dir. Polanski), the 1970s cinema saw a flourish of nefarious possessed-children: think of Regan in *The Exorcist* (1973, dir. Friedkin), Damien in *The Omen* (1976, dir. Donner), or even the monstrous murderous infant of *It's Alive* (1974, dir. Cohen). So, in that late 1970s background, couldn't little Barry be just another of those demonic juvenile fiends? The film narration is calibrated so as to keep the mood unstable and the viewers dubious as to the visitors' scopes for most of the time.

The music has a key role in sustaining this ambiguity, providing itself contrasting hints—when the vacuum cleaner gets 'possessed', the score foregrounds a tuba solo that, if close attention is paid, sounds a bit comical and thus seems to be isomorphic with Barry's perspective on the events.[13] At the same time, it gradually transforms to help disclose the answer to the pending question 'What do they want from us?' The first quarter of the film has little music, besides tone clusters, atonal episodes, and chromatic *ostinati*. Then, as Roy gets more and more fascinated by the visitors, some melodic fragments begin to emerge—as in the night scene in which Roy contemplates his clay mountain—and the score gets increasingly more tonal. Fulfilling a macro-emotive function, music gradually changes from harsh atonalism to romantic tonalism as the viewers are brought closer and closer to the reassuring answer to their curiosity. A first full statement of a tonal melody (I call it the 'Awe Motif') is heard the moment Roy arrives in front of the mountain where the final rendezvous with the extraterrestrials is to take place. However, at this point tonal music continues to share the stage with atonality and clusters—the uncertainty is not resolved yet. Finally, only in the last sequence, we have the musical denouement: 'It starts really when the extra-terrestrials appear from the mother-ship: here the tone-clusters involve all the twelve notes of the chromatic scale. Then you take one strand away, then another, so the music grows more and more consonant, until you end up with a pure, liturgical E major', explains Williams (Elley 1978b, p. 23). When the abducted people—and little Barry—disembark from the mother-ship perfectly safe and sound, the dissonance is permanently replaced by consonance, atonality with tonality. The emotion moment of the reunion redirects and finally stabilises the mood on the positive side of the spectrum. Our curiosity is finally satisfied: now it is clear that there is nothing to be afraid of.

Here, for the first time, we hear the five-note motif not as a diegetic series of electronic timbres, but warmly played by celli in the non-diegetic score. The choice of the celli, with their human-like timbre, is an apt one to contrast the non-human electronic timbre we previously heard—think of the creepy repetition of the electronic tones coming out from Jillian's phone during the kidnapping scene. The gradual passage of the music from clusters, to atonality, and finally to tonality, the presentation of increasingly longer fragments of the 'Awe Motif' during the second half of the film, and the celli rendition of the five-note motif are the devices that build the score's overarching macro-emotive function. All these elements have been designed and developed so as to lead to a musical denouement—firm stabilization of tonality, presentation of the 'Awe Motif' in its complete form, and non-diegetic celli rendition of the five-note Motif—during the sequence that required the strongest emotional response, that of the meeting of earthlings and extraterrestrials. The 'pleasure of recognition' and the soothing feeling given by the arrival of the long-awaited tonality are transferred from the music onto the macro-configuration of the sequence. The music is a major force in helping the film render its explicit meaning unambiguous: universal communication is possible and extraterrestrials are not to be feared because they are not necessarily warmongering. 'We are not alone…*fortunately.*'

There is still one musical element to be considered: the quotation of the 'When You Wish upon a Star' song (music by Leigh Harline, lyrics by Ned Washington) from Disney's *Pinocchio* (1940, dir. Luske and Sharpsteen). In his formalistic study of the score, Tom Schneller has come to some findings similar to mine and provided more insightful musicological information than I have. For example, he remarks that what I have called 'Awe Motif' is based on the 'Fate is Good' musical segment in 'When You Wish upon a Star.' In my view, his analysis is still more concerned with the music rather than with the interaction of the music with the film, notwithstanding the laudable words with which he opens his article: 'Musical analyses of film music tend to be concerned with the individual components of a film score (the various theme and leitmotifs), rather than with the way these components map onto the overarching narrative trajectory to reinforce the form of the film as a whole' (Schneller 2014, p. 98). His is still a *film-music* analysis, not a *film/music* analysis. Consider two points. He starts from the premises that 'The overall form of some of the most famous and effective film scores displays a kinship not only to opera, but the symphonic tradition as well' (Schneller 2014, p. 98). He explains, with Carl Dalhaus, that while Classical music (that is, eighteenth century music) is based on an 'architectonic' form, Romantic music (that is, nineteenth century music) is based on a 'logical' form, and then he sets to show how: 'The large-scale thematic form process at work in [the *Close Encounters*] score is best understood by analogy with the concept of "teleological genesis" [which] involves the emergence over the course of a piece of an extended melodic idea that develops gradually out of motivic fragments' (Schneller 2014, p. 99). Teleological genesis is what I have elsewhere called the technique of 'gradual disclosure of the main theme,' fulfilling a 'macro-emotive' function in the film (Audissino 2014b, p. 126). Schneller's focus is on the score—the teleological genesis is something happening within the score structures in terms of logical development of musical fragments, as similarly happened in most nineteenth-century *absolute musik*. My focus is on what the score does within the film: it presents the theme in fragments, gradually, in order to build an overarching emotional thread across the film that is set to pay off in a particularly important moment in the narrative. It is not so much a matter of organising a logical musical structure in the score as a matter of organising an effective emotional arch over the film and obtaining an effective pay-off in a crucial scene.

Coming to the narration's ambiguity about the visitors' intentions, Schneller's analysis individuates two conflicting poles, the 'Dies Irae' and the *Pinocchio* song 'When You Wish upon a Star,' representing respectively the two poles between which the film narration undulates—terror and wonder: 'In *Close Encounters*, the 'Dies Irae' functions as a musical red herring. By using a motive that is culturally encoded as a portent of impending doom, Williams prods the viewer into expecting the worst' (Schneller 2014, p. 106). Actually, I think not many viewers would identify the 'Dies Irae' in the 'Mystery Motif'—a music scholar certainly would, or a person with some musical background. What I think really creates negative expectations in the layperson viewer is the use of atonality in accordance with the norms of the sci-fi genre. I have traced the collaboration of the music with the film's narration in the creation of this conflictual terror/wonder mood mostly by pinpointing the shifts from atonality to tonality, which comes to be identified with the uncertainty about the aliens' intentions and nature (bloodthirsty monsters = atonality; peaceful visitors = tonality). Similarly, I suspect that even fewer would discern that the 'Awe Motif' is based on the *Pinocchio* song—I confess I did not—and therefore I am not convinced that the function of 'When You Wish upon a Star' is that of incarnating the wonder side of the narrative. I think tonality as opposed to atonality does. Even the composer himself acknowledges that it is not for everyone to spot the musical reference: '"When You Wish upon a Star" was in *Close Encounters*, disguised, for the sense of mystique....Most people don't even notice it, and that's all right, too. It may be just a kind of artistic conceit, I suppose, but it has some meaning to us' (in Schneller 2014, p. 108). Schneller's analysis is insightful but still comes from a score-centric perspective, and it shows. A music analyst tends to focus on the score and on musical elements that people with a medium-high musical education, not a casual viewer, would notice. A film analyst, on the contrary, would focus more on the superficial aspects of the music that most people would notice and, more importantly, on its interplay with the other cinematic devices.

Having said so, what is a more likely function of the quotation of 'When You Wish upon a Star' in the film? Since said quotation might not be recognisable by everyone, its function has to do with the interpretation side of the viewer's activity, not the comprehension—which requires, at least in a Hollywood mainstream film, devices that are clearly noticeable and understandable. The musical quotation of the *Pinocchio* song offers us access to the film's implicit meaning, the missed grasp of which does not impede the comprehension and superficial appreciation of a film. In the Director's Cut—as well as in the Special Edition—Roy is introduced while playing with toy trains at home and ardently trying to convince his unenthusiastic family to go see *Pinocchio* at a local theatre. Our first understanding of his fondness for the Disney cartoon is that Roy is a childlike man. The first thing that we have seen of him is that he is a toy-train enthusiast, and the reference to *Pinocchio* initially appears to be a way to reinforce and contextualise this characterisation—a device with a 'realistic motivation': a childlike man is likely to enjoy cartoons. It may also have a 'transtextual' and an 'artistic motivation' perfectly in line with the New Hollywood poetics: the film director makes an authorial intervention by quoting another film, another film that is particularly relevant to him. However, the *Pinocchio* reference is more than that, it also has an overarching 'compositional motivation.'[14] It is in the finale, when Roy is finally chosen among all the other volunteers to fly away with the extraterrestrials, that we can perceive a stretched musical rendition of 'When You Wish Upon a Star.' Why? Here is Williams' explanation:

> The idea to incorporate 'When You Wish upon a Star' was Spielberg's. I think for him, it had something to do with the innocence of childhood and Walt Disney's music, especially *Pinocchio*, that we all loved as children. He wanted to attach that childhood innocence to a feeling of nostalgia that would affect an audience. So, in a situation that is alien—completely remote from our experience—seeing these creatures and their machines but hearing something very familiar, 'When You Wish upon a Star,' you feel safe and at home. (Lace 1998, online)

This makes sense, compositionally—the *Pinocchio* narrative motif presented verbally at the beginning of the film (set-up) is reprised musically at the end (pay-off), thus closing the circle. It also makes sense as a micro-emotive function—the familiar tune, through the 'pleasure of recognition,' reinforces the tonal music at the end of the film, further reassuring that everything is fine. However, the music here performs a connotative cognitive function as well.

Why is Roy so attached to *Pinocchio* and not, say, to *Bambi*? Is there something specific in the *Pinocchio* narrative that makes it particularly telling here, or is it a random choice and it could have been any other Disney cartoon? In the original 1977 version, the scene that introduces us to Roy's family is quite different. There is no reference to the Disney film in the dialogue—here the father is not trying to talk his family into choosing *Pinocchio* over a match of miniature golf—but the scene opens with a detail of a music-box, with Pinocchio and Jiminy Cricket figurines, chiming 'When You Wish upon a Star'. Then we cut to a toy train track where the engine and wagons derail. Then we cut to a close-up of Roy watching the train wreck with a mix of disappointment and existential *ennui*, the Pinocchio carillon faintly winding down in the background. Spielberg had also considered to include the original song itself, sung by Cliff Edwards, in the finale, instead of the orchestral quotation, but the cards from a test screening discouraged him to do so (Royal 2000, pp. 96–97). As the song was soon removed, so the family scene was modified later for the Special Edition probably because it gave away too conspicuously the centrality of the *Pinocchio* symbolism. The new version of the family scene replaced the too obtrusive musico-visual reference—the detail of the Pinocchio music-box opened the scene and could not *not* be seen—with a more elegant and casual verbal reference to *Pinocchio* being played at a local theatre. The symbolic importance of *Pinocchio* became more covert and less compelling, to the point that it can be seen merely as a device to characterise Roy as a man-child. All these changes around the references to *Pinocchio* attest to its role as a fundamental symbol in the narrative, and Spielberg himself acknowledges it, saying that the Roy character is similar to Pinocchio in his quest to become a real man (in Durwood 1977, p. 118). If, during the film, we observe closely how the spaceships emerge from the night sky—little luminous points that look like stars but then suddenly move forward and grow bigger and brighter—and compare their apparitions with those of the Blue Fairy in Disney's *Pinocchio* we will notice a striking resemblance: in her apparitions, the Blue Fairy initially looks like the Wishing Star. In particular during the arrival of the first spaceships at the Devil's Mountain, both the visuals and the music—with a similar tone of celestial awe—are reminiscent of the first arrival of the Blue Fairy in the Disney film. Figure 8.1 demonstrates the meaningful parallel between the two arrivals: that of the Blue Fairy and that of the extraterrestrials.

Roy is a childlike man chained to a dull job, caged in a monotonous family routine and forced to live in a society that kills his imagination. The encounter with the extraterrestrials gives a welcome twist to his life and a refreshing hope for something better than just being a cog in the social machine. Like Pinocchio (a wooden puppet wishing to become a real boy) Roy wants to quit his puppet-like life and fulfil his real Self. The extraterrestrials are his Blue Fairy and, indeed, it is precisely when he fulfils his wish and is given the opportunity to fly away with them, that Williams's score suggests the link between Roy and Pinocchio by quoting 'When You wish upon a Star.' The film's implicit meaning is that a man living only on materialistic routine and social obligations is like a wooden puppet. In order to be a real man, a further, spiritual dimension, which the extraterrestrial heavenly messengers symbolise, is required.[15] The connotative cognitive function of the music (we are prompted to ask ourselves: Why the *Pinocchio* tune?) helps disclose this subterranean thematic level.

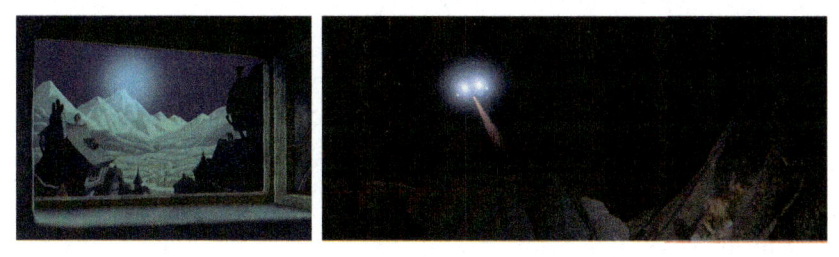

Fig. 8.1 Comparison between *Pinocchio* and *Close Encounters of the Third Kind*

E.T. The Extraterrestrial (1982)

E.T. is a sort of variation on themes from *Close Encounters*, and the music is equally central. Perhaps 'John Williams' best work for Spielberg' (Freer 2001, p. 117), the score is so interconnected with the narration's design as to become the film's soul, or as Spielberg puts it: 'John Williams is *E.T.*' (Spielberg 1982). The film further develops the key theme of *Close Encounters* (extraterrestrials are good, meeting with them can change one's life for better, etc.) with some important differences.[16] First of all, *Close Encounters* is a visually compelling high-profile production featuring spectacular optical effects by *2001*'s Douglas Trumbull; *E.T.* is designed as a kind of intimate, emotional suburb drama. While *Close Encounters* depicts extraterrestrial civilization meeting human civilization on a global scale, *E.T.* is about an individual extraterrestrial and his private encounter with an individual boy. While *Close Encounters* originated from extensive research into reported episodes of encounters with visitors from outer space and Spielberg's long-time fascination for extraterrestrial life,[17] the idea for *E.T.*, reportedly, came suddenly, emerging from childhood fantasies. Spielberg recounts:

> While working on *Raiders*, I had the germ of an idea. I was very lonely, and I remember thinking I had nobody to talk to. My girlfriend was in California, so was George Lucas. Harrison Ford had a bad case of the *turistas*, I remember wishing one night that I had a friend. It was like, when you were a kid and had grown out of dolls or teddy bears or Winnie the Pooh, you just wanted a little voice in your mind to talk to. I began concocting this imaginary creature, partially from the guys who stepped out of the mother ship for ninety seconds in *Close Encounters* and then went back in, never to be seen again. Then I thought what if I were ten

years old again…and what if he needed me as much as I needed him? Wouldn't that be a great love story? (in Sragow 2000, p. 110)

A great love story. While *Close Encounters* is about universal communication, *E.T.* is basically about universal love. The communication theme is now secondary, since love can clear such hurdles; Elliott and E.T. can share their feelings telepathically.

The narration does not play on the ambiguity about the visitor's intents either; after a brief atonal-music beginning—right over the opening titles—a gentle melody ('E.T. Motif') played by the piccolo opens the narrative over a shot of a starry night sky: 'The flute is the instrument of fairy tales [and] the solitude of the solo suggests to us the upcoming exclusion or abandonment of one of the characters of the film (because of the absence of the group, the absence of the orchestra)' (Tylski 1999, online). Then, the extraterrestrials disembark from a spherical comic book-like spaceship in a forest reminiscent of Disney's *Bambi* (1942, dir. Hand). The music, presenting the 'Forest Theme,' is solemn, hymn-like, and sounds as if it were played by a pipe organ, with a reverent 'churchly' quality: 'After a brief rest, a bell can be heard for the first time as we are shown a low-angle shot of the forest, the enormous tree trunks simulating the pillars of a great cathedral' (Tylski 1999, online). Music produces a mood of mystery, not fear, around the outer-space creatures. On the contrary, threatening, dark music is introduced when some cars arrive on the site and human officers—whose faces are kept off-screen—start searching around with their pocket torches. The narration and the score make a point clear: unlike *Close Encounters*, the narrative here is focused on the extraterrestrials—particularly on E.T.—and the menacing creatures are the humans, who are accordingly kept unseen as the extraterrestrials were kept unseen in *Close Encounters*. This upside-down perspective is evident later in the film when the authorities in spacesuits break in Elliott's house to seize E.T., accompanied by atonal music—a sequence that closely mirrors Barry's kidnapping in *Close Encounters*, only with reversed roles.

Apart from these local micro-emotive interventions functional to align us with E.T. and Elliott (warm tonal music) and distancing us from the authorities (cold, non-tonal music), the global macro-emotive function of the score is, again, to sustain the overarching trajectory of the narration and the development of the central theme: the love between the extraterrestrial and the boy. As in *Close Encounters* the music prolongs the ambiguity and then helps elaborate the fact that the aliens are good creatures, so in *E.T.* the score is designed to accompany the gradual growth of the friendship between Elliott and E.T. and to lead it to the proper emotive climax. This is achieved through one of Williams's preferred compositional strategies: the 'gradual disclosure of the main theme.' Williams starts by presenting a thematic fragment early in the film, followed later by a longer one—say, a half phrase—and finally unfolds the whole theme typically in a key scene that requires a strong emotive response:

> We may have the first few notes of this emotional theme suggested early on, then three or four more notes and finally the whole theme. So that finally when you hear it all, there is something vaguely familiar about it. You've been prepared for four reels to actually hear this melody. It isn't presented to you immediately in its complete form. It is suggested here, it's done a little bit frighteningly over here, with a little uncertainty there, and finally expressed harmonically and intervallically in some way that you feel comfortable with it. (in Bouzereau 2002)

The main theme ('Flying theme') is heard piecemeal along the first part of the film—the first occurrence being E.T.'s making some clay balls magically levitate—and it is presented in its entirety and in a full-orchestra rendition only during the famous bicycle flight over the moon. The emotional impact of the scene is the result of the macro-emotive function of the score, prepared throughout the previous scenes by the carefully incremental disclosure of the theme: 'What is so important is an hour and a half or ten reels of preparation to that moment....So, to the audience, you've created an expectancy to deliver something that's not only very emotional but is also inevitable. It's a moment that had to happen' (in Stock 2006). The pleasure given to viewers by the recognition of the already-heard fragments, and by the appearance of the theme in its long-awaited complete form, produces in the flying sequence an uplifting sense of fulfilment. This, along with the ascending configuration and expanding quality of the musical intervals employed (ascending fifth, then ascending octave) is what makes the flying sequence so exhilarating, awe-inspiring and moving.[18]

The final fifteen-minute sequence—the boys helping E.T. flee from the scientists' facilities, their bicycles chased by the police, the bicycles taking off and flying over a Californian sunset, the landing in the forest, the arrival of E.T.'s mother-ship and the sorrowful parting of the two intergalactic friends—is one the musical highlights in the score. The visual action is continuously propelled and punctuated by the score—for example, note groupings in the score mimic the pedal strokes of the boys' bicycles. The music fulfils a temporal perceptive function, by heightening the speed of the chase with its fast tempo, and consolidating the linear direction and consistency of the fast-paced editing sequence with the coherent and propelling micro-configuration of the music. It also fulfils a spatial perceptive function, by mimicking the up-and-down-the-hill flow of the bicycle chase with corresponding up-and-down musical phrases, but also having musical accents when a bicycle hits a bump in the road, or highlighting some important visual detail—like, earlier in the sequence, the sudden musical excitement that points our attention to the withered flower that instantly regenerates, anticipating E.T.'s resurrection.

> That sequence involved a lot of specific musical cues. An accent for each speed bump of the bicycles; a very dramatic accent for the police cars; a special lift for the bicycles taking-off; sentimental music for the goodbye scene between E.T. and Elliott; and finally, when the spaceship takes off, the orchestra swells up and hits an accent as the spaceship whooshes away. So you can imagine in the space of that fifteen minutes of film how many precise musical accents are needed and how each one has to be exactly in the right place. I wrote the music mathematically to configure with each of those occurrences and worked it all out. (in Bouzereau 1996)

Contrary to the common practice, the musical piece for this long sequence was recorded free of visual constraints, as if it were a concert piece, and then it was the editing to be readjusted to conform to the musical flow (Bouzereau 1996).

This remarkable cine-musical sequence was recently modified. The 2002 edition—released for the film's twentieth anniversary—presents additions and trimmings that ended up impairing some of its thematic and formal qualities. One of the most notable was the replacement of the guns with walkie-talkies in the boys/police chase, out of concerns for political correctness.[19] This had a double impact. On the one hand, it diminishes the dramatic contrast between the threatening and armed authorities and the defenceless boys. In the 1982 edition, when the boys reach the road blockade, we are led to believe that the federal agents are ready to shoot—a detail of a shotgun being set in position is shown when the bicycles are, seemingly, approaching the end of their escape, caught by surprise by the police cars closing the road. But then this is followed by an intense close-up of Elliott and then of E.T., and finally by the unexpected magical take off of the bicycles, which leaves the onlooking authorities totally puzzled and impotent. The thematic point of this whole sequence is that a bunch of kids defeat the authorities *and their weapons* by using *other weapons*: fantasy and a faith in the miraculous power of love. Without the guns and rifles, and in particular without that shotgun detail just before the take off, the sequence loses much of its dramatic force and the theme 'boys' weapons vs adults' weapons' is drastically washed out. Spielberg might have been concerned and have had second thoughts about showing a federal agent ready to open fire on a boy, but that juxtaposition of the detail of the shotgun and the close-up of the boy was a powerful 'attractional' moment in an Eisensteinian way. The *montaž*[20] of those two images produced a visual 'shock' that, through the conceptual power of film editing, communicated the repressive power of the authorities and the real danger that the boys were facing. The replacement of the weapons with the walkie-talkies simply made the whole *montaž* collapse, along with the stronger meaning it carried.

But this not only impacted on the thematic level. The replacement of the gun caused a slight shortening of the sequence; the detail of the shotgun had to be removed altogether, since a detail of a walkie-talkie would have been pointless. Trimming the editing meant that the music track had to be trimmed too. This resulted in a quite audible music edit; where previously a dark note by the trombones dramatically highlighted the detail of the shotgun being prepared and charged it emotionally (spatial-perceptive and micro-emotive functions combined), now we hear an edit that has removed that musical measure and spliced the loose ends. The specificity of this scene precisely consisted in its free musical flow and in a rare reverse *modus operandi*; music was freely recorded and then the edit was adapted to the music. With the 2002 edition this specificity is lost.[21]

After taking into consideration the function of the music locally, we can now turn to the bigger picture and examine how the score supports the narration globally. *E.T.* has a score that possesses a high structural cohesiveness, a strong 'teleological genesis,' to use Schneller's perspective. This is mainly the product of a network of leitmotifs associated to each character and idea. 'E.T.'s Motif' is heard on the opening shot of the starry night sky and is reprised each time the score refers to the extraterrestrial. The 'Forest Theme' is heard during the opening scene of the mother-ship landing in the woods, and it is reprised either each time E.T. talks about his home or when his vital necessity to go back home is mentioned. The forest is where E.T. got lost, it is where he places his transmitter, and it is the meeting-point where the mother-ship will eventually come back to rescue him. One gentle theme for harp and strings (the 'Friendship Theme') is heard when Elliott shows E.T. around his room and each time their friendship moves one step forward. A propulsive 4/4 action 'Chase Theme' is heard when the boys cycle around and prominently during the final escape. A dark menacing motif embodies the authorities, and mysterious atonal motif in triplets is used during the suspense scenes, mostly at the beginning of the film. The theme that stands out more is the one known as the 'Flying Theme.' But Williams's words suggest that it should be called differently:

> In *E.T.* there's a theme for the little alien creature and for the little boy Elliott....And that theme is kind of like a love theme. It's not sensual in the way a love theme would be, but it develops as their relationship develops. It starts with a few notes, they look at each other—a little bit uncertain. And it grows and becomes more confident, and more lyrical as E.T. goes away....In that scene their theme or love theme, whatever you call it—the Elliott-E.T. Theme—come back. It's like, in a way, a moment in opera when two lovers are being separated. I built to that kind of musical denouement. (in Zailian 1982)

A love theme for 'a great love story.' Quite appropriately, This 'Love Theme' gradually replaces the 'Friendship Theme' when the relationship between the boy and the alien evolves into something deeper, and its fragments become more complete as their reciprocal love grows stronger—'E.T., I love you!', says the mourning Elliott before his (apparently) dead friend, the music tenderly playing the 'Love Theme.' The score is, as in *Close Encounters*, a major force in sustaining the narrational plan and reinforcing its explicit meaning: telling the growth of a love story between an earthling boy and his extraterrestrial friend.

Yet, the music, once again, suggests more by performing a connotative cognitive function. The 'Love Theme' is not just linked to love, but it is also presented during the miracle scenes: when E.T. heals Elliott's wound and when he resuscitates the dying flowers; when the boys' bicycles escape gravity and take off in a Californian sunset; when E.T. comes back to life. In these moments, the score seems to hint at the film's implicit theme: the immense power of love, which is what makes miracles possible.[22] As love can be tender and intimate but can also be very powerful—E.T.'s love makes the bicycle fly and Elliott's love makes E.T. come back to life—so the 'Love Theme' is soft and graceful during the sentimental moments, but it is imposing and vigorously orchestrated during the spectacular bicycle flights. I mentioned that the score is particularly cohesive because its leitmotivic network presents strong musical connections between one leitmotiv and the others. If we analyse the leitmotivs, we can see that each one of those involved in the love-relationship with the extraterrestrial has a recurrent trait: an ascending perfect-fifth leap. The ones most prominently associated with this love-relationship—'E.T.'s Motif', the 'Friendship Theme' and the 'Love Theme'—even markedly open with the very same perfect-fifth leap. Figure 8.2 presents the major themes and motifs in the *E.T.* score, highlighting the recurrence of the perfect-fifth leap in all of them:

In *Close Encounters of the Third Kind* the ascending perfect-fifth interval closed the five-note 'Communication Motif' but, we said, because of the nature of this musical interval it sounded more like an opening than a closure. Ian Freer wrote, about the connection between the two films, that '*E.T.* was going to start where *Close Encounters* left off' (Freer 2001, p. 109). It is interesting how this is exactly what happens with the music. While the central musical motif of *Close Encounters* closed with an ascending perfect fifth, all the major themes and motifs in *E.T.* open with an ascending perfect fifth. It is indeed as if the former film started a narrative that is then picked up and further developed by the latter.

This shared perfect fifth in the *E.T.* musical catalogue is quite noticeable and a number of analyses have pointed this out, but they all have focussed on the score and have not explained how this musical 'communion' amongst the leitmotivs relates to the film.[23] Tom Schneller, in his already cited article, has also studied the overall design of the *E.T.* score. He stresses the musical kinship that all the themes and motifs share, and explains it on the grounds that they are all based on the 'E.T. motif.' He also provides musico-formal insights into these transformations: 'As E.T. and Elliott get to know each other, Williams introduces a warm, lyrical melody based on a transformation of the E.T. motive. The ascending fifth is retained, but in place of the "alien" Lydian fourth,

Fig. 8.2 Ascending perfect fifth in the *E.T.* score, transcription from *E.T. The Extraterrestrial*, John Williams music published by USI B Music Publishing (1982 BMI), administered by Songs of Universal [Used in compliance with the U.S. Copyright Act, Section 107]

the melody now descends by whole step to a "familiar" diatonic fourth.' (Schneller 2014, p. 102). Again, he focusses on the music within the score's musical system, not on the music within the film's formal system. What does this shared ascending perfect fifth mean *within* the film? I would rather say that all the themes and motifs *share* the perfect-fifth interval, rather than that they are all based on the 'E.T. Motif.' Both statements are true, of course, but Schneller's is concerned with the teleological development of the score—all themes are logical developments of an original musical idea, the 'E.T. Motif.' From a film scholar's perspective, and to connect the score and its musical design to the film itself, the origin of and explanation for the perfect fifth that all musical themes and motifs share has to be searched and can be found in the film itself. If we pay attention to the first sequence, we can notice that when E.T.'s fellow creatures telepathically connect with each other, they emit a distinct sound while their heart lights up: the sound is an *ascending perfect fifth*.[24] The film establishes the ascending perfect fifth from the very beginning as the sound of the heart. Consequently, in the score this musical interval is consistently reprised to symbolize love. Its recurrence in the musical network is the reflection of the love network that embraces all the characters and that points to the film's implicit meaning: the miraculous power of universal love, which makes the bicycles fly and E.T. come back to life. As in *Close Encounters*, the film's implicit meaning is unveiled through music. And while in *Close Encounters* the openness and universality of the ascending perfect-fifth leap symbolised universal communication, in *E.T.* it symbolises universal Love.

Conclusions

Close Encounters and *E.T.* stand out as perhaps the most celebrated film-music achievements of the Steven Spielberg and John Williams duo. Williams's scores for these two films, though stylistically diverse have in common the foregrounded position of the music and its central role in the overall narrational strategy. Moreover, their narrative trajectories are specular and possess a similar strategy of gradually incremental degree of communicativeness—the quantity of narrative information that narration shares with the viewers.[25] In *Close Encounters* the narration draws a trajectory of incremental clarification of the space visitors' intentions and moves from a starting point of lack of communication/unclear communication (between the aliens and the earthlings but also between the narration and the viewers about whether the extraterrestrials are good or bad) to a final point of total and open communication (aliens and earthlings eventually communicate and the narration finally reveals the visitors' nature and scope). Similarly, in *E.T.*, the narration moves from a starting point of mutual fear and uncertainty between the earthling Elliott and the extraterrestrial E.T., which soon evolves into a strong friendship, to a final point of total symbiosis and empathy between the boy and the space creature. *Close Encounters* paints the large picture of a global extraterrestrial visit that the authorities strive to keep hidden from the common people. Specularly, *E.T.* narrates an extraterrestrial visit on much more local a scale and with more intimate a tone. And the situation is here inverted: the extraterrestrial is kept hidden from the authorities by common people, or better, by kids. In *Close Encounters*, the mysterious and threatening characters whose faces we cannot see for most of the narrative are the extraterrestrials; specularly, in *E.T.* the mysterious and threatening characters whose faces we cannot see are the adult earthlings.

In terms of analysis, I have favoured the interpretation of the 'implicit meaning' over the deconstruction of the 'symptomatic meaning.' The principal difference is that a film's implicit meaning is generally something within the author's intentions, while symptomatic meanings may be something constructed by the interpreter, and hence potentially incurring in over-interpretation—a 'made meaning,' to quote Bordwell's controversial meta-criticism of the most common heuristics of film interpretation (Bordwell 1989, p. 21).[26] In other words, while Spielberg himself acknowledges the escapist implicit meaning of *Close Encounters* (in McBride 1997, p. 283), I seriously doubt he meant E.T. to be a 'walking phallus.' In terms of disciplinary perspective, as a film scholar I have focussed on music as a cinematic device operating within the film's formal system, not as music per se within a score. I have shown how music contributes to the production of the emotional response of the viewers, not only in the single moments (micro-emotively) but also throughout the narrative arch (macro-emotively), and how it is also the key to help our interpretation of the thematic level (cognitive function).

Notes

1. The other film in the trilogy is the horror film *Poltergeist* (1982, dir. Hooper). Even if the rumour about Spielberg having in fact ghost-directed the film was questioned by Warren Buckland (Buckland 2006,

pp. 154–173), who through statistical/stylistic analysis is prone to attribute it to Hooper, nevertheless the film bears strong Spielbergian imprints, since he wrote and produced it.
2. Kolker (1988, p. 140) compares *Close Encounters of the Third Kind* to a sort of Hollywood version of Leni Riefenstahl's *Triumph of the Will* (1935), the propaganda film documenting the 1934 Nazi party rally in Nuremberg. The film is also charged with authoritarianism—with music being highly complicit with that—in Lerner (2004).
3. On Spielberg's films and American society, see also Wasse (2010, in particular pp. 101–136).
4. The film is also analysed in terms of universal communication and barrier-breaking pursuit of knowledge in Engel (2002).
5. On the perfect-fifth in Williams's music see Audissino (2014b, pp. 75, 154–158).
6. On music/colour synaesthetic associations, see Cook (1998, pp. 24–41).
7. On the use of music in *Jaws*, see Biancorosso (2010) and Audissino (2014b, pp. 104–118).
8. Tonal music revolves around a central tone, the tonic, which orients the development of the musical phrases and imposes a hierarchy on all the other steps of the scales in relation to the tonic. Thus the listener has a way to get oriented within a tonal piece and his listening experience is characterized by anticipations and expectations that he is drawing as the music flows. Atonal music offers much fewer, if any, anchoring points to orient and guide the listener's expectations and this can result in a sense of frustration, disorientation, and anxiety—as we have no idea of where the music is heading to. On this, see Meyer (1956, pp. 163–166) in particular. Tonal music is the most familiar as it has a longer tradition (and thus by learning one has had more chances to familiarize with it). Yet the tone relations within the diatonic scales of the tonal system are based on the harmonic series that physically constitutes any tone, so the tonal system is the more natural one. On this point, see Sloboda (1999, pp. 253–255).
9. See Rózsa (1989, p. 192).
10. The *ostinato* is the prolonged repetition of a musical fragment. Since it is obsessively repetitious, it causes the musical flow to sound mechanically stuck on the same portion and not 'naturally' developing into something else—think of a turntable needle that gets fastidiously stuck. The constant repetition creates anxiety because of the 'principle of saturation:' see Meyer 156, pp. 135–138. On *ostinatos* and their narrative functions, see Miceli (2009, pp. 620–621). K. J. Donnelly discusses *ostinatos* as creating a 'terror of stasis' in Donnelly (2014, p. 120). On the history of the use of *ostinatos* in film music see Moormann (2012).

11. Good-extraterrestrial themed films and TV programmes are *Mork and Mindy* (1978–1982, prod. Glauberg, Marshall, McRaven), of course *E.T. the Extraterrestrial* (1982, dir. Spielberg) and its clone *Mac and Me* (1988, dir. Raffill), *Starman* (1984, dir. Carpenter), Alf (1986–1990, prod. Patchet, Fusco), *Howard the Duck* (1986, dir. Huyck) and **Batteries not Included* (1987, dir. Robbins), just to name a few.

12. Yet, as pointed out in Gordon (2008, p. 68): 'Chances Are' is a 'promise of love', its lyrics talking about reading the signs of a person falling in love with another. So, the use of the song subtly suggests that all these (seemingly scaring) signs we see in the kidnapping scene are not to be read as scaring. The extraterrestrials have good feelings for the earthlings, and they have just come to pay a visit and make acquaintance.

13. In both Williams's film and concert music, the tuba is typically used in comical or caricaturally grotesque passages: it is used in the 'Jubba the Hutt' theme in *Return of the Jedi* (1983, dir. Marquand), during the benevolent delinquential antics in *Fitzwilly* (1967, dir. D. Mann), doubling the oboe in the 'March of the [comical] Villains' in *Superman the Movie* (1978, dir. Donner), and the Concerto for Tuba (1985) has a light-hearted humorous tone. For malevolent characters Williams would rather use trombones—for example, the Voldemort theme in *Harry Potter and the Sorcerer's Stone* (2001, dir. Columbus)—or dramatic horns—for example, the Kylo Renn motif in *Star Wars: The Force Awakens* (2015, dir. Abrams).

14. On the meaning of Pinocchio in *Close Encounters* and in Spielberg's cinema in general, see Audissino (2010, pp. 23–36).

15. Amongst the many interpretations, I think the more appropriate for the film is the Jungian. In *Close Encounters* the aliens and their meaning closely remind of Jung's 'Puer Aeternus' archetype: Jung (1980, pp. 151–181). A reading along these lines has been made in Bittanti (2002). Moreover, Jung himself wrote about the psychological meaning of UFOs, which makes his theory directly connected with the topic at hand here: see Jung (2002). For Lacanians, it is worth mentioning that Jung is re-read with Lacanian lenses in White and Wang (1999).

16. My analysis is based on the 1982 original version, not on the 2002 'Special Edition.'

17. One of Spielberg's teenage films, *Firelight* (1964), dealt with such a theme and can be considered a low-budget precursor of *Close Encounters*.

18. This can be seen as a case of sentimentality at work. We experience sentimental emotions when we face an event—either sad or joyful—on which we perceive we have little or no control. 'The outcomes that elicit sentimental emotions are changes for better or for worse in the protagonist's life....The sentimental aspect is a response to a change in an inner

process, that is, an abrupt giving up of coping effort or expectation.... The action tendency in sentiment is to yield to the overwhelming' (Tan and Frijda 1999, p. 55). Weeping, the typical emotional venting in such circumstances is the emotional effect of our surrendering to events that are sensed as bigger than us. There are three main emotional themes that are likely to provoke sentimental reactions: the 'separation-reunion theme,' the 'justice in jeopardy' theme and the 'awe-inspiration' theme (ibid.). Each of these is featured in E.T.: the 'separation-reunion' theme can be spotted, of course, in the film's finale and when the authorities seize E.T. (combined in this case with the 'justice in jeopardy' theme, from Elliott's perspective), while the 'awe-inspiration' theme is at work in the miracle scenes, the flight scene being the foremost.

19. On the trimming of the 2002 edition, see Travers (2002).
20. I use here the original Russian spelling because the Westernised version—montage—has come to indicate mostly the montage sequences, while I refer to the original conception of editing being able to produce ideas by creating new sense from two juxtaposed images.
21. Spielberg himself, in 2011, seems to have changed his mind and regretted what he did with the 2002 edition: 'When people ask me which E.T. they should look at, I always tell them to look at the original 1982 E.T. If you notice, when we did put out E.T. we put out two E.T.s. We put out the digitally enhanced version with the additional scenes and for no extra money, in the same package, we put out the original '82 version.' I always tell people to go back to the '82 version.' (Quint' 2011, online). As a matter of fact, from 2002 to 2012 the 1982 was quite hard to find on DVD, only featured in a limited-edition three-DVD box set. For the 30th Anniversary Blu-ray disc the original version has finally resurfaced.
22. Tolerance, acceptance, universal love, and the power of imagination are recurrent Spielbergian themes, mostly associated with childhood, either incarnated by children or by childlike adults. Actually, childhood and the power of imagination can be considered a central theme in Spielberg's cinema: see Friedman (2006, pp. 31–39). On these themes in association with another typically Spielbergian theme, flight, see Audissino (2014a).
23. The common perfect-fifth was noticed in Douglas 2013. The The composer Weiwei Miao presented a conference paper (Miao 2014) that similarly traced all these relations amongst the leitmotivs but without any mention as to how they are related to what happens in the film.
24. It can be clearly heard at 00.03.30 in the 1982 Version, DVD 3, Collector's Edition, Universal Home Video, 2002, 907 028 2.
25. 'Although a narration has a particular range of knowledge available, the narration may or may not communicate all that information' (Bordwell 1985, p. 59).

26. For example, Nigel Morris applies to *E.T.* a typical Levi-Straussian binary reading of the film, listing a series of oppositional couples (Morris 2007, pp. 92–93). This is one of the most exploited heuristics amongst those presented by Bordwell (1989, p. 81). The problem is that, as often happens with Grand Theory and its tools, this is a rather weak analytical tool that is not guaranteed to say much about the film itself. It is possible to find out binary opposition in almost everything—light/darkness, Nature/Culture, high/low, fast/slow—and it is not so much the film that is interrogated through an analytical instrument as the film being bent to the analytical category chosen by the analyst.

References

Audissino, Emilio. 2010. *L'infanzia nel cinema di Steven Spielberg*. Imperia: Ennepi Libri.

Audissino, Emilio. 2014a. Bicycles, Airplanes and Peter Pans: Flying Scenes in Steven Spielberg's Films. *CINEJ Cinema Journal* 3 (2): 104–120.

Audissino, Emilio. 2014b. *John Williams's Film Music. 'Jaws,' 'Star Wars,' 'Raiders of the Lost Ark,' and the Return of the Classical Hollywood Music Style*. Madison, WI: University of Wisconsin Press.

Biancorosso, Giorgio. 2010. The Shark in the Music. *Music Analysis* 29 (1–3): 306–333.

Bittanti, Marco. 2002. 'Il futuro ha un cuore antico. La fantascienza e il "puer aeternus." In *Incubi e meraviglie. Il cinema di Steven Spielberg*, ed. Enzo Alberione, 41–49. Milan: Unicopli.

Bordwell, David. 1985. *Narration in the Fiction Film*. Madison, WI: University of Wisconsin Press.

Bordwell, David. 1989. *Making Meaning Inference and Rhetoric in the Interpretation of Cinema*. Cambridge, MA: Harvard University Press.

Bouzereau, Laurent. 1996. John Williams Interview. *E.T. The Extraterrestrial*, CD booklet, expanded edition. MCA, MCAD-11494.

Bouzereau, Laurent. 1998a. *The Making of Close Encounters of the Third Kind*. Documentary. Columbia TriStar Home Entertainment.

Bouzereau, Laurent. 1998b. 'When You Wish Upon a Note…' CD booklet, *Close Encounters of the Third Kind. The Collector's Edition Soundtrack*. Arista, 07822-19004-2.

Bouzereau, Laurent. 2002. *The Music of 'E.T.' A Discussion with John Williams*. Documentary. Universal Home Video.

Britton, Andrew. 2009. Blissing Out: The Politics of Reaganite Entertainment [1986]. In *Britton on Film. The Complete Film Criticism of Andrew Britton*, ed. Barry Keith Grant, 97–154. Detroit, MI: Wayne State University Press.

Buckland, Warren. 2006. *Directed by Steven Spielberg: Poetics of the Contemporary Hollywood Blockbuster*. New York: Bloomsbury Academic.
Combs, Richard. 2000 [1977]. Primal Scream: An Interview with Steven Spielberg. In *Steven Spielberg Interviews*, ed. Lester D. Friedman, and Brent Notbohm, 30–36. Jackson, MS: University Press of Mississippi.
Cook, Nicholas. 1998. *Analysing Musical Multimedia*. Oxford: Clarendon Press.
Donnelly, K.J. 2014. *Occult Aesthetics: Synchronization in Sound Film*. Oxford and New York: Oxford University Press.
Douglas, Andrew. 2013. A Brief Guide to its Musical Themes and Some Suggestions as to Their Origins [1989]. *Soundtrack* 8: 32: page unknown. Now on *Run Movies*, 5 August, Online. http://www.runmovies.eu/et-the-extra-terrestrial. Accessed 20 Sept 2016.
Durwood, Thomas (ed.). 1977. *Close Encounters of the Third Kind: A Document of the Film*. Kansas City: Ariel Books.
Elley, Derek. 1978a. The Film Composer: 3. John Williams, Part I. *Films and Filming*, July, 20–24.
Elley, Derek. 1978b. The Film Composer: 3. John Williams, Part II. *Films and Filming*, August, 30–33.
Engel, Charlene. 2002 [1996]. Language and Music of the Spheres. Steven Spielberg's *Close Encounters of the Third Kind*. In *The Films of Steven Spielberg. Critical Essays*, ed. Charles L.P. Silet, 47–56. Lanham, MD: Scarecrow Press.
Entman, Robert, and Francie Seymour. 1978. Close Encounters with the Third Reich. *Jump Cut* 18: 3–6.
Freer, Ian. 2001. *The Complete Spielberg*. London: Virgin Publishing.
Friedman, Lester D. 2006. *Citizen Spielberg*. Urbana: University of Illinois Press.
Gordon, Andrew M. 1980. Close Encounter of the Third Kind. The Gospel According to Steven Spielberg. *Literature/Film Quarterly* 8 (3): 156–164.
Gordon, Andrew M. 2008. *Empire of Dreams. The Science Fiction and Fantasy Films of Steven Spielberg*. Lanham, MD: Rowman & Littlefield.
Jung, Carl G. 1980 [1951]. The Psychology of the Child Type. In *The Archetypes and the Collective Unconscious*, Collected Works of C.G. Jung, vol. 9, Part 1, trans. and ed. R.F.C. Hull, 151–181. Princeton, NJ: Princeton University Press.
Jung, Carl G. 2002 [1958]. *Flying Saucers: A Modern Myth of Things Seen in the Skies*, trans. R.F.C. Hull. Abingdon: Routledge.
Kendrick, James. 2014. *Darkness in the Bliss-Out: A Reconsideration of the Films of Steven Spielberg*. London and New York: Bloomsbury.
Kolker, Robert Phillip. 1988. *A Cinema of Loneliness: Penn, Kubrick, Scorsese, Spielberg, Altman*, 2nd ed. Oxford and New York: Oxford University Press.

Lace, Ian. 1998. *The Film Music of John Williams. Music Web International,* Online. www.musicweb-international.com/film/lacejw.htm. Accessed 21 Sept 2016.

Lerner, Neil. 2004. Nostalgia, Masculinist Discourse and Authoritarianism in John Williams' Scores for *Star Wars* and *Close Encounters of the Third Kind*. In *Off the Planet. Music, Sound and Science Fiction Cinema*, ed. Philip Hayward, 96–108. Eastleigh: John Libbey Publishing.

McBride, Joseph. 1997. *Steven Spielberg: A Biography*. New York: Simon and Schuster.

Meyer, Leonard B. 1956. *Emotion and Meaning in Music*. Chicago and London: University of Chicago Press.

Miao, Weiwei. 2014. An Eclectic Analysis of E.T. The ExtraTerrestrial (1982). Paper Presented at the 'Music and the Moving Image IX Conference' (New York University, 30 May–1 June). Friday 30 May.

Miceli, Sergio. 2009. *Musica per film. Storia, Estetica, Analisi, Tipologie*. Lucca and Milan: LIM-Ricordi.

Moormann, Peter. 2012. Composing with Types and Flexible Modules: John Williams' Two-Note Ostinato for *Jaws* and its Use in Film-Music History. *Journal of Film Music* 5 (1–2): 165–168.

Morris, Nigel. 2007. *Empire of Light. The Cinema of Steven Spielberg*. London and New York: Wallflower Press.

Quint. 2011. AICN Exclusive: Spielberg Speaks! *Jaws* Blu-Ray in the Works with No "Digital Corrections!" *Ain't It Cool News*, 3 June, Online. http://www.aintitcool.com/node/49897. Accessed 20 Sept 2016.

Royal, Susan. 2000 [1982]. Steven Spielberg in His Adventure on Earth. In *Steven Spielberg Interviews*, ed. Lester D. Friedman and Brent Notbohm, 84–106. Jackson, MS: University Press of Mississippi.

Rózsa, Miklós. 1989. *A Double Life. The Autobiography of Miklós Rózsa, Composer in the Golden Years of Hollywood*. New York: Wynwood Press.

Schneller, Tom. 2014. Sweet Fulfillment: Allusion and Teleological Genesis in John Williams's *Close Encounters of the Third Kind. The Musical Quarterly* 9 (1): 98–131.

Sloboda, John. 1999. *The Musical Mind. The Cognitive Psychology of Music*, new ed. Oxford and New York: Oxford University Press.

Spielberg, Steven. 1982. Liner Notes. *E.T. The Extraterrestrial*, Original Soundtrack Album. MCA, MCLD 19021.

Sragow, Michael. 2000 [1982]. A Conversation with Steven Spielberg. In *Steven Spielberg Interviews*, ed. Lester D. Friedman, and Brent Notbohm, 107–119. Jackson, MS: University Press of Mississippi.

Stock, Francine. 2006. *The Film Programme*, interview with John Williams. Radio broadcast. BBC Radio 4. 14 April.

Tan, Ed S., and Nico H. Frijda. 1999. Sentiment in Film Viewing. In *Passionate Views. Film, Cognition and Emotion*, ed. Carl Plantinga and Greg M. Smith, 48–64. Baltimore, MD: Johns Hopkins University Press.

Taylor, Philip. 1999. *Steven Spielberg: The Man, His Movies, and Their Meaning*, 3rd ed. London: B. T. Batsford.

Thompson, Kristin. 1988. *Breaking the Glass Armor. Neoformalist Film Analysis*. Princeton, NJ: Princeton University Press.

Travers, Peter. 2002. E.T. The Extraterrestrial. *Rolling Stones*, 14 March, Online. https://web.archive.org/web/20090114114318/http://www.rollingstone.com/reviews/movie/5948461/review/5948462/et_the_extraterrestrial. Accessed 5 Dec 2016.

Tylski, Alexandre. 1999. Scene Study: E.T. (1982). A Dark and Brilliant Overture. *Film Score Monthly*, 3 August, Online. http://www.filmscoremonthly.com/daily/article.cfm/articleID/2642/Scene-Study-E.T.-1982. Accessed 20 Sept 2016.

Wasser, Frederick. 2010. *Steven Spielberg's America*. Cambridge UK and Malden MA: Polity.

White, Daniel, and Alvin Y. Wang. 1999. Through the Dark Mirror: UFOs as a Postmodern Myth? *CTheory*, 1 June, Online. http://ctheory.net/ctheory_wp/through-the-dark-mirror-ufos-as-a-postmodern-myth. Accessed 14 Sept 2016.

Zailian, Marian. 1982. John Williams: Master of Movie Scores. *San Francisco Examiner-Chronicle*, 18 July.

CHAPTER 9

Recapitulation and Final Thoughts

In the 'Introduction' I had set this research question at the basis of this book: 'How can we analyse music in films from a film scholar's perspective, be as discipline-specific as possible, and take into account a gamut as large as possible of the types and range of agency that music can have?' I think that the application of Neoformalism to the task is a good answer. Neoformalism comes from Film Studies and is an analytical approach specifically designed to be applied to films; it has a strong concern for stylistic features (and hence for the technique proper to the medium), which makes it more discipline-specific than other broader approaches that are shared with other branches in the Humanities—for example, Critical Theory or Psychoanalysis; given its interest in forms and style, it is suitable to address all the roles that music can have, from sophisticate 'commentaries' to the humbler 'accompaniment.' Moreover, this is a full-fledged application of Neoformalism to the analysis of music in film: while a cognitive-theory approach has long been applied to the study of film music—see, for example, Jeff Smith's work[1]—Neoformalism sensu stricto has never been to such extent. To address music, I have enhanced the Neoformalist framework with elements borrowed from Leonard B. Meyer's musicology. Meyer's theories provide a psychological and not too musicologically technical way to account for how we make sense of and affectively respond to music, and also offer valuable concepts to account for music's ability to translate images, ideas, and feelings into its own language—which is a fundamental power for film music. The chosen overarching framework is Gestalt Psychology, as it offers a fruitful conceptualisation of how music and visuals cooperate: not by addition but by multiplication, creating with their fusion a perceived audiovisual configuration that is not simply a layering or a sum of elements but a fusion, a new product that transcends the configurations of the single factors.

Blending these theories and approaches, I have conceptualised and offered examples of how film music can be analysed as to its relation with the film's form, that is, the reciprocal interaction of a stylistic level, a narrative level, and a thematic level. I have designed a set of guidelines that should point the analyst's attention to what music does in films, indicating three areas of functions that music can perform—emotive, perceptive, and cognitive function. This set of analytical tools cover the transparent, less evident 'accompaniment' functions (emotive and perceptive functions) as well as the often more complex and foregrounded 'commentary' function (cognitive function). The set of functions is not prescriptive; it is like a compass: it gives some orientation but it is up to the analyst to decide what direction to take and where to linger.

The solidity of this three-function set can be sustained by the fact that, even if I have framed it within a Gestalt-based theorisation, it remains valid also when theorised within a Cognitive-Psychology framework—say, the 'Congruence-Association Framework' (Cohen 2013). For example, as regards the spatial-perceptive function, neuro-cognitive evidence demonstrates that different pieces of music make us focus our visual attention on different parts of the screen space, depending on the congruence of the music with the visual action (Mera and Stumpf 2014; Wallengren and Strukelj 2015). Or, as regards the cognitive function, music is proved to be able to stabilise the meaning of a situation that in the visuals alone is ambiguous.[2] What Meyer called 'metaphoric mimicry' has been reformulated as 'cross-domain feature correspondence' in cognitivist terms (Eitan 2013, p. 166).[3] The entire set of functions could find empirical basis in the cognitivist literature.[4] The set of functions also satisfies the research question (treating music as a device within the film's system from the discipline-specific perspective of Film Studies) because it could be applied to analyse the agency of any other device besides music; a lighting pattern or an editing match can also have emotive, perceptive, and cognitive function. This applicability to non-musical devices too ensures that music is indeed treated like one of the cinematic devices that construe the film's system.

A criticism against my work may derive from my use of 'old' theories: Leonard B. Meyer, Gestalt, and Neoformalism. I have already defended this choice. The 'old' theories I have employed were never adapted, combined, and applied to the study of music in film, and their combination works. An even stronger criticism can arise from the very fact that I have chosen Neoformalism. As we have seen, the biggest risk that is liable to occur with Neoformalism is to see the viewer as a logical abstraction predictably responding to stimuli. Says Robert Stam: 'Cognitive theory [on which Neoformalism is based] allows little room for the politics of location, or for the socially shaped investments, ideologies, narcissisms, and desires of the spectator, all of which seem too irrational and messy for the theory to deal with. Why do some spectators love, and others hate, the *same* films?' (Stam 2000, p. 241). But it must also be said that often *too much* room has been allowed, and a risk of the opposite nature may present itself: films being exclusively studied as object of identity appropriation and cultural usage.[5] Most of such critical attacks seem to descend (more or less explicitly) from Neoformalism's 'guilt' of not being politically engaged with the deconstruction (and denunciation) of hidden messages, but only concerned with forms and style. In Carroll's words:

> Cognitivists [and Formalists], unlike proponent of the Theory, tend to believe that there are aspects of cinematic reception that can be studied independently of questions of political or ideological consequences....But proponents of the Theory, on the other hand, presuppose that every aspect of cinema is implicated in ideology....To stamp one's feet and to insist that every dimension of film must have an ideological dimension...is simply dogmatic.' (Carroll 1996, pp. 49–51)

In the recent James Buhler presentation of Formalism and Neoformalism, the more or less explicit accusations of ahistoricism and socio-political disengagement present themselves once again: '[F]ormalism accepts the intentional fallacy, which presumes that intention matters only to the extent that it has been realized in the material; and if it has been realized in the material than there is no reason to appeal to the category, or indeed to history' (Buhler 2014, p. 202). Neoformalism might indeed accept the 'intentional fallacy' but this can simply be a counterbalance for an opposite long-standing trend, what could be called 'hidden-intention fallacy'—films *must* be 'read' only against the grain and the *real* intention is not the one openly realized in the material. Bordwell amusingly exemplifies this with a 'parable' that is worth quoting as completely as possible:

> On a Summer day, a father looks out at the family lawn and says to his teen-aged son: 'The grass is so tall I can hardly see the cat walking through it.' The son slopes off to mow the lawn, but the interchange has been witnessed by a team of live-in social scientists....One sees it as typical of the American household's rituals of power and negotiation. Another observer construes the remark as revealing a characteristic bourgeois concern for appearances and pride in private property. Yet another…insists that the father envies the son's sexual proficiency and that the feline image constitutes a fantasy that unwittingly symbolizes (a) the father's identification with the predator; (b) his desire for liberation from his stifling life; (c) his fears of castration (the cat in question has been neutered); or (d) all of the above. Now if these observers were to propose their interpretations to the father, he might deny them with great vehemence, but this would not persuade the social scientists to repudiate their conclusions. They would reply that the meanings they ascribed to the remark were involuntary, concealed…. The social scientists have constructed a set of *symptomatic* meanings, and these cannot be demolished by the father's protest. Whether the sources of meaning are intrapsychic or broadly cultural, they lie outside the conscious control of the individual who produces the utterance. (Bordwell 1989, pp. 71–72)

Against-the-grain interpretation still wins more favour than with-the-grain analysis. The only part of my Neoformalist analysis of John Williams's neoclassicism that was appreciated in an otherwise dismissive review (Halfyard 2015) was the one in which I *deconstruct* 'Marion's Theme' from *Raiders of the Lost Ark* (1981, dir. Spielberg) as masculinist—a passing remark that I made to point out that further interpretations of the film's music were possible, but my interest was for the analysis of music's formal contribution.

As early as 1981, a review saw the newborn Neoformalism as a potential danger, 'detrimental' to the academic community:

> [I]t leads to criticism which is limited to stylistic analysis....*Film Art* proposes to be an introductory textbook on film as an art form, yet does not cover film as a cultural force, a social phenomenon or a medium capable of expressing serious themes....There is little doubt that film scholars have traditionally been 'too' concerned with thematic interpretation at the expense of film form, but to reverse the situation is to regress. If scholars

continue to restrict their concern to form, we will see a new generation of film students trained only as technicians rather than as interpreters in the humanities. (Salvalaggio 1981, pp. 45, 51, 52)[6]

More than thirty years later, we can say that this has not happened. Neoformalism continues to provide effective tools for the study of the history of film style (Burnett 2008), and is deemed pedagogically stimulating too for film students (Blewitt 1997), but has not become an hegemonic orientation at all:

> Whereas in relation to other art forms—including painting, music, and dance—formalism has been a fairly dominant, mainstream view, in relation to film, formalism is a minority view overshadowed by a strong interpretive tradition. Moreover, it is not a minority view because it has gone largely unnoticed; on the contrary, formalism in its contemporary guise is seen by many film scholars as a threatening force to be vigorously resisted. (Thomson-Jones 2011, p. 131)

I think that, since there are already many instances of 'readings' that give more importance to how films are used and to their socio/cultural significance, the presence of a few 'analyses' that give more importance to how films are built and their aesthetic significance is not detrimental but a healthy pluralistic counterbalance. And, as I have claimed in the 'Introduction,' I think that we in Film Studies should be 'interpreters' but also 'technicians,' scholars who can also deal with the discipline-specific technicalities of this art-form, as happens with Arts or Music Studies. Neoformalism is discipline-specific, interested in technicalities and—contrary to what is stated by its detractors—does *not* belittle interpretation but connects it with formal analysis. I do not claim that Neoformalism is *the* perfect approach. There is not a perfect approach, as any approach is biassed in some way. As Robert Stam puts it: 'The danger of cognitivism [and Neoformalism] is to reduce meaning, to see film reception as *only* perceptual and cognitive process....The danger of the other side, that of Grand Theory in the Barthesian-Lacanian tradition, is perhaps the opposite, to inflate meaning' (in Quart 2000, p. 41). Every research endeavour should start with a question; and bearing in mind that there is no *perfect* approach and that each has its limits and biasses, one has to look for *the good* approach for her/his specific research question, the one that proves the most suitable to find a satisfactorily answer.

Depending on the task, one might need a hammer on one occasion and a screwdriver on other. Only, we should possess a tool box as rich and varied as possible, in order to find what we need for any task that can be presented to us. The purpose of this study was to offer an alternative to the present scenario, in which I see the musicological and hermeneutic approaches as the majority. My aim was to expand the current toolbox of analytical tools. What I wished to propose here was not a revolutionary theory—something 'ground-breaking' or 'cutting-edge', to use the bombastic lingo of academic marketing—but a 'modest approach' (Thompson 1988, p. 9) that can be fruitfully applied by those interested in stylistics and film form. But I would not be surprised that my proposal may sound irritatingly provocative to some—like a Swiftian 'modest proposal'—or appear dull, frustrating, 'pseudo-scientific' (as one peer-reviewer for a journal article once called my approach) or simplisticly descriptive to those more concerned with hermeneutics and deconstructionism. Academic 'ideologies' and disciplinary boundaries aside, my wish is that the findings presented in this study can be of some use for both the disciplines involved. To film scholars, the proposed analytical categories can be handy guidelines to talk about music in film, and offer a view of film music as a cinematic device that can be handled with more confidence, as discussion of film music doesn't require here specialistic analysis of the musical text (the score). To musicologists and music theorists, this approach may provide a way to deepen their understanding of and insights into the ways in which music interacts with the other cinematic elements. After all, music on the pages of a score is not film music. It really becomes *film* music once coupled with the visuals and the other sound components.

Notes

1. To cite a couple, Smith (1999) and Smith (1996).
2. Music influences the judgement of a visual situation that per se can be ambiguously interpreted as either friendly or aggressive: see Bolivar et al. (1994).
3. On 'cross modal relations', see also Kendall and Lipscomb (2013) and Iwamiya (2013).
4. Cognitive-Psychology studies have shown that music can modify the interpretation of an image; draw the attention to a specific element of the image rather than to another; modify the perception of the speed of the visual action; help fix images in the memory; strengthen the closure effect of an episode; project on the images its emotional content and even,

although paradoxical it might seem, make the narrative world seem more real than it would seem without music. Most of these experiments are presented and explained in Cohen (1994) and Tan et al. (2013).
5. A provocative example of the potential excesses of this ethnographic/culturalist approach is Kennett (2008).
6. A reply is in Bordwell and Thompson (1982).

REFERENCES

Blewitt, John. 1997. A Neo-Formalist Approach to Film Aesthetics and Education. *Journal of Aesthetic Education* 31 (2): 91–96.

Bolivar, Valerie J., Annabel J. Cohen, and John C. Fentress. 1994. Semantic and Formal Congruency in Music and Motion Pictures: Effects on the Interpretation of Visual Action. *Psychomusicology* 13 (Spring/Fall): 58–59.

Bordwell, David. 1989. *Making Meaning: Inference and Rhetoric in the Interpretation of Cinema*. Cambridge, MA: Harvard University Press.

Bordwell, David, and Kristin Thompson. 1982. Neoformalist Criticism: A Reply. *Journal of the University Film and Video Association* 34 (1): 65–68.

Buhler, James. 2014. Ontological, Formal, and Critical Theories of Film Music and Sound. In *The Oxford Handbook of Film Music Studies*, ed. David Neumeyer and James Buhler, 188–225. Oxford and New York: Oxford University Press.

Burnett, Colin. 2008. A New Look at the Concept of Style in Film: The Origins and Development of the Problem-Solution Model. *New Review of Film and Television Studies* 6 (2): 127–149.

Carroll, Noël. 1996. Prospects for Film Theory: A Personal Assessment. In *Post-Theory. Reconstructing Film Studies*, ed. David Bordwell and Noël Carroll, 37–68. Madison, WI: University of Wisconsin Press.

Cohen, Annabel (ed.). 1994. *Psychomusicology* 13 (Spring/Fall).

Cohen, Annabel. 2013. Congruence-Association Model of Music and Multimedia: Origin and Evolution. In *The Psychology of Music in Multimedia*, ed. Siu-Lan Tan, Annabel J. Cohen, Scott D. Lipscomb, and Roger A. Kendall, 17–47. Oxford: Oxford University Press.

Eitan, Zohar. 2013. How Pitch and Loudness Shape Musical Space and Motion. In *The Psychology of Music in Multimedia*, ed. Siu-Lan Tan, Annabel J. Cohen, Scott D. Lipscomb, and Roger A. Kendall, 165–191. Oxford: Oxford University Press.

Halfyard, Janet K. 2015. John Williams's Film Music: Jaws, Star Wars, Raiders of the Lost Ark, and the Return of the Classical Hollywood Music Style by Emilio Audissino (Review). *Music, Sound, and the Moving Image* 9 (2): 231–236.

Iwamiya, Shin-ichiro. 2013. Perceived Congruence Between Auditory and Visual Elements in Multimedia. In *The Psychology of Music in Multimedia*, ed.

Siu-Lan Tan, Annabel J. Cohen, Scott D. Lipscomb, and Roger A. Kendall, 141–164. Oxford: Oxford University Press.

Kendall, Roger A, and Scott D. Lipscomb. 2013. Experimental Semiotics Applied to Visuals, Sound, and Musical Structures. In *The Psychology of Music in Multimedia*, ed. Siu-Lan Tan, Annabel J. Cohen, Scott D. Lipscomb, and Roger A. Kendall, 48–65. Oxford: Oxford University Press.

Kennett, Chris. 2008. A Tribe Named Chris: Pop Music Analysis as Idioethnomusicology. *Open Space Magazine* 10: 1, Online. http://the-open-space.org/issue-10. Accessed 9 Feb 2017.

Mera, Miguel, and Simone Stumpf. 2014. Eye-Tracking Film Music. Music and the Moving Image 7 (3): 3–23.

Quart, Alissa. 2000. David Bordwell Blows the Whistle on Film Studies. *Lingua Franca* 10 (March): 36–43.

Salvalaggio, Jerry L. 1981. The Emergence of a New School of Criticism: Neo-Formalism. *Journal of the University Film Association* 33 (4): 45–52.

Smith, Jeff. 1996. Unheard Melodies? A Critique of Psychoanalytic Theories of Film Music. In *Post-Theory. Reconstructing Film Studies*, ed. David Bordwell and Nöel Carroll, 230–247. Madison, WI: University of Wisconsin Press.

Smith, Jeff. 1999. Movie Music as Moving Music: Emotion, Cognition, and the Film Score. In *Passionate Views: Film, Cognition, and Emotion*, ed. Carl Plantinga and Greg M. Smith, 146–167. Baltimore, MD: Johns Hopkins University Press.

Stam, Robert. 2000. *Film Theory An Introduction*. Malden, MA: Blackwell.

Tan, Siu-Lan, Annabel J. Cohen, Scott D. Lipscomb, and Roger A. Kendall (eds.). 2013. *The Psychology of Music in Multimedia*. Oxford: Oxford University Press.

Thompson, Kristin. 1988. *Breaking the Glass Armor Neoformalist Film Analysis*. Princeton, NJ: Princeton University Press.

Thomson-Jones, Katherine. 2011. Formalism. In *The Routledge Companion to Philosophy and Film*, ed. Paisley Livingston and Carl Plantinga, 131–141. Abingdon and New York: Routledge.

Wallengren, Ann-Kristin, and Alexander Strukelj. 2015. Film Music and Visual Attention: A Pilot Experiment using Eye-Tracking. *Music and the Moving Image* 8 (2): 69–80.

Filmography

*Batteries not Included (Matthew Robbins, 1987, USA).
1941 (Steven Spielberg, 1979, USA).
2001: A Space Odyssey (Stanley Kubrick, 1968, UK/USA).
9 1/2 Weeks (Adrian Lyne, 1986, USA).
Abominable Dr. Phibes, The (Robert Fuest, 1971, UK/USA).
Adventures of Robin Hood, The (Michael Curtiz, William Keighley, 1938, USA).
Adventures of Tintin, The (Steven Spielberg, 2011, USA/New Zealand).
Alf (Tom Patchet, Paul Fusco, 1986–1990, TV Series, USA).
American Graffiti (George Lucas, 1973, USA).
Apartment, The (Billy Wilder, 1960, USA).
Arsenic and Old Lace (Frank Capra, 1944, USA).
Artist, The (Michel Hazanavicius, 2011, France/USA/Belgium).
A Woman Is a Woman (*Une femme est une femme*, Jean-Luc Godard, 1961, France).
Bachelor in Paradise (Jack Arnold, 1961, USA).
Badlands (Terrence Malick, 1973, USA).
Bambi (David D. Hand, 1942, USA).
Best Years of Our Lives, The (William Wyler, 1946, USA).
Bigamist, The (*Il bigamo*, Luciano Emmer, 1956, Italy).
Big Sleep, The (Howard Hawks, 1946, USA).
Birth of a Nation, The (David Wark Griffith, 1915, USA).
Breaking Bad (Vince Gilligan, 2008–2013, TV Series, USA).
Breathless (*À bout de souffle*, Jean-Luc Godard, 1960, France).
Brief Encounter (David Lean, 1945, UK).
Butch Cassidy (George Roy Hill, 1969, USA).
Caddyshack (Harold Ramis, 1980, USA).

Captain Blood (Michael Curtiz, 1935, USA).
Casablanca (Michael Curtiz, 1942, USA).
Castle (Andrew W. Marlowe, 2009–2016, TV Series, USA).
Citizen Kane (Orson Welles, 1941, USA).
Clockwork Orange, A (Stanley Kubrick, 1971, UK/USA).
Close Encounters of the Third Kind (Steven Spielberg, 1977, USA).
Closet Land (Radha Bharadwaj, 1991, USA).
Conversation, The (Francis Ford Coppola, 1974, USA).
Crimson Peak (Guillermo del Toro, 2015, USA/Canada).
Day the Earth Stood Still, The (Robert Wise, 1951, USA).
Dead Silence (James Wan, 2007, USA).
Deserter (*Dezertir*, Vsevolod Pudovkin, 1933, Soviet Union).
Dishonored (Joseph Von Sternberg, 1931, USA).
Double Indemnity (Billy Wilder, 1944, USA).
Duel (Steven Spielberg, 1971, USA).
East of Eden (Elia Kazan, 1955, USA).
Eroica (Simon Cellan Jones, 2003, TV film, UK).
E.T. The Extraterrestrial (Steven Spielberg, 1982, USA).
Exorcist, The (William Friedkin, 1973, USA).
Firelight (Steven Spielberg, 1964, USA).
Fitzwilly (Delbert Mann, 1967, USA).
Five Easy Pieces (Bob Rafelson, 1970, USA).
Forbidden Planet (Fred M. Wilcox, 1956, USA).
Fury (Fritz Lang, 1936, USA).
Gentlemen Prefer Blondes (Howard Hawks, 1953, USA).
Gone with the Wind (Victor Fleming, 1939, USA).
Gospel according to St. Matthew, The (*Il Vangelo secondo Matteo*, Pier Paolo Pasolini, 1964, Italy/France).
Grande Illusion, La (Jean Renoir, 1937, France).
Great Silence, The (*Il grande silenzio*, Sergio Corbucci, 1968, Italy/France).
Green Berets, The (John Wayne, 1968, USA).
Hangmen Also Die! (Fritz Lang, 1943, USA).
Hangover Square (John Brahm, 1945, USA).
Harry Potter and the Sorcerer's Stone (Chris Columbus, 2001, USA).
Harum Scarum (Gene Nelson, 1965, USA).
Hateful Eight, The (Quentin Tarantino, 2015, USA).
Hook (Steven Spielberg, 1991, USA).
Hotel Rwanda (Terry George, 2004, UK/South Africa/Italy).
Howard the Duck (Willard Huyck, 1986, USA).
Informer, The (John Ford, 1935, USA).
Inland Empire (David Lynch, 2006, France/Poland/USA).
Intolerance (David Wark Griffith, 1916, USA).

Investigation of a Citizen Above Suspicion (*Indagine su un cittadino al di sopra di ogni sospetto*, Elio Petri, 1970, Italy).
Irreversible (Gaspar Noé, 2002, France).
It's Alive (Larry Cohen, 1974, USA).
It Started in Naples (Melville Shavelson, 1960, USA).
Ivan the Terrible—Part I (*Ivan Groznyy*, Sergei M. Eisenstein, 1945, Soviet Union).
Jaws (Steven Spielberg, 1975, USA).
JFK (Oliver Stone, 1991, USA).
Joyeux Noël (Christian Carion, 2005, France/Germany/Belgium/UK).
Killers, The (Robert Siodmak, 1946, USA).
Kind Hearts and Coronets (Robert Hamer, 1949, UK).
King of Kings (Nicholas Ray, 1961, USA).
Kuhle Wampe (Kuhle Wampe Oder: Wem Gehört die Welt? Slatan Dudow, 1932, Germany).
Lady in the Lake (Robert Montgomery, 1947, USA).
Laura (Otto Preminger, 1944, USA).
Lawrence of Arabia (David Lean, 1962, UK/USA).
Legend of Lylah Clare, The (Robert Aldrich, 1968, USA).
Letto a tre piazze (Steno [Stefano Vanzina], 1960, Italy).
Life Boat (Alfred Hitchcock, 1944, USA).
Lost Highway (David Lynch, 1997, USA/France).
Mac and Me (Stewart Raffill, 1988, USA).
Macaroni (*Maccheroni*, Ettore Scola, 1985, Italy).
Making of Close Encounters of the Third Kind, The (Laurent Bouzereau, 1997, USA).
Man with the Golden Arm, The (Otto Preminger, 1955, USA).
McCabe & Mrs Miller (Robert Altman, 1971, USA).
Memento (Christopher Nolan, 2000, USA).
Metropolis (Fritz Lang, 1927, Germany).
Million, The (*Le Million*, René Clair, 1931, France).
Modern Times (Charles Chaplin, 1936, USA).
Mork and Mindy (Joe Glauberg, Garry Marshall, Dale McRaven, 1978–1982, TV Series, USA).
Mulholland Drive (David Lynch, 2001, USA/France).
Music of 'E.T.' A Discussion with John Williams, The (Laurent Bouzereau, 2002, USA).
Night of the Living Dead (George Romero, 1968, USA).
Night Walker, The (William Castle, 1964, USA).
North by Northwest (Alfred Hitchcock, 1959, USA).
October (*Oktyabr*, Sergei M. Eisenstein, 1928, Soviet Union).
Of Men and Mice (Lewis Milestone, 1939, USA).

Omen, The (Richard Donner, 1976, USA).
Once Upon a Time in the West (*C'era una volta il west*, Sergio Leone, 1968, Italy/USA).
On the Waterfront (Elia Kazan, 1954, USA).
Ordet (Carl Theodor Dreyer, 1955, Denmark).
Parallax View, The (Alan J. Pakula, 1974, USA).
Pauline et Paulette (Lieven Debrauwer, 2001, Belgium/France/Netherlands).
Pinocchio (Hamilton Luske, Ben Sharpsteen, 1940, USA).
Poltergeist (Tobe Hooper, 1982, USA).
Psycho (Alfred Hitchcock, 1960, USA).
Pulp Fiction (Quentin Tarantino, 1994, USA).
Quintet (Robert Altman, 1979, USA).
Raiders of the Lost Ark (Steven Spielberg, 1981, USA).
Rat Race, The (Robert Mulligan, 1960, USA).
Reservoir Dogs (Quentin Tarantino, 1992, USA).
Return of the Jedi (Richard Marquand, 1983, USA).
Rope, The (Alfred Hitchcock, 1948, USA).
Rosemary's Baby (Roman Polanski, 1968, USA).
Saving Private Ryan (Steven Spielberg, 1998, USA).
Scarface (Howard Hawks, 1932, USA).
Sea Hawk, The (Michael Curtiz, 1940, USA).
Seashell and the Clergyman, The (*Le coquille et le clergyman*, Germaine Dullac, 1928, France).
Seven Year Itch, The (Billy Wilder, 1955, USA).
Shootist, The (Don Siegel, 1976, USA).
Soldier Blue (Ralph Nelson, 1970, USA).
Something Evil (Steven Spielberg, 1972, TV film, USA).
Sorry, Wrong Number (Anatole Litvak, 1948, USA).
Starman (John Carpenter, 1984, USA).
Star Wars (George Lucas, 1977, USA).
Star Wars: The Force Awakens (J.J. Abrams, 2015, USA).
Stella Dallas (King Vidor, 1937, USA).
Strike (*Stachka*, Sergei M. Eisenstein, 1924, Soviet Union).
Superman the Movie (Richard Donner, 1978).
Suspicion (Alfred Hitchcock, 1941, USA).
Swindle, The (*Il bidone*, Federico Fellini, 1955, Italy).
Tales that Witness Madness (Freddie Francis, 1973, UK).
Taxi Driver (Martin Scorsese, 1976, USA).
Three Colors: Blue (Krzysztof Kieslowski, 1993, France/Poland/Switzerland).
Titanic (James Cameron, 1997, USA).
Treasure of the Sierra Madre, The (John Huston, 1948, USA).
Triumph of the Will (*Triumph des Willens*, Leni Riefenstahl, 1935, Germany).

Trouble with Harry, The (Alfred Hitchcock, 1955, USA).
Twisted Nerve (Roy Boulting, 1968, UK).
Umbrellas of Cherbourg, The (*Les parapluies de Cherbourg*, Jacques Demy, 1964, France).
Vertigo (Alfred Hitchcock, 1958, USA).
Witches of Eastwick, The (George Miller, 1987, USA).
Women, The (George Cukor, 1939, USA).
Zodiac (David Fincher, 2007, USA).

Index

0-9
1941, 80
2001: A Space Odyssey, 196, 197
9½ Weeks, 167

A
Abbate, Carolyn, 19, 55, 56
Abominable Dr. Phibes, The, 127
Absolute Musik, 2, 19, 201
Accompaniment, 26–30, 33, 47, 58, 85, 126, 165, 223, 224
Adorno, Theodor W., 24, 28, 87
Adventures of Robin Hood, The, 17, 145, 150
Adventures of Tintin, The, 109
Affective congruence, audiovisual, 120
Agogics, 108
Aha, phenomenon, 115, 121
Ahistoricism, accusation of, 225
Aleatoric, music, 97
Alexandrov, Grigory, 27
Alf, 216
Altman, Rick, 28, 33, 37, 49
Amplification, 47
American Graffiti, 167
Ancrage, 114, 152
Anderson, Leroy, 9, 118
Anempathetic effect, 162–166, 198–199
Apartment, The, 84, 134, 142, 143, 146, 158
Arnheim, Rudolf, 26, 103
Arsenic and Old Lace, 174
Artistic motivation, 84, 90, 128, 129, 160, 202
Artist, The, 77, 99, 126
Asynchronism, 26, 28, 47
Atonal, music, 96, 196, 198, 199, 206, 207, 215
Austin, John, 32
A Woman Is a Woman, 129, 150

B
Bachelor in Paradise, 160
Background, 4, 6, 27, 28, 31, 33, 56, 71, 74, 75, 102, 105, 126, 137, 162, 171–173, 177, 195, 197, 199, 201, 203
Badlands, 59
Balázs, Béla, 37, 103

Bambi, 203, 206
Basinger, Kim, 167
*Batteries not Included, 216
Bazin, André, 26
Bellour, Raymond, 4
Benveniste, Émile, 33, 72
Berio, Luciano, 97
Bernstein, Leonard, 48
Best Years of Our Lives, The, 55
Biancorosso, Giorgio, 4, 34
Bigamist, The, 160
Big Sleep, The, 4
Birth of a Nation, The, 7
Bordwell, David, 7, 10, 59, 67–69, 76–80, 82, 85, 88, 100, 104, 105, 119, 121, 149, 151, 217, 218
Bource, Ludovic, 126
Branigan, Edward, 51
Breaking Bad, 84, 167
Breathless, 83
Brecht, Bertolt, 2
Brief Encounter, 147, 149, 152
Brooks, Mel, 128
Browne, Nick, 74
Buckland, Warren, 37, 178, 214
Buhler, James, 18, 33, 225
Burch, Noël, 68
Butch Cassidy, 127

C

Caddyishack, 126
Cage, John, 97
Cano, Cristina, 87
Canonical, story format, 104, 105, 130
Canudo, Ricciotto, 26
Captain Blood, 173
Carroll, 72, 75
Carroll, Noël, 57, 75, 110
Casablanca, 168
Casetti, Francesco, 33, 37

Castle, 134, 137, 138
'Chances Are', 216
Chandler, Raymond, 38, 174
Chatman, Seymour, 59, 89
Chion, Michel, 28, 36, 37, 49, 50, 162
Chromaticism, music, 23, 196
Citizen Kane, 72, 111, 147
Clair, René, 26
Clockwork Orange, A, 166, 167
Close Encounters of the Third Kind, 4, 37, 191, 192, 212
Closet Land, 25
Clusters, music, 195, 196, 199, 200
Cognitivism, 72, 73, 75, 88, 105, 106, 115, 120, 227
Cohen, Annabel J., 87, 90, 120
Comment, 5, 7, 8, 10, 26, 27, 37, 74, 85, 114, 142, 145, 150, 165, 167, 233
Communications, model, 31–35, 45, 46, 48, 51, 53, 56–59, 69, 70, 72, 89, 114, 161, 162, 163
Communicativeness, narration, 213
Commutation, Tagg's, 178
Complementation, Cook''s, 46, 114
Compositional motivation, 83, 84, 129, 203
Comprehension, narrative, 79, 89, 142, 149
Configuration, 85, 101–103, 106, 107, 110–112, 116–118, 132, 133, 136, 138, 139, 144, 148, 161, 167, 170, 177, 179, 180, 182, 186, 207, 224
Conformance, 46, 47, 48, 86, 116, 117
Conformance, Cook's, 47, 86, 114
Congruence-Associationist Framework, 224
Connotation, 7, 32, 76, 97, 112, 144, 145, 159, 168–170

INDEX 239

Connotative cognitive function, 144, 145, 148–150, 158, 166, 173, 196, 203, 204, 210
Consonance, music, 108, 200
Constructivism, 72, 73–74, 77, 105
Contest, 46, 116
Contest, Cook's, 47, 48, 86, 115, 117
Contingent universals, 73, 99
Conversation, The, 198
Cook, Nicholas, 24, 46, 116
Copland, Aaron, 49, 87
Counterpoint, 26
Counterpoint, audiovisual, 28, 31, 47, 54, 115, 116, 165, 166
Crawford, Joan, 174
Crimson Peak, 137
Criticism, of Neoformalism, 70, 75
Culturalism, 37
Curiosity, narrative, 118, 121, 195, 197–200

D

Dalhaus, Carl, 201
Day the Earth Stood Still, The, 196, 197
Dead Silence, 71
Deconstructionism, 53, 228
Defamiliarisation, 71, 86
Deleuze, Gilles, 52
Denotations, 114, 141
Denotative cognitive function, 141, 148–150
Deserter, 26, 144, 149, 165
Designative meaning, 97
Deus ex machina, 128
'Deutschlandlied', 169
Device, 20, 23, 52, 58, 59, 75, 78, 82–84, 86, 88, 95, 110, 111, 116, 117, 118, 125, 127–129, 131, 132, 137, 139, 141, 144, 149, 150, 158, 159, 160, 164, 171, 172, 186, 192, 195, 196, 198, 200, 202, 204, 214, 224, 228
Devol, Frank, 148
Diatonic music, 18, 108
Diegetic music, 33–35, 56, 58, 61, 129, 138, 141, 162, 163, 165, 169
'Dies Irae', 196, 201
Dishonored, 140, 141
Dissonance, music, 108, 147, 148, 196, 200
'Die Wacht am Rhein', 168–171
Dominance, 47, 48, 111
Dominant, 25, 31, 45, 82, 83, 85, 134, 149, 193, 194, 227
Donnelly, K. J., 4, 37, 49, 103, 120, 215
Double Indemnity, 79
Duel, 198
Dujardin, Jean, 126

E

E.T. The Extraterrestrial, 4, 152, 191, 192, 193, 194, 214, 216
East of Eden, 53
Economical, motivation, 127, 128
Ehrenfels, Christian von, 100, 101
Eichenbaum, Boris, 69
Eisenstein, Sergei M., 61, 103
Eisler, Hanns, 2, 9, 24, 87
Embodied, meaning, 97, 119
Emotion moment, 131, 132, 135, 197, 198, 200
Emotive function, 130, 132, 133, 147, 148, 158, 173, 180, 183, 196, 200, 203, 207, 209
Endogenous motivations, 127, 128
Eroica, 24
Excess, 143, 159, 162, 186, 229
Exogenous motivations, 127

Exorcist, The, 199
Expectations, music, 96, 97, 129, 135, 175, 201, 215
Explicit meaning, 80, 81, 149, 150, 192, 200, 210

F
Fabula, 79, 80, 126
'Faccetta nera', 168
Fairbanks, Douglas, 126
Fantastical Gap, 34, 35, 57, 58, 129, 157, 159, 161, 162
Filmmind, 57
Firelight, 216
Fitzwilly, 216
Five Easy Pieces, 25
Flinn, Caryll, 2, 31
Flynn, Errol, 137, 160
Forbidden Planet, 196
Formalism, 53, 68–70, 74, 76, 104, 225, 227
Frampton, Daniel, 55
Franklin, Peter, 24
Freud, Sigmund, 30, 51, 72, 83
Friedhofer, Hugo, 2, 55
Functional analysis, 23, 60, 86, 87, 101
Fury, 174

G
Gable, Clark, 143
Gault, Berys, 73
Gender Studies, 25
Genette, Gérard, 37
Gentlemen Prefers Blondes, 80
Gestalt, 49, 50, 95, 100–112, 115, 116, 118, 119, 223–225
Godard, Jean-Luc, 35, 76, 83, 84, 128, 129, 150
Gombrich, Ernst, 68
Gomery, Douglas, 151
Gone with the Wind, 81, 109, 133, 135
Gorbman, Claudia, 2, 20, 31, 33, 38, 55, 87, 152, 163
Gospel according to St. Matthew, The, 128
Gradual disclosure of the main theme, 136, 201, 207
Grand Theory, 51–53, 56, 60, 68, 74, 88, 99, 218, 227
Great Silence, The, 176
Green Berets, The, 81
Grice, Paul, 50
Grodal, Torben, 131

H
Habitualisation, 70, 71
Hangmen Also Die!, 9
Hangover Square, 163
Harry Potter and the Sorcerer''s Stone, 193, 216
Harum Scarum, 25
Hateful Eight, The, 174
Hazanavicius, Michel, 126, 127
Heldt, Guido, 51
Hermeneutics, 35, 228
Herrmann, Bernard, 21, 27, 47, 126, 127, 131, 145
Historical materialistic narration, 149
Hitchcock, Alfred, 18, 21, 25, 51, 81, 109, 126, 127, 139, 145, 174
Hitler, Adolf, 145
Hook, 111, 112
Horner, James, 127
Hotel Rwanda, 71
Howard the Duck, 216
Huron, David, 96

I

Ideology, 29, 31, 74, 76, 77, 80, 225
Implications, music, 45, 96, 97, 134, 169
Implicit meaning, 7, 80–82, 89, 192, 202, 204, 213, 214
Inaudibility, 31
Inference, 73, 79, 115
Informer, The, 186
Inland Empire, 80, 232
Insights, 103, 104, 211, 228
Interdisciplinarity, 9
Interpretation, 7, 8, 23, 30, 32, 34, 37, 45, 48, 51–53, 57, 68, 70, 74–76, 81, 82, 86, 89, 99, 113, 116, 117, 126, 141, 144, 150, 151, 159, 160, 166, 177, 178, 186, 191, 192, 202, 214, 216, 226–228
Intolerance, 10, 232
Intradiegetic, 37, 38, 161
Investigation of a Citizen Above Suspicion, 177, 233
Invisibility, editing, 83, 106
Irreversible, 79, 233
Isomorphism, 102, 103, 105–107, 110–113, 115–117, 120, 144
It started in Naples, 143, 233
It's Alive, 199
Ivan the TerriblePart I, 85, 233

J

Jaws, 4, 21, 33, 126, 158, 195, 197, 215, 233
Jazz, 134, 143, 174, 183, 186
Jennings, Will, 127
JFK, 193, 233
Joyeux Noël, 179, 233
Jung, Carl G., 53

K

Kalinak, Kathryn, 2, 25, 27, 36, 45, 46, 54, 137, 186
Kassabian, Anahid, 5, 24, 25, 37, 61
Killers, The, 111, 233
Kind Hearts and Coronets, 137, 233
King of Kings, 196
Koffka, Kurt, 119, 120
Köhler, Wolfgang, 101–103, 106, 107, 110, 111, 115, 116, 119, 120, 144
Korngold, Erich W., 145, 150, 152, 160, 162, 174, 185
Kracauer, Siegfried, 37
Kubrick, Stanley, 166, 196, 232
Kuhle Wampe, 9, 233
Kulezic-Wilson, Danijela, 3, 50

L

Lacan, Jacques, 29–31
Lady in the Lake, 174
Lang, Fritz, 2, 9, 10, 61, 127
Langer, Susanne K., 103
Larsen, Peter, 4
Laura, 157–159
Lawrence of Arabia, 186
Legend of Lylah Clare, The, 148
Legrand, Michel, 181
Lehman, Frank, 22
Leitmotiv, 22, 28, 37, 109, 126, 161, 162, 169, 211, 217
Lemon, Jack, 89
Lerner, Neil, 37, 196
Letto a tre piazze, 141
Levinson, Jerrold, 34, 35
Life Boat, 159
Limeliters, The, 168
Lissa, Zofia, 87, 90
Lohengrin, 142
Loren, Sophia, 144

Lost Highway, 79
Lubitsch, Ernst, 127

M
Mac and Me, 216
Macaroni, 142, 148
Macro-configuration, 114, 116–118, 120, 132, 133, 136, 139, 141, 144, 147, 148, 164, 166–168, 173, 177–179, 185, 196, 200
Macro-emotive function, 132–135, 147, 148, 180, 183, 186, 199, 200, 201, 206, 207
Mancini, Henry, 2, 160
'Marseillaise', La, 169–171
Man with the Golden Arm, The, 134
Mastroianni, Marcello, 160
Mathis, Johnny, 199
McCabe & Mrs Miller, 176, 179
McGurk effect, 49, 50
Memento, 79
Merleau-Ponty, Maurice, 60
Metadiegetic, 33, 35, 37, 38
Metaphoric mimicry, 112, 137, 195, 224
Metaphor model, 46, 47
Metropolis, 61
Metz, Christian, 29, 37
Meyer, Leonard B., 95, 96, 98, 103, 112, 114, 118, 119, 135, 223, 225
Miceli, Sergio, 28, 35, 36, 209, 215
Mickey-mousing, 30, 47, 137
Micro-configuration, 114, 116, 117, 118, 125, 131, 132, 136, 139, 141, 143, 144, 164, 166, 167, 168, 173, 185, 208
Micro-emotive function, 132–134, 136, 146–148, 158, 173, 180, 196, 203, 209
Million, The, 26

Modern Times, 71
Modernistic music, 24, 195
Modifier, music, 110
Monroe, Marilyn, 128, 146
Montage, 55, 78, 85, 110, 114, 140, 141, 147, 217
Monteverdi, Claudio, 132
Mood, 61, 77, 98, 106, 107, 112, 119, 130–135, 143, 147, 149, 167, 180, 197–200, 202, 206
Moormann, Peter, 21, 215
Mork and Mindy, 216
Morricone, Ennio, 18, 28, 175
Mr Mulliner Speaking, 38
Mulholland Drive, 51, 83
Münsterberg, Hugo, 26
Musicals, 25, 33, 150, 162
Muzak, 126

N
Nagari, Benjamin, 53
Narmour, Eugene, 96
Narration, 6, 51, 55, 57–59, 72, 79–82, 117, 118, 128, 134, 136–138, 140–144, 149, 150, 152, 162, 164, 171–173, 175, 180, 192, 193, 197–199, 201, 202, 205, 206, 209, 210, 213, 214, 217
Narrative level, 21, 38, 78, 79, 82, 88, 129, 161, 224
Narrator, 32–34, 38, 54, 57, 59, 72, 79, 89, 129, 161–163
Nasta, Dominique, 50, 51
Nattiez, Jean Jacques, 19
Neoformalism, 59, 60, 67–70, 72–77, 79, 83, 85, 86, 88, 89, 95, 99, 100, 104, 105, 110, 125, 223, 225–227
Neo-Riemannian theory, 18

Neumeyer, David, 2, 8, 11, 18, 35, 50, 87
Nicholson, Jack, 158, 185
Night of the Living Dead, 71
Night Walker, The, 134, 152
Nondiegetic, 57, 58, 159, 200
Non-separatist conception, 46, 49, 55, 56, 58, 86, 111
North by Northwest, 139
Nostalgia, 31, 109, 168, 183, 203
Novak, Kim, 127
Nutcracker, The, 140

O

October, 61
Of Men and Mice, 49
Omen, The, 199
Once upon a Time in the West, 61
Onomatopoeic music, 9, 137
On the Waterfront, 48
Opera, music, 19, 20, 52, 56, 61, 173, 201, 210, 214
Ostinato, music, 21, 22, 96, 141, 196, 215

P

Parallax View, The, 198
Parallelism, 8, 26, 28, 30, 35, 47
Parallelism, audiovisual, 37
Parametric form, 90
Parker, Roger, 19
Pasolini, Pier Paolo, 128
Passacaglia, 141
Pauline et Paulette, 139
Peirce, Charles S., 29
Penderecki, Krzysztof, 195
Perception model, 53, 58–60, 69, 72, 86, 95, 162, 164
Phenomenology, 50, 53, 55, 57, 59, 60

Pinocchio, 200–204, 216
Plantinga, Carl, 89, 119, 186
Poetics, 53, 77, 84, 203
Poetika Kino, 69
Polarisation, audiovisual, 120, 198
Poltergeist, 214
Prägnanz, Law, 101, 106
Prendergast, Roy M., 2, 48, 90, 151, 185
Primary parameters, music, 108
Procedural schemata, 73
Profilmic, 52, 61, 78
Projection, 5, 47, 61
Prokofiev, Sergei S., 85
Prototype, 73, 126, 130
Psycho, 21, 51, 133, 145, 163, 164, 174
Psychoanalysis, 29–31, 35, 53, 72, 77, 81, 88, 99, 223
Psychomusicology, 1, 95
Pudovkin, Vsevolod, 26, 144, 165
Pulp Fiction, 79

Q

Quintet, 186

R

Rachmaninov, Sergei V., 146, 152
Raiders of the Lost Ark, 22, 136, 138, 226
Raksin, David, 158
Rat Race, The, 143
Realistic motivation, 58, 83, 84, 128, 129, 202
Receiver, 32, 72
Redner, Gregg, 52, 53, 86
Referential meaning, 80, 81
Reservoir Dogs, 174
Return of the Jedi, 216
Rope, The, 25

Rosar, William H., 5
Rosemary's Baby, 199
Rossini, Giacchino, 61, 166, 167
Rota, Nino, 25
Rózsa, Miklós, 111, 196, 215

S
Sabaneev, Leonid L., 1
Saccadic eye movement, 106
Sadoff, Ronald, 86
Saving Private Ryan, 4, 56
Scarface, 80
Schemata, 73
Schenkerian analysis, 18, 36, 96
Schneller, Tom, 36, 200, 211, 213
Scriabin, Alexander, 194
Sea Hawk, The, 160
Seashell and the Clergyman, The, 80
Seashore, Carl E., 95
Secondary parameters, music, 108, 110, 120
Semiotics, 29–32, 35, 50, 51, 68, 89
Sender, 32, 33, 54, 58, 72
Separatist conception, 29, 36, 45, 46, 48, 50, 51, 54, 55, 59
Set-up/pay-off, 84
Seven Year Itch, The, 146, 149
Shklovsky, Viktor, 69, 70, 71, 77
Shootist, The, 176
Similarity/difference test, 46, 116
Skaters' Waltz, The, 4
Sloboda, John, 95, 96, 194, 215
Smith, Gregg M., 130, 197
Smith, Jeff, 57, 120, 159, 223
Smith, Murray, 8
Sobchack, Vivian, 57, 60
Soldier Blue, 197
Something Evil, 198
Sonnenschein, David, 165, 166
Sontag, Susan, 119
Sorry, Wrong Number, 141

Spatial perceptive function, 136, 137, 138, 140, 147, 152, 160, 208, 224
Spielberg, Steven, 4, 191, 214, 216, 217
Spottiswoode, Raymond, 87
Stalin, Joseph, 70
Stam, Robert, 73, 75, 225, 227
Starman, 216
Startle reflex, 147, 198
Star Wars, 18, 21, 24, 37, 193, 216
Star Wars: The Force Awakens, 18, 21, 24, 193, 216
Steiner, Max, 133, 135, 174, 186
Stella Dallas, 131
Stilwell, Robynn, 5, 6, 25, 34, 35, 57, 110, 157, 159
Stinger, 132, 133, 147, 198
Strike, 10, 76, 77, 118, 130, 142, 161
Style, 7, 31, 37, 52, 61, 68, 78, 79, 82, 83, 96, 126, 137, 150, 160, 162, 167, 183, 192, 223, 225, 227
Stylistic level, 78, 82, 88–90, 224
Superman The Movie, 193, 216
Suspicion, 109, 177
Swindle, The, 160
Symptomatic meaningful, 81, 82, 141, 145, 150, 214, 226
Synchresis, 49
Synchronism, 26, 47, 49
Syuzhet, 79, 149

T
Tagg, Philip, 19, 178
'Take My True Love by the Hand', 168
Takete/maluma experiment, 106
Tales that Witness Madness, 164
Tarantino, Quentin, 174, 176
Taxi Driver, 145, 148
Tchaikovsky, Piotr I., 109, 140

Template, 73, 80, 104, 159, 164
Temporal perceptive function, 138–141, 208
Thematic level, 78, 80, 88, 89, 90, 141, 204, 209, 214, 224
Thompson, Kristin, 10, 36, 52, 60, 67, 69, 71, 73, 77, 82, 84, 89, 100, 104, 197, 228
Three Colors: Blue, 53
'Threnody for the Victims of Hiroshima', 195
Tierney, Gene, 158
Titanic, 127
Tonal music, 96, 97, 194, 199, 203, 215
Transtextual motivation, 84, 127, 129, 196
Traviata, 21
Treasure of the Sierra Madre, The, 142
Triumph of the Will, 215
Trouble with Harry, The, 18
Truffaut, François, 191
Trumbull, Douglas, 205
Twisted Nerve, 164
Tynyanov, Yury, 69, 83

U

Umbrellas of Cherbourg, The, 181
Unconsummated symbol, music, 103

V

Valentino, Rudolph, 126
Ventriloquist effect, 49
Vertigo, 126, 127, 149, 174
'Volga Boatmen', The, 142

W

Wagner, Richard, 20, 37, 142
Waldteufel, Émile, 4
Walker, Elsie, 53
Waxman, Franz, 141
Wertheimer, Max, 120
Wierzbicki, James, 5, 37, 61
Williams, John, 4, 28, 136, 158, 191, 205, 213, 226
Witches of Eastwick, The, 158–160
Wittgenstein, Ludwig, 50
Women, The, 174
Woodehouse, P.G., 38

Y

Yacavone, Daniel, 34
'You Can Leave Your Hat On', 167

Z

Zodiac, 58

Printed in Great Britain
by Amazon